T0301610

Cost–Benefit Analysis and Evolutionary Computing

TRANSPORT ECONOMICS, MANAGEMENT AND POLICY

Series Editor: Kenneth Button, *Professor of Public Policy, School of Public Policy, George Mason University, USA*

Transport is a critical input for economic development and for optimizing social and political interaction. Recent years have seen significant new developments in the way that transport is perceived by private industry and governments, and in the way academics look at it.

 The aim of this series is to provide original material and up-to-date synthesis of the state of modern transport analysis. The coverage embraces all conventional modes of transport but also includes contributions from important related fields such as urban and regional planning and telecommunications where they interface with transport. The books draw from many disciplines and some cross disciplinary boundaries. They are concerned with economics, planning, sociology, geography, management science, psychology and public policy. They are intended to help improve the understanding of transport, the policy needs of the most economically advanced countries and the problems of resource-poor developing economies. The authors come from around the world and represent some of the outstanding young scholars as well as established names.

 Titles in the series include:

Financing Transportation Networks
David Levinson

Transportation Networks and the Optimal Location of Human Activities
A Numerical Geography Approach
Isabelle Thomas

European Union Port Policy
The Movement Towards a Long-Term Strategy
Constantinos I. Chlomoudis and Athanasios A. Pallis

Structural Change in Transportation and Communications in the Knowledge Society
Edited by Kiyoshi Kobayashi, T.R. Lakshmanan and William P. Anderson

Globalisation, Policy and Shipping
Fordism, Post-Fordism and the European Union Maritime Sector
Evangelia Selkou and Michael Roe

Cost–Benefit Analysis and Evolutionary Computing
Optimal Scheduling of Interactive Road Projects
John H.E. Taplin, Min Qiu, Vivian K. Salim and Renlong Han

Cost–Benefit Analysis and Evolutionary Computing

Optimal Scheduling of Interactive Road Projects

John H.E. Taplin
Professor of Information Management and Transport,
University of Western Australia

Min Qiu
Senior Lecturer in Information Management and Transport,
University of Western Australia

Vivian K. Salim
Research Scientist, Transport Futures Team,
Australian Commonwealth Scientific and Industrial Research
Organisation

Renlong Han
Research and Development Officer in Traffic Modelling,
Main Roads Western Australia

TRANSPORT ECONOMICS, MANAGEMENT AND POLICY

Edward Elgar
Cheltenham, UK • Northampton, MA, USA

Published by
Edward Elgar Publishing Limited
Glensanda House
Montpellier Parade
Cheltenham
Glos GL50 1UA
UK

Edward Elgar Publishing, Inc.
136 West Street
Suite 202
Northampton
Massachusetts 01060
USA

A catalogue record for this book
is available from the British Library

ISBN 1 84542 421 2

Printed and bound in Great Britain by MPG Books Ltd, Bodmin, Cornwall

Contents

Figures

Tables

Abbreviations

AADT	Annual average daily traffic
BC	Base cost
BPR	Bureau of Public Roads
CBD	Central business district
CBR	California bearing ratio
CESA	Cumulative equivalent standard axles
CNDP	Continuous network design problem
CULWAY	A type of culvert strain gauge
DNDP	Discrete network design problem
DEF	Falling weight deflection
Div	Divisible
DUE	Deterministic user equilibrium
ED	Euclidean distance
ESA	Equivalent standard axle
FWD	Falling weight deflection
GA	Genetic algorithm
GDP	Gross domestic product
GF	Growth factor
HDM	Highway Development and Management
HIAP	Highways Investment Analysis Package
Indiv	Indivisible
IRI	International roughness index
IRR	Internal rate of return
MCA	Multi-criteria analysis
MINLP	Mixed-integer non-linear program
MNDP	Mixed network design problem
MSN	Modified structure number
NDP	Network design problem
NPV	Net present value
OD	Origin-destination

PIARC	World Road Association
PMX	Partially mapped crossover
RAM	Random access computer memory
RM	Routine maintenance
SLK	Straight line kilometres
SNC	Structural number for pavement strength
SP	Sub-project
STOCH	An algorithm for assigning traffic devised by Dial (1971)
SUE	Stochastic user equilibrium
TTC	Travel time cost
UB	User benefit
VHT	Vehicle hours of travel
VKT	Vehicle kilometres travelled
VOC	Vehicle operating cost

Preface

The purpose of writing this book is to show how evolutionary computing in the form of genetic algorithm enables cost benefit analysis to be extended to cover the previously intractable problem of selecting from an overwhelmingly large number of possibilities the best set of future road projects and scheduling them in the best possible way. The book is based on the experience gained in substantial exploratory applications to optimize investment in regional roads, in urban roads and in road maintenance.

The innovations in methodology reported here would have been infeasible only a few years ago because the search procedure is so extensive. When the models were developed and applied they imposed heavy burdens on computing resources but the rapid gains in computer capacity subsequently – in keeping with 'Moore's Law' – have reduced this difficulty to a minor matter. Thus it is timely to present the approach and method in the belief that others, particularly road planners, will be in a position to adapt the procedures to their own professional needs.

A considerable part of the text covers analytical issues that are important in the development of the genetic algorithms and the subsidiary but crucial travel and traffic assignment models. However practically oriented readers should be able to use the material selectively in formulating their own applications.

It has been our objective to produce a fully integrated treatment of the subject, not a collection of papers. The four authors have contributed jointly. Nevertheless Chapters 7, 8 and 9 summarize the PhD studies of three of us, the particular author being mentioned at the beginning of each of these chapters.

To avoid excessive interruptions to the flow of the text only a limited number of references have been included within it. However there is a full list of references at the end of each chapter.

Finally we wish to acknowledge the help and support given by Main Roads Western Australia and the Australian Research Council.

John H.E. Taplin
Min Qiu
Vivian K. Salim
Renlong Han

1. Introduction

Access to good roads is a major service provided by government to the community. This service may be seen as simply meeting transport demands but it is also a contribution to the general objective of maximizing community welfare. The government needs to maintain and upgrade existing roads and sometimes construct new ones in an efficient, equitable and environmentally sustainable way. It may do the work through its own agencies or outsource all or part to the private sector.

Whatever the method of doing the work, keeping the road network in good order requires continuous review and development. At the planning stage transport policy objectives are developed or interpreted, road passenger and freight demands are predicted, the existing road inventory is investigated and gaps between future road needs and the existing supply are assessed. This stage should provide a forward plan which identifies road projects that are justified on the basis of economic, social and other criteria. Planning at this level focuses on long-term road needs and does not necessarily consider financial consequences.

Actions to implement the plan are identified in the subsequent project programming stage when financial and other constraints are taken into account. The outcome is a project construction timetable which specifies the funds to be allocated to each project over a period of years. Budget limitations make it impossible to include all identified projects in the timetable. After project programming comes the final stage which covers design and construction, the focus being on engineering details.

These stages become a rolling process. In each round of the process the impacts of the projects already implemented are used to update the planning database and sometimes projects which were left out of the previous timetable are now included.

GENETIC ALGORITHM: THE NEW PLANNING TOOL

It is our contention that genetic or evolutionary algorithms can radically improve road planning. Such algorithms are becoming so familiar that they need little introduction, but Chapter 4 is devoted to explaining how a genetic algorithm works. Recently reported applications in the transport field include optimizing the sequence of aircraft departures and optimizing three-dimensional highway alignments. This book will show that genetic algorithm can solve the previously insoluble problem of optimally selecting and timetabling road projects.

The applications start with the case of selecting new road projects from 34 possibilities in a rural area and optimally scheduling their construction. This involves finding the best among an astronomical number of selection and sequencing possibilities. The second application is in an urban area with 56 potential projects and correspondingly more possibilities which are complicated by the need to take account of morning and evening peaks.

The third application deals with maintenance. In many countries the major road engineering task has become prevention of system decline. Networks have been expanded to such an extent that controlling or reversing the aggregate deterioration has become the dominant task. Maintenance does not take the form of a limited number of well-defined projects but rather a continuum of activities which are individually fairly small and also heavily influenced by the time elapsed since previous work.

Maintenance planning is in terms of many small road sections or segments – 319 in the application reported in Chapter 9. But planning by segments means that the maintenance work to be implemented depends upon the time since the last treatment. This is incorporated in the solution procedure but the number of possibilities makes it a large computation task. Whereas one might tend to think that maintenance planning is a matter of reacting to emerging needs, it turns out that rigorous optimization of the forward maintenance plan gives a far better result.

THE GENERAL PLANNING PROBLEM

Many professionals have felt some degree of unease about formal methods of selecting projects and ordering them into a construction timetable. Planning engineers have found it necessary to amend such timetables to take account of the impacts of projects on each other or some other system effect that could be improved by reordering. They have generally been right to make changes if these were intended to remedy the inadequacy of any attempt to rank projects according to stand-alone evaluations.

Another difficulty arises when a whole programme of projects is evaluated: there is no way of knowing how much better an alternative programme might be. Experimentation with alternatives is likely to make some improvement but there is still no telling how much more the schedule could be improved. The task is to select the best complete investment timetable. A group of projects may be included in various ways in many potential schedules and the aim is to select the right schedule.

An unfortunate effect of these difficulties has been to cast doubt on the evaluation methods themselves, whereas the fault lies not with the methods but with incomplete application. The problem is the inability to assess alternative construction schedules rigorously. Our purpose is to present a rigorous but manageable method of selection and scheduling which takes full account of interactions. This means choosing among all possible schedules and timetables. The computations are substantial but can be done readily with the current generation of desk computers.

We raise no objection to the normal procedures used to evaluate road projects as far as they go. A standard package estimates traffic impacts using a suitable algorithm to assign and reassign traffic throughout the network in each year of the assessment period. Furthermore these procedures can be used to evaluate a whole programme of projects, taking account of all projected traffic responses. The task addressed here is to go further by simultaneously selecting the projects and ordering them into an optimal construction sequence. Naturally this must employ the existing system and network techniques but it must do a great deal more.

Much of the discussion will be about selecting and scheduling projects in large networks but the same fundamental problems arise in a small network. Determining a sequence of road projects in the network represented in Figure 1.1 would run up against the responsiveness of driver route selection to even small changes in road conditions. These responses make the outcome from each potential project sequence unique and assessing every possible sequence of only ten projects would require an analyst to consider more than three million cases. This is infeasible and an efficient search method is needed.

Questions Addressed

Here are some of the questions about optimal scheduling of interactive road projects that are considered in this book.

- What is different about a programme optimizing approach to road investments?
- How difficult is it computationally?
- How are standard evaluation methods and criteria incorporated?
- How are planning and budget constraints handled?
- What is genetic algorithm and how is it used to select and schedule projects?
- How is traffic generation and assignment handled?
- To what extent can standard software be used in optimization?

- How is the method applied to regional road networks?
- How is it applied to urban road networks?
- How is it used to optimize maintenance?
- To what extent does the method give the decision maker latitude to choose between solutions of similar merit?

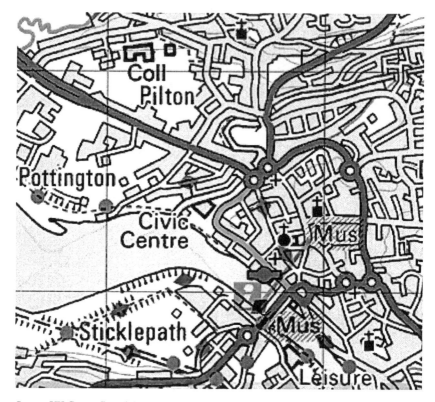

Source: UK Crown Copyright

Figure 1.1   Central Barnstaple, England

Traffic Interactions between Projects

At the most basic level the analyst must face up to the effects that projects have on each other. Adding or improving road links changes the pattern of network traffic. A project on a link not only affects traffic on substitute and complementary links but also on others not obviously related to it. Moreover the traffic impact of the project is affected by the construction of projects on other links. The benefits from the various projects are not additive.

Traffic interaction is obvious in congested cities but it also occurs in uncongested networks. The example in Figure 1.2 has been constructed to illustrate the fact that the net benefit is not the simple sum of separately calculated project benefits. The 10 000 vehicles per day between A and B use Route 1 (link 1) and Route 2 (links 2 and 3). There are three potential projects:

(a)   Upgrade link 2 to increase vehicle speed from 60 to 80 km/hr
(b)   Upgrade link 3 to increase speed from 80 to 100 km/hr
(c)   New Route 3 (link 4) 25 km long with vehicle speed of 120 km/hr.

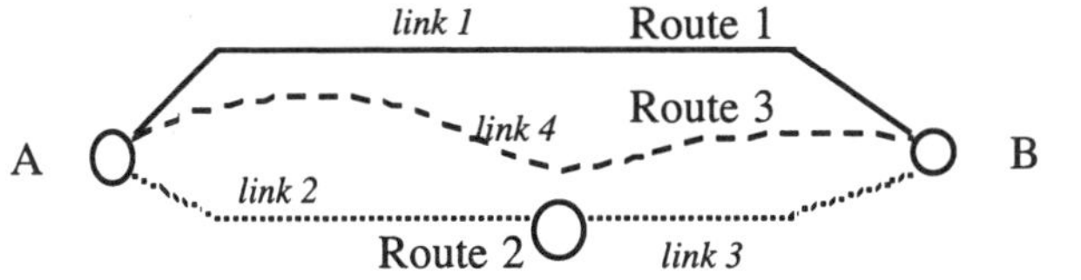

			Without project			With project completed		
Link	Route	Project	Length (km)	Speed (km/hr)	Travel time (hr)	Length (km)	Speed (km/hr)	Travel time (hr)
1	1	–	20	80	0.25	–	–	–
2	2	(a)	10	60	0.17	10	80	0.13
3	2	(b)	8	80	0.10	8	100	0.08
4	3	(c)	–	–	–	25	120	0.21

Source: Qiu, 2000

Figure 1.2   Network to illustrate interactions between road projects

Starting with the network, projects and data in Figure 1.2, traffic volumes have been calculated by assuming stochastic network loading with a multipath logit traffic assignment model in which the taste parameter θ is set to 1.0. The results are shown in Table 1.1. Chapters 5 and 6 deal with the estimation and use of such models. Project benefit in this example is the difference in total vehicle-hours between base and project cases. The following conclusions can be drawn from Table 1.1.

1. The joint benefit is not equal to the sum of the benefits from separate projects:
   • Joint benefit from (a) + (b) + (c) on links 2, 3 and 4 is 376 vehicle-hours whereas individually these projects would give an apparent sum of 481.
   • The joint benefit from (a) + (b) on links 2 and 3 is 313 vehicle-hours whereas individually these projects would give an apparent sum of 309.

2. The benefit from a project is greater when substitutes are not constructed than when they are. Project (c) on link 4 and (a) + (b) on links 2 and 3 are substitutes. The benefit from (c) is 172 without the substitute projects and 63 with them.
3. The benefit from single projects is smaller without complementary projects than with them. Projects (a) and (b) on links 2 and 3 are complements: the benefit from them jointly is 313 whereas singly the benefits are 209 and 99, making a slightly smaller total of 309.

Table 1.1   Vehicle time benefits from projects based on Figure 1.2

Case	Route	Time (hour)	Traffic (vehicles)	Vehicle hours	Benefit (hrs) = Base minus Project
Base	1	0.25	5042	1260	
	2	0.27	4958	1322	
				2583	–
Project (a)	1	0.25	4938	1234	
	2	0.23	5062	1139	
				2373	209
Project (b)	1	0.25	4992	1248	
	2	0.25	5008	1235	
				2483	99
Project (c)	1	0.25	3305	826	
	2	0.27	3250	867	
	3	0.21	3445	718	
				2411	172
Projects (a)+(b)	1	0.25	4888	1222	
	2	0.21	5112	1048	
				2270	313
Proj. (a) + (b)+ (c)	1	0.25	3238	809	
	2	0.21	3387	694	
	3	0.21	3375	703	
				2207	376

Note: Traffic has been calculated by a logit assignment model: $X_i = T.\exp\theta t_i / \sum_{\forall j \in L} \exp\theta t_j$ where X_i is traffic volume on route i, T is total traffic between centroids A and B, t_j is travel time on route j and $\theta\ (= -1)$ is a taste or distribution parameter.

Limited Capacity to Enumerate Project Sequences

When the number of interactive projects is small it may be possible to find the optimum construction timetable by enumerating all possible project sequences and choosing the one giving the highest value of the assessment criterion. However when the number of potential projects is moderately large the number of possible sequences becomes extremely large and it is impossible to use enumeration to find the optimum timetable, as shown in Table 1.2.

Table 1.2   Time to evaluate outcomes of possible project sequences

Number of projects, P	Number of possible project sequences, P!	Hours required to evaluate all possible project sequences
4	24	0.007
8	40 320	11.2
10	3 628 800	1 008
12	479 001 600	133 056
16	20 922 789 888 000	5 811 886 080

Note: The estimate of required time is based on the assumption that it takes one second to schedule the projects and calculate the costs and benefits.

It can be seen (Table 1.2) that when the number of potential projects is ten the number of possible sequences is more than 3.6 million and it would take a computer about 1000 hours to find the optimum timetable by enumeration. In reality there are likely to be many more than ten projects to be scheduled. The time required for enumeration becomes unacceptable and efficient search methods for the optimum project construction timetable are needed.

SCHEDULING INTERACTIVE ROAD PROJECTS

The naive approach to getting value for money is to rank all projects according to rate of return, benefit–cost ratio or other criterion. The evaluations required to do this are expected to take full account of traffic effects throughout the network and would give good results if the projects were independent. Improvements on this method of ranking are considered in Chapter 2.

Generally projects do affect each other to a greater or lesser degree and it is no good simply to implement them in apparent order of merit and hope that they will combine well. The interactions mean that the separate evaluations are no longer correct and can lead to serious misdirection of investment. The following two examples are simple illustrations of the problem of finding the best project sequence.

Major Road Projects

Table 1.3 shows road projects scheduled into a construction timetable on the basis of separate evaluations. Project 21 has the highest ranking and project 6 the lowest. Seventeen projects are completely scheduled into the five-year construction timetable and one partially (project 17) while seven are omitted because of limited funds. If these projects were truly independent then Table 1.3 would be the correct schedule to maximize benefits.

Table 1.3   Road construction timetable based on simple rank order

Project Ranking: $21 \rightarrow 8 \rightarrow 1 \rightarrow 12 \rightarrow 20 \rightarrow 2 \rightarrow 18 \rightarrow 4 \rightarrow 15 \rightarrow 25 \rightarrow 10 \rightarrow 7 \rightarrow 9 \rightarrow 3 \rightarrow 16 \rightarrow 5 \rightarrow 24 \rightarrow 17 \rightarrow 13 \rightarrow 14 \rightarrow 22 \rightarrow 19 \rightarrow 23 \rightarrow 11 \rightarrow 6$

Proj. No.	Cost $m	Year 1	Year 2	Year 3	Year 4	Year 5	Completed, $m
1	3		3				3
2	5		5				5
3	10				10		10
4	15			15			15
5	7					7	7
6	8						
7	6				6		6
8	18	13	5				18
9	3				3		3
10	4				4		4
11	21						
12	2		2				2
13	5						
14	26						
15	6			6			6
16	9				1	8	9
17	8					3	3
18	14		6	8			14
19	6						
20	9		9				9
21	17	17					17
22	22						
23	1						
24	12					12	12
25	7			1	6		7
Budget ($m)		30	30	30	30	30	150

However it is highly likely that they are not independent and a corrected schedule would either rearrange the first 18 projects or would both rearrange and replace one or more when interactions were taken into account. But the real difficulty is that anything approaching a complete search for the best sequence of the 25 projects is an impracticable task as Table 1.2 indicated.

Maintenance and Renewal Projects

The selection of road maintenance treatments, routine maintenance, patching, resealing, overlaying or reconstruction depends on roughness (Figure 1.3). The usual assessment is based purely on the surface condition of the road and has little to do with travel demand or interaction between projects. In theory the maintenance treatment is determined when roughness reaches a certain value on the international roughness index (IRI, from 0 to 10).

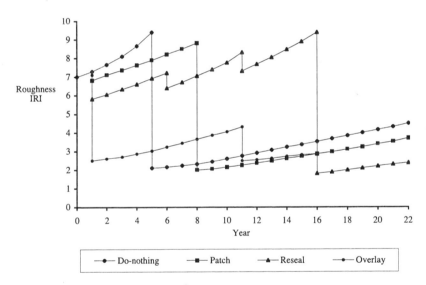

Source: Han, 2002

Figure 1.3   Maintenance treatments at different roughness levels

However when network effects are considered, one segment in relatively better condition might be found to require treatment before another one in worse condition. This is illustrated in Figure 1.4 by a simple rural network comprising nine 5-kilometre segments. Four of them (segments 6 to 9) are in good condition but the other five (segments 1 to 5) are in bad condition with roughness values greater than 4.0. The figures in brackets are average annual daily traffic (AADT) and roughness (IRI). The problem is to determine which of the segments is most deserving of maintenance expenditure. If road condition is the key criterion then segment 4 is the prime candidate. If the busiest road deserves attention first then segment 1 or 2 or 3 are more deserving.

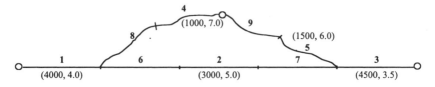

Source: Han, 2002

Figure 1.4   Hypothetical network (daily traffic and roughness in brackets)

Even if one road only is considered it is still difficult to tell which one of segments 1, 2 or 3 should be maintained first or when and how to maintain each segment to maximize benefits. The reason is that they are all related to each other and under a budget constraint the amount to spend on one segment depends on the expenditure on the others. There is a trade-off between traffic and segment condition, a trade-off between roads and a trade-off between time and space, even in a simple network. Without loss of generality this simple network can be extended to a real road network; maintenance treatments for all links determined only by heuristic methods are certainly not optimal for an entire network.

THE POTENTIAL OF EVOLUTIONARY COMPUTING

When the problem of schedule selection with project interactions has been addressed previously it has usually been done with some form of mathematical programming. In some cases this is adequate but there may be so much complexity, discontinuity and non-linearity that the problem becomes exceedingly difficult. This has been the position with multiple road projects where any rearrangement of project sequence produces radical changes in vehicle route choices throughout the network. Any change of this kind has a substantial effect on project benefits. Mathematical programming to schedule roadwork is discussed in Chapter 2.

    The invention of evolutionary computing, particularly genetic algorithm, has made available a new way of searching efficiently for the best system solution. Some mathematicians have reservations about the method because it is a form of computer-aided search which does not use gradient techniques. That means there is no guarantee that the solution is precisely optimal. Conversely the search is unlikely to be trapped by some discontinuity or at a sub-optimum. Production of a series of search results ensures that no reasonable possibility has been missed. In fact a great merit of the method is that it gives a variety of good solutions, sometimes differing appreciably in the details of work to be done, so that the decision maker can choose a programme which is about as good as any other but preferable on wider grounds.

Finding the best investment schedule for the whole system does not involve any departure from established evaluation criteria. They are applied across the whole schedule of projects. Each potential schedule generated in the course of the genetic algorithm search is assessed by a combination of traffic assignment and cost–benefit or multi-criteria evaluation. These topics are discussed in Chapter 3 and subsequently.

Other Potential Network Applications

There are other cases where a high degree of network interactiveness would make it difficult to select the best sequence of investments. A possible case is the emerging and proposed network of hydrogen filling stations in the California Hydrogen Highway plan. The sketch map in Figure 1.5 gives a general indication of the 2010 plan for such filling stations. Determining the optimum sequence of their construction would best be done with genetic algorithm. The location of even one new filling station could be expected to change the pattern of hydrogen car adoption and the locations where drivers would choose to refuel.

OUTLINE OF THE BOOK

There are three main parts in the book. The first comprises Chapters 2, 3 and 4 which deal with the issues in finding an optimal programme of projects, including the genetic algorithm search method. The second part, Chapters 5 and 6, deals with traffic modelling. The third major part comprises Chapters 7, 8, 9 and 10, which present applications of genetic algorithm to three large real-world problems as well as a hypothetical case designed to show how spreadsheets with an add-in can be used to solve a problem of moderate size.

Chapter 2 reviews some practical procedures already used to allocate investment to a road network and goes on to consider mathematical programming models designed to optimize such allocations, including the network design problem (NDP).

Chapter 3 opens with a brief review of the essentials of project evaluation and gives particular attention to user benefits. The discussion of genetic algorithm to select project schedules indicates the way in which evaluation criteria are incorporated and then reviews the problems and constraints that must be taken into account when a project sequence is transformed into a real construction timetable.

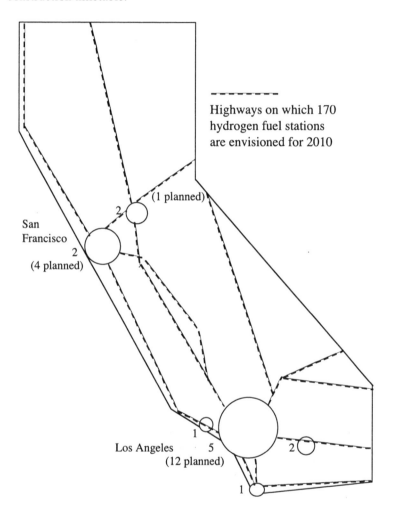

Highways on which 170 hydrogen fuel stations are envisioned for 2010

(1 planned)

San Francisco
2
(4 planned)

1

Los Angeles   5
(12 planned)

2

1

Source: Based on State of California, 2004

*Figure 1.5   California: existing and currently planned hydrogen fuel
                 stations and highways where another 170 are envisioned*

Chapter 4 presents the essentials of genetic algorithm operations, emphasizing those aspects on which the modeller needs to make decisions. The magnitudes of the search parameters are considered and the chapter ends with a brief discussion of the use of the idle time of a set of networked computers to accelerate genetic algorithm solution.

Chapter 5 deals with theoretical issues in traffic modelling and the formulation of models to represent user responses to changes in a road network. Urban traffic modelling is given specific attention.

Chapter 6 goes from theory to practice and deals with the estimation of rural and intercity traffic models. First it deals with the calibration of a combined traffic generation and assignment model. Then it presents an already estimated model and suggests a simple way of calibrating it for a new situation.

Chapter 7 presents the results of a study to optimize regional road investment. Convergence of the genetic algorithm solution is considered and the importance of having a number of similar solutions is addressed.

Chapter 8 presents the results of a large study to optimize an urban road investment programme. The big difference from the rural case is that congestion and time-of-day impacts are taken into account. Assessing for three times of day multiplies the whole computation task by almost three.

Chapter 9 presents the results of an even larger study to optimize the maintenance and renewal programme in a rural road network. In this case the elements of the genetic algorithm chromosome are not projects but road segments. Thus each potential solution is a sequence of segments that is transformed into a maintenance programme by a heuristic which takes account of the road condition at that time.

Chapter 10 shows how a spreadsheet workbook with a genetic algorithm add-in can find an optimal multiple project road investment timetable for a small network using a full traffic generation and assignment model.

Chapter 11 provides a review and raises some general issues and problems.

REFERENCES AND FURTHER READING

Berechman, J. (1995), 'Transport infrastructure investment and economic development', in Banister, D. (ed.), *Transport and Urban Development*, London: E&FN Spon, 17-35.

Bristow, A.L. and J. Nellthorp (2000), 'Transport project appraisal in the European Union', *Transport Policy*, **7**, 51-60.

Capri, S. and M. Ignaccolo (2004), 'Genetic algorithms for solving the aircraft-sequencing problem: the introduction of departures into the dynamic model', *Journal of Air Transport Management*, **10**, 345-351.

Coombs, H.M. and D.E. Jenkins (1994), *Public Sector Financial Management*, 2nd edition, London: Chapman & Hall, University and Professional Division.

Dickey, J.W. (1983), *Metropolitan Transportation Planning*, 2nd edition, Washington, DC: Hemisphere Publishing Corporation and McGraw-Hill Book Company.

Han, R.L. (2002), *Genetic Algorithm to Optimise the Allocation of Road Expenditure Between Maintenance and Renewal*, PhD thesis, University of Western Australia.

Jong, J-C. and P. Schonfeld (2003), 'An evolutionary model for simultaneously optimizing three-dimensional highway alignments', *Transportation Research Part B*, **37**, 107-128.

Janson, B.N., L.S. Buckels and B.E. Peterson (1991), 'Programming route improvements to the national highway network', *Transportation Research Record 1305*, Washington, DC: Transportation Research Board, 243-254.

Qiu, M. (2000), *Optimising a Road Project Construction Timetable for Rural Roads*, PhD thesis, University of Western Australia.

Roberts, P.O. (1971), 'Selecting and staging additions to a transport network', in Meyer, J.R. (ed.), *Techniques of Transport Planning*, vol. 1, Washington, DC: Brookings Institution, Transport Research Program, 251-276.

Salim, V.K. (2000), *Genetic Algorithms for the Evaluation and Scheduling of Urban Road Projects in Optimal Network Design*, PhD thesis, University of Western Australia.

State of California (2004), California Hydrogen Highway http://www.hydrogenhighway.ca.gov/.

2. Approaches to Scheduling Interactive Road Projects

It is well understood that adding or improving road links changes the pattern of network traffic. A project affects traffic not only on substitute and complementary links but also on others not obviously related to it. Moreover the traffic impact of the project is affected by projects elsewhere. It was noted in Chapter 1 that standard packages can take full account of such traffic impacts by assigning and reassigning traffic throughout the network in each year of the assessment.

However it is a sometimes confusing fact that normal road project evaluations which do take account of traffic interactions can still lead to the wrong conclusions. This will result if projects and their interactions are assessed one at a time and then ranked according to the individually calculated measure of benefit. When the procedure is extended to evaluating a whole schedule of projects the result will be correct in itself but there is still the problem of selecting from the huge number of such potential schedules as indicated in Chapter 1 (See Table 1.2).

A number of procedures or packages recognize this scheduling problem and use approximate methods to improve the selection and ordering of projects. In 1976 the problem of road investment selection and programming was seriously addressed in a series of US Transportation Research Board publications. Assessment of multiple alternative improvements was incorporated in the Highway Investment Analysis Package (HIAP) which worked on successively best marginal additions to the programme.

The following short review starts with a shifting base method using similar principles to HIAP. It has been applied to a problem already solved by genetic algorithm in order to test how closely it can approach the best available solution. This is followed by brief presentations of methods used in COBA (a version of cost–benefit analysis) and HDM-4 (Highway Development and Management) and concludes with a short discussion of the 'network design problem' and mathematical programming for scheduling road projects.

QUASI-OPTIMIZING WITH A SHIFTING BASE CASE

In order to provide a test of the extent to which a good procedure can fall short of the best, the urban investment study reported in Chapter 8 was subsequently reworked by a simpler method. The problem is to optimize the selection and scheduling of road projects on a freeway, two parallel arterial roads and three intersecting arterials (portion shown in Figure 2.1). The study network has 782 nodes, 2 335 links and 11 928 origin-destination pairs.

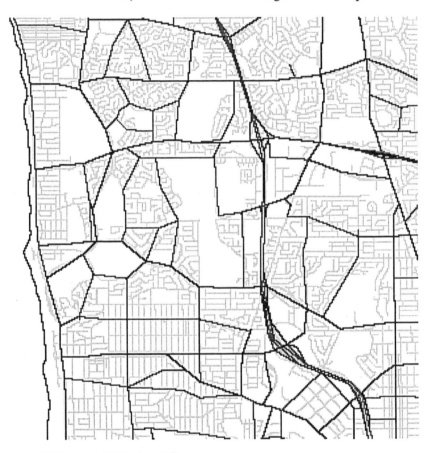

Source: Main Roads, Western Australia

Figure 2.1   Study corridor: freeway with parallel and intersecting arterials

The shifting base study used a rolling procedure. Projects were evaluated in diminishing bundles, taking account of the projects already implemented. Initially separate benefit–cost ratios were calculated for all potential projects and those with the highest ratios were notionally implemented in the first year up to the annual budget limit. In other words the projects with the best independently calculated benefit–cost ratios were allocated to the first year. If any selected project was not fully implemented due to the budget limit then it continued into the next year. In each subsequent year the network already improved by projects constructed in preceding years became the base and projects were re-evaluated. In each study year of every case a full traffic assignment was carried out.

The process was repeated to the end of the planning period. (It would stop earlier if there were no project left with benefit–cost ratio greater than one.) In this way a complete investment schedule was generated by selecting the projects in updated rank order until the budgets were exhausted.

Weakness in the Early Years

Figure 2.2 shows the genetic algorithm (GA) solution of Chapter 8 compared with the shifting base results. The results of ranking by independent ('naive') benefit–cost ratio are also shown. Benefits provide the appropriate comparison because the amounts of investment are identical.

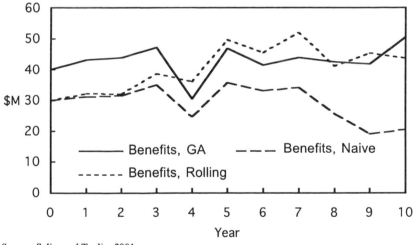

Source: Salim and Taplin, 2001

Figure 2.2   Annual benefits: alternative methods of scheduling projects

It is in the first four years that the benefits from the shifting base method clearly fall short; they are little better than the benefits from the naive ranking method. This relative failure in the early years is crucial because authorities are likely to follow a policy of re-evaluating all projects every few years, the planning horizon being extended as new information arrives and new forecasts are made.

In subsequent years there were benefit reversals because of the timing of freeway and other large project completions. In the longer term to year 30 (not shown) the accumulated benefits from the shifting base case remained below those of the genetic algorithm solution. The shifting base method gave fairly good results but its weakness was in being limited to interactions between consecutive bundles of projects whereas the genetic algorithm solution accounted for interactions between projects across all time periods.

To sum up, the shifting base method implements the apparently best value for money projects first. These are then removed from consideration and the remaining candidate projects are re-evaluated for the next planning year. However the order and sequence of subsequent projects is extremely important and the shifting base method cannot cope with this.

Although planners and policy makers plan for many years into the future, these plans are not static. As new information and data are brought to bear the planning process is repeated and existing plans are modified. Thus the crucial part of a plan is in its initial years and this is when the shifting base result falls short by about 25 per cent (Figure 2.2). The first year of the schedule determined by this method is its weakest because it is identical to naive ranking by benefit–cost ratio. It improves gradually but not until about the fourth year does it begin to be appreciably better than naive ranking.

REGIONAL ROAD PLANNING WITH COBA

The British COBA system of evaluating road projects provides for comprehensive evaluations of programmes of projects. Our comments focus on this aspect. The following quotation from the COBA Manual (2002) Vol. 13 Sect. 1 Ch. 4 Part 3 gives an indication of the way in which this procedure deals with interactions:

> ...where the planning of schemes is interrelated there arises a question of how to appraise a package of schemes which may be complementary or offering competing solutions to a traffic, operational or environmental problem. This is a strategic evaluation problem often referred to as the 'Scheme in Route' issue which involves the economic appraisal of a complete scheme strategy and the contribution made by its component sections.

The expression 'scheme in route' is important. The Manual goes on to say that the following matters need to be addressed:

- The optimal extent of the strategy and its overall economic worth.
- Priority ranking of start dates for sections of the strategy.
- Appraisal of the component sections within the strategy.
- Precise design standards and alignments for each component.

It also notes that clearly impracticable options should not be appraised.

The method of handling strategic evaluation problems is indicated by a schematic example in the Manual. There are four components in the notional strategy: A, B, C and D which may be competing, complementary or neutral with respect to each other. These give the following 15 strategy combinations on the assumption that all the schemes start in the same year:

A	A + B + D	B + C + D
A + B	A + C + D	C
A + C	B	C + D
A + D	B + C	D
A + B + C	B + D	A + B + C + D

Evaluation of each strategy combination involves modelling present and future traffic flows for each composite configuration.

The Manual takes the case where A + C + D has a higher net present value (NPV) than any other combination and considers which section of this strategy should be built first. It notes the possibility that the 'best' phasing may be to complete the strategy all at once. For other cases it goes on to say that the 'component which offers the highest NPV should be undertaken first. It is therefore necessary to test each scheme independently against the base "Do-Minimum" network that excludes all the other elements of the strategy to establish that section which delivers the highest NPV.'

At this stage the procedure is similar to our shifting base case presented at the beginning of the chapter, as indicated in the COBA Manual (2002) Vol. 13 Sect. 1, 4.9:

> If it is established that scheme A should be given priority then clearly it will form part of the network before other schemes in the strategy become operational. A is, therefore, added to the 'Do-Minimum' network against which C and D are tested respectively in order to establish which one of these schemes takes precedent over the other.

Exclusion and Isolation Analysis

The next step is to assess the worth of each component of the strategy. The incremental exclusion and isolation analysis is designed to check against possible overprovision and ensure that the best value for money is obtained, taking account of other schemes in the surrounding area. A particular section may be neutral with respect to the strategy or be in competition with other components, so leaving the strategy NPV unchanged or increased if it is not built.

Exclusion analysis

Each component is treated as a 'missing link' in the preferred strategy. Each link is appraised against a do-minimum base network which changes through time. In the example given in the Manual, it is assumed that the start dates for the preferred strategy A + C + D have been established as year 0, year 5 and year 10 respectively. The exclusion test for A is illustrated in Figure 2.3.

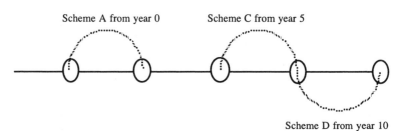

Do Minimum for Scheme A

Scheme C from year 5

Scheme D from year 10

Do Scheme A

Scheme A from year 0   Scheme C from year 5

Scheme D from year 10

Source: COBA Manual, 2002, vol. 13, section 1, Chapter 4, part 3, Figure 4/2

Figure 2.3   Exclusion analysis for scheme A

The economic appraisal of A is with respect to a base do-minimum network which includes scheme C from year 5 and D from year 10 onwards over the appraisal period (upper portion of Figure 2.3).

When scheme C is tested, it is done against a do-minimum network that includes A from year 0 and D from year 10. The exclusion test for D is against a do-minimum comprising A from year 0 and C from year 5.

Appraisal starts in the opening year of the first scheme, A in the example, and the final appraisal is 30 years after the opening of the last scheme, D in the example. Each test gives the NPV of the preferred strategy without the contribution of one of its components, indicating the NPV foregone if that section were not built. If a section is complementary to others then the NPV of the strategy with and without the excluded section will change significantly.

Isolation analysis
Each component is appraised against a do-minimum network which does not change through time and incorporates only those schemes that have an earlier start date. Thus A is compared in isolation to the do-minimum network in year 0, C is compared to a base network including A from year 0, while D is compared to a base network including A from year 0 and C from year 5.

The COBA Manual goes on to explain that isolating each section in turn shows the economic worth of a scheme if later sections in the strategy are not built. If sections are largely neutral with respect to each other then the action of isolating a section should not substantially change the NPVs of previous sections. If D complements the services of A and C then its implementation will improve the NPVs of A and C significantly. This technique shows how sensitive a scheme's benefits are to the assumption that the strategy will be completed.

The Significance of Interactions

The interactions mean that the overall strategy result is not simply the sum of the NPVs of the individual sections – the point we illustrated in Chapter 1, Table 1.1. The scheme in route analysis should normally give the results for component sections in exclusion and isolation and also for the strategy as a whole, where the entire strategy has been tested against a do minimum base case (COBA Manual, 2002, vol. 13, sect. 1, part 3, 4.12 to 4.15). The Manual goes on to say:

> ...a scheme that has a positive NPV in isolation is justified economically provided that the other future schemes in the strategy are not actually competing with it. However, on the assumption that the rest of the strategy is in fact completed, a scheme is justified even if it is negative in isolation, provided it is positive in exclusion and that the strategy itself is positive. In such cases, the negative isolation result shows the sensitivity of the scheme's

economic justification to the assumption that the strategy is completed.

This whole procedure is certainly an advance on the shifting base approach because it allows for an initial inclusion in the schedule to be removed subsequently if it does not complement the other elements of the strategy. Such complementarity extends through time.

Traffic in COBA

The main user responses calculated by COBA are route changes. Traffic is reassigned so that some travellers from A to B shift to an alternative route between A and B. User costs are calculated on the basis of a fixed trip matrix with the effects of daily and seasonal flow variations being estimated by formulae for speed/flow, junction delay, accident and vehicle operating cost. On the basis of traffic forecasts the calculations are repeated for each of the 30 years in the evaluation period and benefits are discounted to the base year.

If a scheme or combination of schemes is considered likely to cause a significant response other than reassignment then the use of a fixed trip matrix may be dropped. Examples given are schemes in congested conditions, long inter-urban routes and major estuary crossings. When a fixed trip matrix is not appropriate the user is advised to use variable trip matrix appraisal methods, the TUBA program being recommended (COBA Manual, 2002, Vol. 13, sect. 1, part 1, 3.2). The manual mentions trips being made at different times of day, trips to the same destination being made by a different mode of transport and generation of new trips where there were none previously (including the release of suppressed demand).

WORLD BANK MAINTENANCE PLANNING: HDM-4

The World Bank's HDM-4 is primarily aimed at planning within a single route but it does give some attention to network planning and optimization. The following comments are based on the HDM-4 Overview and Software User Guides (2000). They are two of the five manuals comprising the suite of HDM-4 maintenance management package documentation. The package is made available through the World Road Association (PIARC).

The focus is on pavement condition but the package provides a capacity for strategy analysis covering entire road networks. It deals with categories defined by factors affecting pavement performance and user costs. A road network matrix may be classified according to traffic, pavement type, pavement condition, environment or climatic zones and possibly functional classification. The Overview notes that it is possible to model individual road sections in the strategy analysis application but suggests that, because most road authorities are responsible for thousands of kilometres of roads, it is cumbersome to model individual segments (HDM-4, 2000, Vol. 1, 5.1).

Taking the example of high, medium and low traffic, two pavement types and good, fair and poor pavement condition, the Overview suggests that 18 (= 3 x 2 x 3) representative pavement sections could be used in a strategy analysis but says there is no limit to the number of representative sections. A more detailed road network matrix can be expected to give more accurate results. 'Strategy analysis may be used to analyse a chosen network as a whole, to prepare medium to long range planning estimates of expenditure needs for road development and conservation under different budget scenarios' (HDM-4, 2000, Vol. 1, 5.1). Suggested applications are:

- Medium to long-term forecasts of funding required to meet specified maintenance standards.
- Forecasts of long-term road network performance under varying levels of funding.
- Optimal allocation of funds to defined budget heads such as routine maintenance, periodic maintenance and development (capital).
- Optimal allocation of funds to sub-networks, for example by functional road class or by administrative region.
- Policy studies such as impact of changes to the axle load limit, pavement maintenance standards, energy balance analysis, sustainable road network size, evaluation of pavement design standards, etc.

Traffic in HDM-4

For each project alternative the user can define not only generated but also diverted traffic and there is a traffic diversion facility to model it. The AADT values are specified when defining normal traffic for the project and traffic diversion is specified by period and traffic type (HDM-4, 2000, Vol. 3, 7.14.4). In one of the examples, constructing a bypass causes 'significant redistribution of traffic between existing roads and the new road' but only a limited part of the network is considered (HDM-4, 2000, Vol. 1, Appendix C.6). Traffic flow patterns may be defined by time of day and season. Speed-flow types are specified in whatever detail is required.

Strategy Planning

Optimization under budget constraints is available for life-cycle analysis or a constrained multi-year forward programme. When a budget is being optimized for a life-cycle analysis, budget periods can be inserted, appended and deleted. However only one budget period is possible when optimizing a budget for a constrained multi-year forward programme.

A medium- to long-term investment strategy is executed for a set of sections, the optimization criterion and budget constraints being defined for each strategy analysis. 'The investment alternative is a combination of maintenance and improvement standards that are applied to a section.' The network matrix option allows for definition of a number of representative sections using aggregate parameters to represent the road network being analysed. (HDM-4, 2000, Vol. 3, 9.3).

An example

The example in the Overview is a network comprising 4267 km of paved roads and 3145 km of unpaved (gravel) roads (HDM-4, 2000, Vol. 1, Appendix A). The condition of the paved network is 22.3 per cent good, 36.2 per cent fair and 41.5 per cent poor. The standards for maintenance and network improvement comprise:

- Widening all paved roads with volume to capacity ratio greater than 0.8.
- Rehabilitation (structural overlay) of all paved roads in poor condition.
- Resealing (surface dressing) paved roads when surface deterioration exceeds 30 per cent.
- Reactive routine maintenance on paved roads comprising patching potholes immediately, sealing cracks, edge repairs and so on as required.
- Upgrading gravel roads carrying more than 250 vehicles per day to paved surface.
- Regravelling when the remaining gravel thickness falls below 50 mm.
- Grading gravel roads with medium traffic twice a year, and grading once a year for gravel roads carrying less than 100 vehicles per day.
- Routine maintenance to shoulders, drainage ditches, road markings and roadside furniture.

The objective is to determine the required funding to meet the standards and to monitor the effect of budget constraints on the long-term network performance trends. The steps in the HDM-4 procedure are:

- Create the representative road network matrix using the Strategy application.
- Define the characteristics of the vehicles that use the road network
- Specify traffic growth rates.
- Assign the maintenance and improvement standards to the road network matrix together with their unit costs.
- Run the HDM-4 Strategy application to determine the total budget requirement.
- Carry out constrained budget analyses.
- Review reports and graphs of the analyses conducted.

Results of the analysis of the example indicate that the ideal maintenance and improvement standards specified by the policy would require approximately US$56.2 million per year for the paved road network and US$21.2 million per year for the unpaved road network (based on the unit costs of the various road works). If only 50 per cent of the required funding were available this would result in a 54 per cent loss in road user benefits (compared with road user costs for the routine and recurrent option).

Program analysis
This is done to prioritize a long list of road projects at link level into a multi-year work programme subject to budget constraints. The analysis compares life cycle costs in the with and without project cases. Whereas strategy analysis groups road segments with similar characteristics, programme analysis deals with individual links and sections that are unique physical units. In both cases the problem is to find the combination of treatments that optimizes the objective function under the budget constraint. The HDM-4 programme analysis can be used to prepare a multi-year rolling programme subject to resource constraints. The incremental NPV–cost ratio is used as the ranking index to maximize benefits from each additional unit of expenditure.

HDM-4 Strategy Planning of the Estonian Road Network

This case study of network strategy in Estonia was prepared by the Estonian National Road Administration and Technical Centre with assistance and funding by the Finnish National Road Administration (Figure 2.4). The objective was to maximize NPV with a time horizon of 20 years. Unconstrained and budget constrained alternatives were analysed. Figure 2.4 summarizes the unconstrained result and shows average roughness being progressively reduced to an acceptable level.

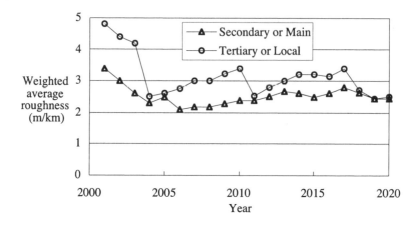

Source: Based on Kalliokoski, 2001

Figure 2.4   Result of unconstrained HDM-4 strategic analysis: Estonia

NEED-BASED PROJECT PRIORITIZATION

Need-based methods in various forms have been used for many years. Recently such a method has been presented as an alternative to cost–benefit analysis for prioritizing and selecting highway improvement projects (Kulkarni et al., 2004). The approach is based on developing a multi-attribute need function that quantifies relative concerns of a highway agency and the travelling public about various physical and operational deficiencies of highway segments. It is argued that cost–benefit analysis has major limitations when applied to a large-scale (statewide) highway construction programme and that these are overcome by a need-based approach. The latter has been implemented in the Kansas statewide highway improvement programme.

APPROXIMATE OPTIMIZATION METHODS: REVIEW

The fundamental problem with approximate methods of optimizing road investment schedules is that there are too many possibilities to examine. As noted in Chapter 1, there are 479 million possible sequences of 12 projects – and there are usually many more potential projects. Any search method, even genetic algorithm, must thread its way through them as efficiently as possible. This means spotting potentially winning sequences and avoiding losers.

It was shown at the beginning of this chapter that the shifting base method suffers from the problem that the early project selections fall seriously short of the optimum even though the modelling method takes full account of all network traffic interactions. Subsequent choices are made by taking preceding ones into account and as the process progresses there is increasing success in finding a winning sequence. However the early errors are serious because road authorities are likely to re-evaluate long-term plans every few years, thus making the early stages crucial.

The COBA method of exclusion analysis does shift the whole investment schedule closer to the optimum. In the example Scheme A has priority (in benefit terms) in the A + C + D strategy but it is still tested by exclusion analysis. This would appear to open the possibility that C and D may diminish A's contribution to NPV to the extent that it may be omitted from the strategy. This is certainly an advance on the shifting base method in which the first project selected cannot be displaced. Nevertheless the sample enumeration of possibilities reflects COBA's use primarily for limited scheduling problems rather than full network optimization.

The HDM-4 approach avoids the problem of multiple potential sequences by simply ranking projects incrementally according to marginal capital efficiency. Again this is akin to the shifting base method of selecting as the next additional project the one that makes the biggest economic contribution to the whole strategy. The HDM-4 focus is on restoration or enhancement of pavement condition including the addition of lanes. The benefit calculations take account of the detailed differences between the pavement impacts of various classes of vehicle and the projected traffic growth on each link. Also the fact that some alternatives include traffic diversion and generation is taken into account but the network is not fully interactive.

The need-based approach is generalized but it appears to take limited account of interactions and therefore falls short of network optimization.

In summary the methods reviewed are considerably better than basing a road programme on separate cost–benefit evaluations. However they do not effectively sort through the millions of possible road project sequences. An optimized selection of investments for an interactive network has been the goal of a long series of theoretical papers dealing with the 'network design problem'.

THE NETWORK DESIGN PROBLEM

The transport network design problem (NDP) has been classified broadly into discrete and continuous cases. The discrete problem was stated by LeBlanc (1975) as follows:

> ...to choose an optimal subset from a set of proposed link additions to an existing road network. The aim is to find that network configuration whose user optimum flows result in the smallest vehicle hours. Associated with each proposed link is a cost of construction; in addition, a budget is given that limits total expenses incurred. Of course, the optimal improvements will be determined by the allowable expenditures.

For each potential link development in the discrete case the decision is either to implement the project or not. The possible increments of road capacity are fixed and predetermined. For his seminal paper, LeBlanc used a branch and bound strategy to solve a problem in Sioux Falls, South Dakota (Figure 2.5), with a network that consisted of 24 nodes, 76 arcs and 552 OD pairs. This has since been used in many other studies as a test network.

To overcome the computational difficulties with a large number of integer variables the NDP has been recast into continuous form. This eliminates the combinatorial nature of the discrete problem and makes it amenable to solution by non-linear programming. The transformed problem can be specified to minimize costs subject to the variation of expenditure on any link. The decision variable not only determines whether a link should be improved but also defines how much improvement is optimal. Investment costs may be represented by convex or concave functions.

An important difference between the two functional types is that the convex investment function favours minor additions to existing capacity while the concave investment function favours large increases in capacity (as in the addition of new links). Hence convex functions reflect increasing user cost due to road or link congestion, while concave functions represent economies of scale. On the Sioux Falls network it was found that the Hooke and Jeeves search method for continuous variables in both convex and concave functions decreases congestion by about 23 per cent, which is more than the 13 per cent obtained from the discrete model. Hence the fractional improvements in practical capacity make a difference in the performance of the traffic network.

However it may be difficult to translate the results into reality. When small fractional improvements to a large number of links are indicated there is the practical problem of substantial start-up costs. In terms of computing efficiency, processing time is decreased when the continuous method is used. An advantage of the alternative discrete model is that it can easily allow for an investment to affect the free-flow speed on arcs while it is not so obvious how this may be achieved in the continuous model. In addition, where the type of investment differs, for example if the competing design alternatives are a transit service or a road capacity improvement, then the discrete model is the feasible method.

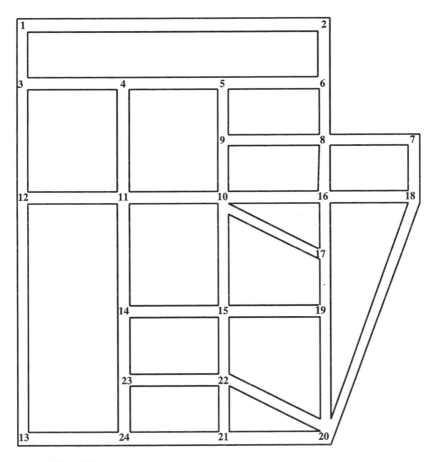

Source: Salim, 2000

Figure 2.5   Test network with 24 nodes in Sioux Falls, South Dakota

Solution Methods

The NDP may be formulated as a bi-level programming problem. The upper level is to minimize the total user and construction costs with respect to adding new roads and increasing the capacities of existing links subject to a construction budget constraint. The lower level of the problem is formulated as either a deterministic user equilibrium traffic assignment problem or a system optimization problem to solve for traffic flows on links.

The upper level of the NDP may be formulated as a discrete network design problem (DNDP), which models the addition of new road links as integer variables, or as continuous with divisible link capacity enhancements (the continuous network design problem, CNDP). A mixture of the DNDP and CNDP may also be used (mixed network design problem, MNDP). Solution of the DNDP needs a branch-and-bound algorithm and is impractical for large problems.

The continuous model makes the problem more tractable mathematically but this has to be balanced against realism. It can be argued that road capacity does vary in a more or less continuous manner with road width, making the CNDP appropriate. This is true in determining road link capacity. On the other hand it may make little sense to improve road capacity in a continuous way: adding two-thirds of a lane to a freeway for example.

SCHEDULING BY MATHEMATICAL PROGRAMMING

As noted in the previous section, mathematical programming has been the preferred approach to the network design problem (NDP). In other studies similar to the road project timetable problem two types of linear program have been used. They have been formulated to select:

- an optimum combination of projects subject to a budget constraint; or
- an optimum combination of projects scheduled in an optimal construction sequence.

Linear and non-linear programming have been used in general project management, particularly for resource allocation and to shorten the duration of a project. These applications can be extended to more than one project so that they are scheduled for completion at minimum cost and subject to jointly imposed resource constraints. Time steps are readily added.

A linear program to determine a road project timetable can be extended to multiple objectives as goal programming. This is akin to multi-criteria analysis (MCA) but with more power to explore relationships between projects. The objective of a goal program is to minimize the sum of weighted deviations from unachievable goals.

This method has been used to optimize the allocation of available funds between a small number of improvements and routine maintenance treatments over an entire highway system and also to select and schedule road projects on the basis of policy goals as well as the usual economic efficiency goals. If decision variables are restricted to integer values then goal and integer programming can be combined.

Budget and other constraints can be imposed when scheduling road projects. A linear program can readily handle project linkages, divisibility of project payoffs, limits to annual expenditure on individual projects, preferred investment profiles over years for individual projects and projects constructed in stages. These constraints can be specified in a linear program because they are all linear.

Linear Programming and Traffic

Non-linearities make road projects difficult to schedule. The traffic speed-flow relationship is nonlinear and so too is the function used to distribute uncongested traffic between alternative routes (as in Table 1.1 of Chapter 1). A mathematical program with non-linear functions can be used to assign traffic to a network of moderate size – but with some difficulty. Adding multiple investment options and time steps to deal with project selection and scheduling increases the computational difficulty. However it may be feasible to deal with the non-linear functions by using successive or piecewise linear approximations.

One way to investigate this issue is to incorporate a traffic assignment procedure as a set of constraints or as a lower-level program through which traveller responses to changes in the road network can be captured (Yang and Bell, 1998). Nevertheless it would be difficult to include traffic assignment in a linear program searching for the optimum project timetable.

A more tractable approach may be to use the result of traffic assignment as an input to the linear program so that some or all projects can be implemented together. The objective in these programs is to maximize the sum of pay-offs contributed by all projects individually, but these contributions are dependent on each other and there is a different traffic outcome for each combination. Separating traffic assignment and the search for the optimum project timetable thus limits the capacity of linear programming to handle project interaction directly.

It might be possible to combine a travel demand model, a project evaluation procedure and a linear program and to repeat them sequentially. The iterative process would use results from the previous linear program to modify project contributions. Nevertheless this repetitive framework could not guarantee convergence of the solution to the optimum because the solution space is non-convex and has many good sub-optima.

A linear program has been specified to handle interaction between two projects in two steps (Shortreed and Crowther, 1976). The first calculates the contribution of each project to the objective function when only that project is implemented. Then the joint contribution of both projects implemented together is calculated and also the difference between the sum of the two independent contributions and the joint contribution.

The second step is to create dummy variables for these differences. When the two projects are implemented together, the dummy variable for the project pair is equal to 1, otherwise 0. This model may deal with the road project timetable problem for several years.

It is theoretically possible to extend this type of model to more than two related projects in a group. The drawback is that it has to enumerate all possible project combinations and then calculate the differences between the sum of the independent contributions and the joint contribution for each of the possible combinations. Since the number of all possible combinations for n projects is 2^n, this model would become computationally intractable when there is an appreciable number of related projects. Another difficulty is that the definition of related projects is arbitrary. The related projects should be defined on the basis of substitutability and complementarity which are not necessarily apparent from the relative locations of projects in the network.

In another version of the linear transport problem, the decision variable is either 1 for building the project or 0 for not building it (Roberts, 1971). The objective is to minimize the sum of total travel and investment costs. The model can elegantly analyse the pay-off interdependencies between projects but the objective function is too simplistic to cope with the objective of maximizing the total net present value of projects included in a timetable. This is more complex than the total of travel and investment costs.

In addition the traffic assignment model used in this linear program is based on all-or-nothing assignment, which is not a good representation of route choice in rural road networks. All-or-nothing assignment implies that travellers always choose the shortest routes; but travellers on uncongested rural roads select a variety of routes which are not always the shortest. To represent this behaviour requires the use of stochastic network loading to assign the traffic. This network planning model is essentially a simplified version of the DNDP where all-or-nothing instead of user equilibrium assignment is used.

Mixed-Integer Non-linear Programming for Road Maintenance

In a recent mathematical programming formulation based on discrete control theory (Ouyang and Madanat, 2004) a non-linear pavement performance model and integer decision variables are incorporated into a mixed-integer non-linear program (MINLP). This pavement rehabilitation model minimizes the life-cycle cost for a finite horizon. It solves the problem of multiple rehabilitation activities in many locations, using empirical models of deterioration and rehabilitation effectiveness.

As illustrated in Chapter 1 Figure 1.3, highway pavement roughness follows a saw-tooth trajectory over time as the pavement deteriorates and is resurfaced. However the maintenance and rehabilitation decisions are governed by budget constraints and resource availability. Whereas the highway authorities allocate resources for rehabilitation at the beginning of a budget year, the deterioration is continuous.

The decision for each pavement segment in each year is whether to rehabilitate and to what degree. The goal is to minimize the net present value of life-cycle costs for the agency and the users over a finite horizon. A branch-and-bound solution is used for this mixed-integer program. Rehabilitation measures are selected sequentially to maximize objective function increases – an optimal increment approach. The total expenditure is divided into multiple single-action problems so that each gives an optimal solution under all constraints.

Starting from the beginning of the planning period, the best combination of time, intensity and facility is chosen. When a facility is selected for an optimal action at a certain time, that year's budget and the facility condition are updated. The steps are repeated and actions are selected until any additional action would decrease the objective function. This specification is less general than in the maintenance optimization of Chapter 9 but is a good approach to the timing of maintenance.

Limitations of NDP and Mathematical Programming Methods

The differences between the full road project scheduling problem and the NDP and mathematical programming approaches can be summarized as follows:

- The objective is to maximize the net present value of projects in a construction timetable for a multiple-year program, whereas the NDP objective is to minimize the total travel and construction costs resulting from new roads and increased capacities of existing links. The optimization in the NDP has usually been limited to one or two time periods.
- In mathematical programming for project scheduling, only all-or-nothing traffic assignment can be incorporated within the program. As traffic assignment is the key to capturing the traveller's route choice behaviour and to investigating interdependence between projects on a road network, failure to use stochastic network loading assignment makes linear programs less relevant to the scheduling of road projects in a rural network. In the urban case, all-or-nothing assignment may be appropriate but speed–flow functions are non-linear.

The project scheduling problem is different from those that can be solved through the NDP or mathematical programming. The problem involves multiple years, complex constraints, responsive travel demand, stochastic traffic assignment or non-linear speed–flow and the objective is to maximize the total net present value of projects.

In the case of a rural road network, mathematical programming for project scheduling can handle a variety of constraints but has limited capability to incorporate a traffic assignment model reflecting traveller route choices. Consequently it cannot properly investigate the interdependencies between projects in searching for the optimum timetable.

BALANCING REALISM AND OPTIMALITY

Optimally scheduling interdependent road projects is a combinatorial programming problem. It can be transformed into a continuous specification – with some degree of approximation and simplification – for solution by linear programming. This approach finds the solution with limited computation and preserves the essence of the original problem to some extent. In other words the problem of optimal road project scheduling can be formulated in various ways depending on study focus and resource availability. The extent to which the solution is close to the true optimum depends on how realistic are the assumptions. Thus the deviations of various solutions from the true optimum depend on the realism of the assumptions, as indicated schematically in Figure 2.6.

For road project scheduling, mathematical programming can handle a range of realistic constraints including limited pay-off interdependence between projects, budgets and project linkages. However its efficiency in finding the optimum may suffer when more realistic assumptions are incorporated, for example strong non-linearity and non-differentiability of the objective function. Realistic modelling of route choice by road users introduces extreme difficulty.

Consequently mathematical programming may be abandoned in favour of heuristic search methods. Even then solving a more complete formulation of the problem of scheduling road projects by a heuristic search method is not necessarily optimal. However an imperfect solution to an adequately specified problem may be much better than an 'optimal' solution to an inadequately specified problem.

A strong motive for using a heuristic method to solve a real-world problem is to avoid oversimplifying the formulation in order to make it amenable to mathematical programming. A further objective is to find better solutions which are not guaranteed to be optimal but preserve the real-world features as much as possible. Though the trade-off between assumption realism and solution optimality is a matter of judgement, heuristic methods have been very successful in scheduling projects for a large road network.

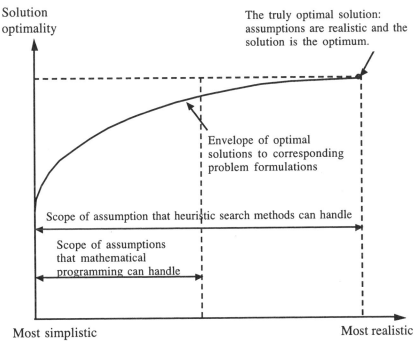

Source: Qiu, 2000

Figure 2.6   Assumption realism versus solution optimality

The intensive computation required by heuristic search methods has previously limited their application to practical problems, but advances in computer technology have virtually eliminated this difficulty. It is now possible to formulate a complex and realistic programming problem, such as a road project construction timetable, and to find the optimal or near-optimal solution with a genetic algorithm.

The next chapter deals with the basics of project evaluation as they are applied to the search for a complete schedule of projects. The latter part of the chapter deals with the effects of constraints and commonly imposed restrictions on the selection and timetabling of projects.

REFERENCES AND FURTHER READING

Incremental Investment Schedules

Gruver, J.E., F.P. Patron, J.H. Batchelder, and R.D. Juster, (1976), 'Highway investment analysis package', *Transportation Research Record 599*, Washington, DC: Transportation Research Board, 13-18.

Juster, R.D. and W.M. Pecknold, (1976), 'Improving the process of programming transportation investments', *Transportation Research Record 599*, Washington, DC: Transportation Research Board, 19-24.

Salim, V.K. and J.H.E. Taplin (2001), 'Optimizing urban road network development policy: comparison of investment timetables determined by genetic algorithm and by separate cost-benefit ratios', *International Journal of Transportation, Privatization and Public Policy*, **1** (1), 3-36.

Network Investment Planning

COBA Manual (2002), *Economic Assessment of Road Schemes*, Department of Transport, Highways Agency, UK, May.

HDM-4 (2000), *Highway Development and Management Series*, Washington, DC: World Bank.

Hegazy, T., A. Elhakeem and E. Elbeltagi (2004), 'Distributed scheduling model for infrastructure networks', *Journal of Construction Engineering and Management*, **130** (2), 160-167.

Kalliokoski, A., Finnish Road Enterprise (2001), 'Case study: network level strategy for paved roads in Estonia', HDM-4 Tutorial for the 5th International Conference on Managing Pavements.

Kulkami, R.B., D. Miller, R.M. Ingram, C-W. Wong and J. Lorenz (2004), 'Need-based project prioritization: alternative to cost-benefit analysis', *Journal of Transportation Engineering* **130** (2).

Roberts, P.O. (1971), 'Selecting and staging additions to a transport network', in Meyer, J.R. (ed.), *Techniques of Transport Planning Vol. 1*, Washington, DC: Brookings Institution, Transport Research Program, 251-276.

Network Design Problem

Abdulaal, M. and L.J. LeBlanc (1979), 'Continuous equilibrium network design models', *Transportation Research B*, **13B**, 19-32.

Boyce, D.E. and B.N. Janson (1980), 'A discrete transportation network design problem with combined trip distribution and assignment', *Transportation Research B*, **14B**, 147-154.

Chan, Y., T.S. Shen and N.M. Mahaba (1989), 'Transportation-network design problem: application of a hierarchical search algorithm', *Transportation Research Record 1251*, Washington, DC: Transportation Research Board, 24-34.

Chang, C. and S. Chang (1993), 'A heuristic algorithm for solving the discrete network design problem', *Transportation Planning and Technology*, **17**, 39-50.

Dantzig, G.B. and S.F. Maier (1979), 'Formulating and solving the network design problem by decomposition', *Transportation Research B*, **13B**, 5-17.

Davis, G.A. (1994), 'Exact local solution of the continuous network design problem via stochastic user equilibrium assignment', *Transportation Research B*, **28B**, 61-75.

Dionne, R. and M. Florian (1979), 'Exact and approximate algorithms for optimal network design', *Networks*, **9**, 37-39.

Friesz, T.L. (1985), 'Transportation network equilibrium, design and aggregation: key developments and research opportunities', *Transportation Research A*, **19A**, 413-427.

Hoang, H.H. (1973), 'A computational approach to the selection of an optimal network', *Management Science*, **19** (5), 488-498.

LeBlanc, L.J. (1975), 'An algorithm for the discrete network design problem', *Transportation Science*, **9**, 183-199

LeBlanc, L.J. and M. Abdulaal (1984), 'A comparison of user-optimum versus system-optimum traffic assignment in transportation network design', *Transportation Research B*, **18B**, 115-121.

LeBlanc, L.J. and D.E. Boyce (1986), 'A bilevel programming algorithm for exact solution of the network design problem with user-optimal flows', *Transportation Research B*, **20B**, 259-265.

Los, M. (1979), 'A discrete-convex programming approach to the simultaneous optimisation of land use and transportation', *Transportation Research B*, **13B**, 33-48.

Melinyshyn, W., R. Crowther, and J.D. O'Doherty (1973), 'Transportation planning improvement priorities: development of a methodology', *Highway Research Record 458*, 1-12.

Pearman, A.D. (1979), 'The structure of the solution set to network optimisation problems', *Transportation Research B*, **13B**, 81-90.

Poorzahedy, H. and M.A. Turnquist (1982), 'Approximate algorithms for the discrete network design problem', *Transportation Research B*, **16B**, 45-56.

Rothengatter, W. (1979), 'Application of optimal subset selection to problems of design and scheduling in urban transportation networks', *Transportation Research B*, **13B**, 49-63.

Salim, V.K. (2000), *Genetic Algorithms for the Evaluation and Scheduling of Urban Road Projects in Optimal Network Design*, PhD thesis, University of Western Australia.

Shortreed, J. H. and R. F. Crowther (1976), 'Programming transport investment: a priority-planning procedure', *Transportation Research Record 574*, Washington, DC: Transportation Research Board, 48-57.

Xiong, Y. and J.B. Schneider (1995), 'Processing of constraints in transportation network design problem', *Journal of Computing in Civil Engineering*, **9** (1), 21-28.

Yang, H. and M.G.H. Bell (1998), 'Models and algorithms for road network design: a review and some new developments', *Transport Reviews*, **18**, 257-278.

Mathematical Programming and Evolutionary Search

Bäck, T., U. Hammel, and H. Schwefel (1997), 'Evolutionary computation: comments on history and current state', *IEEE Transactions on Evolutionary Computation*, **1** (1), 3-17.

Bergendahl, G. (1969), 'A combined linear and dynamic programming model for interdependent road investment planning', *Transportation Research*, **3**, 211-228.

Fogel, L.J. (1995), 'The valuated state space approach and evolutionary computation for problem solving', in Palaniswami, M., Y. Attikiouzel, R.J. Marks, D. Fogel, and T. Fukuda (eds), *Computational Intelligence – A Dynamic System Perspective*, IEEE Press, 129-136.

Ouyang, Y. and S. Madanat (2004), 'Optimal scheduling of rehabilitation activities for multiple pavement facilities: exact and approximate solutions', *Transportation Research A*, **38A**, 347-365.

Sinha, K.C., M. Muthusubramanyam, and A. Ravindran (1981), 'Optimisation approach for allocation of funds for maintenance and preservation of the existing highway system', *Transportation Research Record 826*, Washington, DC: Transportation Research Board, 5-8.

Taplin, J.H.E., M. Qiu, and Z. Zhang (1996), 'Policy-sensitive selection and phasing of road investments with a goal program', *Transport Policy*, **2** (4), 251-256.

Taylor, B.W. and A.J. Keown, (1983), 'An integer goal programming model for solving the capital allocation problem of metropolitan mass transportation agencies', *Transportation Research A*, **17A**, 375-383

Theberge, P.E. (1987), 'Microcomputer linear programming model for optimizing state and federal funds directed to highway improvements', *Transportation Research Record*, 1156, Washington, DC: Transportation Research Board, 1-9.

3. Selection of Project Schedules

It was noted in Chapter 1 that finding the best investment schedule for a whole network does not involve any departure from established evaluation criteria. The brief review in the first part of this chapter will not only remind readers of the essentials of project evaluation methods but also show how these are incorporated into the integrated procedure. The nature of the approach makes net present value the key criterion supplemented by the ratio of benefits to costs, particularly in incremental form. Multi-criteria evaluation can also be incorporated. The latter part of the chapter deals with the effects of constraints and commonly imposed restrictions on the selection and timetabling of projects.

EVALUATION BASICS

The result of an economic evaluation of a single investment proposal or a schedule of them is usually expressed in a summary measure which may be net present value, the ratio of benefits to costs, the rate of return or some kind of weighted sum. We may also ask about winners and losers, about the distribution of benefits and disbenefits. The Pareto criterion that nobody should lose has generally been considered too restrictive, and project acceptance is based on the compensation principle that the gainers should be able to compensate the losers and still be better off.

Compensation is merely hypothetical, so that the actual welfare outcome is uncertain, but it is safe to say that a given benefit or cost usually means more to a poor person than to a rich one. One approximate way of reducing any inequitable effects of project selection is to weight benefits and costs by the reciprocal of the average income or status (or both) of those affected according to their residential locations. Another is to incorporate such distributional effects in a set of weighted multiple criteria.

Standard cost–benefit evaluation also includes some corrections, particularly with respect to taxation, but these are unlikely to affect the selection and ranking of road projects. Such corrections have been explained by a number of writers such as Sugden and Williams (1978). However the selection and ordering of urban road projects may need to take account of environmental and social effects such as severance of a community.

Discounting Future Costs and Benefits

Virtually all forms of economic evaluation weigh the future against the present. It is a matter of how people value future benefits – including benefits to future generations – in relation to current sacrifices as compared with potential returns from alternative investments. The social time preference discount rate is related to the way people value future benefits against present sacrifices, whereas the opportunity cost of capital rate is about alternative investments. The time preference rate is expected to be lower than the opportunity cost rate and a government may compromise between the two when prescribing a discount rate for public projects.

Because most of the costs and benefits of a project ultimately represent withdrawals from or increments to consumption, there is a strong argument for the discount rate to be the consumer's rate of time preference. It has also been suggested that as society becomes more concerned about timing of benefits and costs, and less concerned about economic growth, the time-preference basis will become the more important foundation. However there is no satisfactory way of estimating a social rate of time preference for long-term projects.

Many treasury officials prefer a discount rate based on the opportunity cost of capital rather than on the social rate of time preference. This is seen as ensuring that public investment does not displace higher-yielding private investment. But it can be argued that this is correct only where public provision of facilities completely displaces private provision.

The time preference rate and the government borrowing rate provide an approximate lower limit (say 2-4 per cent) while the market rate and the opportunity cost rate of return give an upper limit (say 7-10 per cent). If one of the lower rates were used as the public discount rate then the opportunity cost of public investment would generally be understated. Conversely a higher rate (7-10 per cent) tends to overstate the opportunity cost of funds taken from the private sector.

These rates are in real terms so that projects are evaluated as if prices will be constant in the future. If the inflation rate is 3 per cent then the market equivalent of a 7 per cent real public sector discount rate would be 10 per cent in the private sector.

A way to allocate efficiently from a fixed budget is to use an equivalent opportunity cost approach. The discount rate is set at the highest internal rate of return available from unfunded projects. This may give a discount rate as high as 10 per cent or even more.

A number of writers take the view that no single discount rate will be satisfactory under all circumstances because discount rates, like all other prices, vary according to the situation and are sensitive to many factors.

The difficulties in selecting a rate have led some governments to establish a uniform or central discount rate, often set at a relatively high level around 10 per cent, to provide a severe test of the merit of alternatives. For example the Chinese government's specification of a real rate of 12 per cent for road projects was in force for more than a decade.

Whatever choice is made, it is advisable to test two or more discount rates. Management then has a basis for judging the sensitivity of the results to the discount rate and is in a position to make a more enlightened decision. If it is not feasible to repeat the whole selection and scheduling procedure at a different discount rate then an alternative test rate can be used to recalculate the net present values of the best solutions in order to test the sensitivity of their ranking to the interest rate.

In some cases there is a practical objection or limitation to the use of a low discount rate. At a low rate the discounted benefits may go on increasing year by year so that the length of the evaluation period will arbitrarily determine the total discounted net benefit. At a higher rate the present value of the benefits will decline in magnitude so that lengthening the evaluation period will not have a decisive effect. This issue arises in Chapter 8.

Social Cost–Benefit Evaluation

In cost–benefit evaluation, costs and benefits are discounted to a suitable base year. Rarely is a future year selected but such a base – requiring compounding instead of discounting or a mixture of both – can be used in order to provide a comparison with some non-quantifiable outcome at a future time. In all other cases the operative word is 'present', meaning a year at or about the commencement of project outlays. The net present value (NPV) comprises the discounted costs less the discounted benefits, the rate of return is the rate that gives a zero NPV, and the benefit–cost ratio is obtained by expressing discounted benefits and associated costs as a ratio to the constrained capital outlay.

While net present value (NPV) can be expressed as the difference between the two sums when benefits and costs are discounted, it can be calculated identically as:

$$NPV = \sum_{t=0}^{n} (Benefit_t - Cost_t)/(1+D)^t \tag{3.1}$$

where *Benefit_t* and *Cost_t* are the benefit and cost in year *t*, *D* is the discount rate and *n* is the analysis period, usually taken to be equal to the longest service life of any capital item in the project being analysed.

There can be no ambiguity about discounting benefits and costs to a single value but projects of different magnitudes may make the NPV misleading because a large project of low capital efficiency might appear to outrank a smaller project of higher capital efficiency. However for a programme of projects, the topic of this book, the selection among mutually exclusive alternative schedules within a fixed budget can be unambiguously based on NPV because the relative magnitude problem does not arise.

The internal rate of return (IRR) is the discount rate which makes the present value of all expected benefits just equal to the present value of all expected costs so that the NPV is zero. Finding the discount rate which makes the NPV zero means satisfying the following:

$$\sum_{t=0}^{n}(Benefit_t - Cost_t)/(1+D)^t = 0 \qquad (3.2)$$

There is a possibility that more than one rate could satisfy this equation; this might occur with large fluctuations in costs and benefits. It is convenient to find the rate of return iteratively within a reasonable range up to about 20 per cent by a trial-and-error procedure. The project or investment programme will be acceptable if the rate of return is greater than a predetermined critical (or 'hurdle') discount rate. When the NPV or benefit–cost ratio is used to assess public sector projects it is useful to calculate the IRR as additional information.

The benefit–cost ratio is widely used by governments as a capital efficiency ratio for setting priorities. The appropriate form is:

$$\frac{B}{C_0} = \frac{\sum_{t=1}^{n}(B_t - C_t)/(1+D)^t}{C_0} = \frac{NPV + C_0}{C_0} \qquad (3.3)$$

In Figure 3.1 the constrained capital input to be evaluated is shown in years 0, 1 and 2. This is discounted to the base year. The rest of the flows including the negative in year 15 (due to renewal) are also discounted to the base year and expressed as a ratio to the discounted constrained capital.

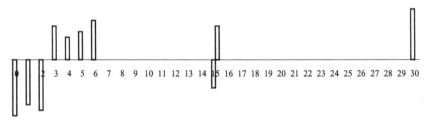

Source: Han, 2002

Figure 3.1   Hypothetical cash and benefit flows over an analysis period

Sometimes there is ambiguity in positioning the annual expense item C_t in the numerator as a deduction from the corresponding gross benefit as shown in equation (3.3) or in the denominator as an addition to the capital investment discounted to year zero. However equation (3.3) is used to evaluate road projects for two reasons:

- The first is that the main issue in cost–benefit analysis of projects is to investigate the efficient allocation of capital to competing alternatives by gauging the pay-off to the investment. The projects compete for the scarce capital and its diversion to an alternative should be the basis against which the net benefit of a project is measured. The repetitive expenses C_t are consequences of the capital invested initially. Thus in the algebraic definition of the benefit–cost ratio, the numerator in equation (3.3) represents the effect of the project and the denominator the cause of the project. Expenses C_t need to be positioned in the numerator as an effect of a project or schedule of projects.
- The second reason is related to the first. One of the effects of a road project is on the level of maintenance; any project will cause some change to maintenance costs. The saving is the difference between maintenance cost without the project and its counterpart with the project. The maintenance saving could be positive or negative. When a project is a new road link, maintenance cost is incurred after the project is completed. This maintenance consumes resources during the life of the project, with no saving of maintenance on the new link and possibly little indirect saving. To be consistent with the definition of maintenance saving, the maintenance cost incurred on the new road link should be treated as a negative benefit, being positioned in the numerator of the benefit–cost ratio.

In summary it is not usually appropriate to take a simple ratio of all benefits to all costs. If this were done then subsequent running or renewal costs would be confused with the constrained capital. The result would be failure to obtain a clear measure of capital efficiency.

The exception is the evaluation of projects where the only expenditure is on maintenance and renewal. In Chapter 9 this is all treated as calling on constrained resources and the benefit–cost ratio for the maintenance only schedule is obtained by putting all of the expenditure in the denominator.

Incremental (or marginal) cost–benefit analysis can be done with a recursive algorithm which allocates each investment increment to the part of the network that will give the largest increase in benefit. The incremental benefit–cost ratio is defined as the added benefit of advancing from one improvement level to the next divided by the corresponding added cost. This method has been used for optimal budget allocation to maintenance, rehabilitation and replacement of bridges. It also provides a rigorous way of testing whether the last budget increment for a complex maintenance programme is warranted.

The Benefits in Practical Terms

The benefits from a road project are calculated by comparing the two alternative states of the road network: with the project (the project case) and without the project (the base case). This is done with respect to relevant evaluation criteria. Major benefits include the saving of travel time and reductions in the costs of vehicle operation, road maintenance and road accidents.

A project which improves the road network allows motorists to spend less time travelling than they would otherwise do in the base case. The saved time is translated into money terms by applying the value of time. The improvement in the network may also reduce costs related to vehicle operation, including fuel consumption, engine oil consumption, tyre wear and vehicle maintenance.

Whether an improved road network will reduce vehicle fuel costs depends on travel speeds allowed in the project and base cases. The improvement normally allows higher speeds. For a given vehicle type, fuel consumption per kilometre decreases with the vehicle travel speed to a certain threshold and then increases with speed. When the vehicle speeds in both project and base cases are below the speed threshold the improvement in the road network reduces fuel consumption. When they are both above the speed threshold the improvement increases fuel consumption.

If the vehicle speed in the base case is below the speed threshold and in the project case it is above, then whether the improvement in the network reduces or increases fuel consumption depends on the actual speeds. The overall saving of vehicle operating costs caused by a road project is determined not only by the magnitude of changes in fuel used but also by engine oil consumption, tyre wear and maintenance.

Road maintenance

A road network improved by a project may not need as much maintenance as it would require in the absence of the project, so that its construction may reduce road maintenance costs, depending on the amounts and types of maintenance required with and without the project. For example sealing an unsealed road may reduce maintenance costs whereas widening or duplication of a road section may increase maintenance costs due to the increase in pavement area.

When a new link is added, it causes extra road maintenance costs, which become an expense rather than a benefit. As discussed in the previous section, a cost–benefit analysis of a road project will treat this expense as a negative benefit of the project rather than as part of the project cost. As explained, the issue here is alternative allocations of scarce project capital.

Accidents

Saving of road accident costs depend on whether improvement in the physical condition of a road actually reduces accidents. The calculation of savings is based on vehicle-kilometres, accident rates by type and road classification, and costs associated with individual accident types. Vehicle-kilometres can be derived from traffic volumes on the network in the presence and absence of the project. However it is not always possible to obtain relevant information on accident rates and costs for a specific area. There are two reasons for this, the first being that the rate at which road crashes occur is influenced by many local factors specific to geographic regions and even to individual roads. This makes it difficult to extend the use of crash statistics from region to region.

The second reason is that it is sometimes difficult to classify information on road accidents in a region with respect to road types and other factors relevant to cost–benefit analysis of road projects. Moreover it is not necessarily valid to assume that improvement in a road's physical condition automatically reduces accidents. In some situations a road project creates unfamiliar physical conditions for drivers and may cause confusion and even accidents if public awareness education in relation to the changed conditions is lacking or inadequate. For these reasons the studies reported in this book omitted savings of road accident costs from the project benefits.

Estimation of User Benefits

Major benefits come from the savings of road user costs. The demand for road use is inversely related to generalized user cost when other influences are held constant. If any kind of restoration or improvement work is done on a road in the network then trips between two centres using this road will change due to the reduced travel cost. Also the improved segment and the routes which include it will have more traffic while the substitute routes will have less. The increased traffic on the improved routes has two components:

- traffic induced or generated by the decreased 'separation' between centres;
- traffic diverted from other routes.

In an evaluation of improvements to a whole road network, any project may induce new traffic and cause a series of diversions between origin–destination trips and routes. The complexity of the responses make it impossible to identify the truly generated and diverted traffic. However such identification is not necessary because the benefits are estimated in the same manner for both cases.

Suppose that generalized user cost before the road improvement is C_0 and initial traffic is q_0. After the improvement the cost becomes C_1 resulting in an increase of traffic to q_1. Then the shaded area shown in Figure 3.2 is the measure of the consumers' gain from a road cost reduction from C_0 to C_1.

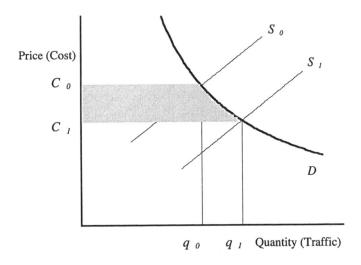

Figure 3.2   Consumers' surplus from changing travel cost and demand

The shaded area in Figure 3.2 represents benefits to both generated and diverted traffic that can be approximated by the rule-of-a-half method. This can be applied to all links in a system. The user benefit (UB) from expenditure on a whole network is estimated as:

$$UB = \frac{1}{2}\sum (q_0 + q_1)(C_0 - C_1) \qquad (3.4)$$

where q is the quantity of traffic and C is the individual user cost experienced by the drivers. The subscripts 0 and 1 refer to the base and project cases. The rule-of-a-half benefit measure is an approximation because it uses a linear path of integration. The method of calculating user benefits depends on the level of aggregation which may be:

- all travel from a particular origin or arriving at a particular destination;
- all travel along a particular route;
- all travel on a link.

When journeys between all origins and destinations are aggregated, equation (3.4) becomes:

$$UB = \frac{1}{2} \sum_{rs} (q_{rs}^0 + q_{rs}^1)(C_{rs}^0 - C_{rs}^1) \qquad (3.5)$$

where q_{rs} represents trips from origin r to destination s and C_{rs} is the generalized cost of travel from origin r to destination s. From equation (3.5):

$$UB = \frac{1}{2} \sum_{rs} (q_{rs}^0 C_{rs}^0 + q_{rs}^1 C_{rs}^0 - q_{rs}^0 C_{rs}^1 - q_{rs}^1 C_{rs}^1) \qquad (3.5a)$$

Let C_k be the cost of travelling along link k. If n is the set of links on routes from r to s then $C_{rs} = \sum_{k \in n} C_k$.

Let V_k be the volume of trips on link k, and N the set of origin-destination pairs between which k is a link so that $V_k = \sum_{rs \in N} q_{rs}$.

If K and M are the sets of links in the base and new networks then:

$$UB = \frac{1}{2} [\sum_{k \in K} (V_k^0 C_k^0 + V_k^1 C_k^0) - \sum_{m \in M} (V_m^0 C_m^1 + V_m^1 C_m^1)] \qquad (3.6)$$

This formulation provides a practical way to calculate road user benefits and has been used in the project scheduling applications.

MULTI-CRITERIA EVALUATION

The multi-criteria evaluation method is designed to overcome a perceived narrowness of evaluation criteria by including effects that are difficult to measure and represent in money terms (Nijkamp et al., 1990). A score, usually based on community consultation, is given to each project on each of a number of criteria. In addition to those effects that can be given money values, criteria may include community access and impacts on such things as flora and fauna, cultural sites and national parks. These criteria are brought into a formal evaluation by attaching to them importance weights which reflect community views and the political insights of policy makers. If the government is not satisfied that its concerns have been fully represented in the resulting weighted scores for projects then weights can be adjusted to take account of relative policy priorities.

It has been found that assessors tend to perceive merit separately from size. If two projects are equally meritorious with respect to a particular criterion and therefore have the same score then the larger will have a greater impact in terms of that criterion. Thus it may be appropriate to weight a project score by its cost or some proportion of it before the importance weights are applied.

Multi-criteria evaluation was not used in the studies reported in later chapters but the method is relevant here because it can be incorporated into a selection and scheduling procedure with genetic algorithm, as outlined below.

GENETIC ALGORITHM AND EVALUATION

The evolutionary approach to selecting projects and determining construction schedules is more robust than non-evolutionary methods, particularly with respect to traffic changes. The following sections deal with the incorporation of evaluation criteria, project interactions and constraints. Although there are other evolutionary methods such as simulated annealing, only genetic algorithm is considered. The actual method is presented in Chapter 4 and the succeeding chapters deal with specific aspects of applying genetic algorithm to road investment problems in various situations.

As already indicated, net present value (NPV) is the appropriate criterion to use with genetic algorithm because a solution is a complete timetable of projects to be implemented within the budget constraints. Alternative solutions generated by the genetic algorithm are directly comparable in terms of NPV because they involve exactly the same budget expenditure and of course they are mutually exclusive.

In each case it is also appropriate to calculate the discount rate which makes the NPV zero. This is the internal rate of return. While NPV is the primary criterion, the benefit–cost ratio for the whole project schedule provides an explicit measure of capital efficiency.

If the discount rate has been set fairly high then it is possible that the NPV will be small or even negative and the benefit–cost ratio slightly less than 1.0. Under these circumstances projects can be dropped one by one working backwards from the last until the remaining investment program becomes viable.

Alternatively the analyst can examine the incremental benefit–cost ratio. The last project is dropped from the best solution in which the fixed budget has already been optimally allocated; the result of the whole program is then recalculated taking account of traffic impacts. Then the amount saved becomes the denominator and the lost benefit the numerator of the marginal benefit–cost ratio for the deleted project. This method is applied in Chapter 9.

The Option of a Multi-criteria Objective Function

An alternative to using standard economic measures is incorporation of multi-criteria evaluation into the objective function of a genetic algorithm. As with NPV the weighted sum for one solution is directly comparable to the weighted sum for any other because they require the same budget and are mutually exclusive. The weights would be predetermined and for some of the criteria each project would be given a fixed score at the outset. The variable traffic impacts would be calculated in the assessment of each possible program as for NPV.

The scores on a criterion such as air pollution would also be variable but to a large extent as a function of traffic. However the polluting effect of traffic in an area with low wind speed would be higher than in an area with high winds and this would have to be taken into account functionally. Other criteria relating to social impacts would also vary. Some such as accessibility would involve calculation for each investment configuration.

In total the calculations for the multi-criteria objective function would be more complex than the simple cost and time calculations for NPV. However the computing time added by the multi-criteria objective function calculations would still be only a small proportion of the time taken by the traffic assignments.

Divisibility of Project Benefits

Although benefits often accrue only after a project is completed, some projects produce partial benefits when they are partly finished. In other words some are benefit divisible and others are benefit indivisible. A comparison of Figures 3.3 and 3.4 illustrates the differences in cost and benefit flows between two such projects. In both cases the construction period is three years.

In evaluating an individual project, ignorance of whether the benefits are divisible or indivisible may not be a serious deficiency because the purpose of such an evaluation is mainly to justify the cost in terms of the benefits from the single project. Competition with others for resources is not necessarily a concern.

On the other hand, when road projects are prioritized and scheduled in a construction timetable, divisibility of benefits becomes an important issue. If two marginal projects *A* and *B* have identical benefit–cost ratios but *A* generates partial benefits during the course of construction while *B* does not then *A* should be constructed first if the annual budget is not enough to construct either of them completely. Another important point is that if a road project is benefit indivisible it is preferable to build it in one year rather than spread its construction over two or more years.

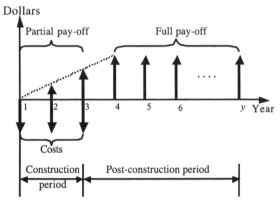

Source: Qiu, 2000

Figure 3.3   Cost and benefit flows: road project with divisible benefits

Thus benefit divisibility is associated with the timing of benefits during the construction and post construction periods. Failure to recognize the issue would result in underestimation of the benefits produced by divisible projects as well as distortion of the sequence of projects in the construction timetable. So long as benefit divisibility is correctly specified, the genetic algorithm can be relied upon to make the right decision.

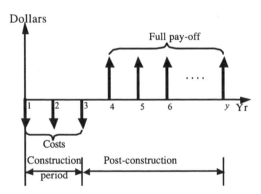

Source: Qiu, 2000

Figure 3.4   Cost and benefit flows: road projects with indivisible benefits

Constraints on a Construction Timetable

The financial plan for construction expenditure can be treated as a series of annual budgets that are not to be exceeded. Although relationships between the parties involved in financial planning are complex, budget preparation is relatively simple. It is common to base a new budget on the previous one with marginal adjustments to reflect new requirements. The analyst generally works within externally determined budgets, which may be constant from year to year or growing at some reasonable rate. This makes the budget profile through time fairly easy to project, especially for the near future.

A limit to annual expenditure on an individual project
If there were no limit to annual expenditure on an individual project a large project with high priority might consume most or all of the budget in a particular year and leave nothing for other projects. This rarely happens because the construction authority prefers to spread expenditure over a range of projects and regions, so that there is a ceiling to annual expenditure on any one project. A convenient way to represent this policy is to express maximum expenditure on any one project as a percentage of the annual budget

In Table 3.1 with individual project expenditure not limited, project 4 uses all of the resources in year 1, leaving nothing for others.

Table 3.1   Project schedule: no limit to yearly expenditure on any project

Project ranking: 4 → 9 → 10 → 6 → 3 → 5 → 8 → 1 → 7 → 2							
Project	Cost	Investment by year ($m)					Total
no.	($m)	1	2	3	4	5	($m)
1	2.10						0.00
2	4.90						0.00
3	10.20			2.38	7.82		10.20
4	15.26	10.00	5.26				15.26
5	6.54				2.18	4.36	6.54
6	7.70		0.08	7.62			7.70
7	4.90						0.00
8	10.60					5.64	5.64
9	2.50		2.50				2.50
10	2.16		2.16				2.16
Budget ($m)		10.00	10.00	10.00	10.00	10.00	50.00

Source: Qiu, 2000

Limiting expenditure on any one of the Table 3.1 projects to 50 per cent
of the annual budget, as in Table 3.2, means that project 4 is no longer the
only one to be scheduled in year 1. Projects 6, 9 and 10 are scheduled in year
1 also. The effect of even further reducing the proportion that can be spent on
any one project is to spread the construction of large projects over more and
more years. It tends to distribute each year's funding over a wider range of
projects and there is a significant impact on the timetable.

Table 3.2   No project to take more than 50 per cent of the annual budget

| Project ranking: 4 → 9 → 10 → 6 → 3 → 5 → 8 → 1 → 7 → 2 | | | | | | | |
| Project no. | Cost ($m) | Investment by year ($m) | | | | | Total ($m) |
		1	2	3	4	5	
1	2.10					0.64	0.64
2	4.90						0.00
3	10.20			2.64	5.00	2.56	10.20
4	15.26	5.00	5.00	5.00	0.26		15.26
5	6.54				4.74	1.80	6.54
6	7.70	0.34	5.00	2.36			7.70
7	4.90						0.00
8	10.60					5.00	5.00
9	2.50	2.50					2.50
10	2.16	2.16					2.16
	Budget ($m)	10.00	10.00	10.00	10.00	10.00	50.00

Source: Qiu, 2000

Preferred investment profiles for individual projects
A related constraint arises from the fact that it is not always desirable to
complete a project in one year because of limitations on some construction
activities and on the availability of labour and equipment. Each of the many
operations in a construction project needs a different period of time to
complete. Attempts to shorten completion times may sometimes jeopardize
construction quality. For example concrete pavement needs 28 days to reach
its full strength and premature exposure to loaded vehicles will cause
structural damage. Moreover relationships between construction activities
vary, some being independent of each other and able to be done in parallel and
some being predecessors for others.

    Project completion can usually be accelerated by arranging for successor
activities to begin some time before their 'predecessors' are finished or, in the

case of a road, by dividing the whole project into several homogeneous sections and constructing them simultaneously. However this is equivalent to what is called 'crashing' in critical path analysis and needs added resources, not only financial but also labour and equipment.

Recognizing the need for an orderly construction process, an authority may have a preferred investment profile for each type of project, based on experience. A profile is a series of proportions of project cost to be spent annually, for example a three-year percentage profile of 30:30:40. In essence the preferred investment profile reflects resource requirements which are governed primarily by engineering constraints.

Table 3.3 shows a modification of the hypothetical example in Table 3.2 to demonstrates how preferred investment profiles or engineering constraints work in scheduling projects. The profiles for projects 3 and 6 act as targets for spreading investment over years. There is a deviation from the project 6 target because there are insufficient funds to satisfy it.

Table 3.3 Imposition of preferred investment profiles for individual projects

Project Ranking: 4 → 9 → 10 → 6 → 3 → 5 → 8 → 1 → 7 → 2

- Any individual project limited to 50% of annual budget and
- Preferred investment profiles for individual projects are different.

Proj. no.	Cost ($m)	Preferred investment profile: actual construction years (% of project cost)			Investment by year ($m)					Sub-total ($m)
					1	2	3	4	5	
1	2.10	100								0.00
2	4.90	100								0.00
3	10.20	30	30	40			2.64	3.48	4.08	10.20
4	15.26	100			5.00	5.00	5.00	0.26		15.26
5	6.54	100						5.00	1.54	6.54
6	7.70	50	50		0.34	5.00	2.36			7.70
7	4.90	100								0.00
8	10.60	100						1.26	4.38	5.64
9	2.50	100			2.50					2.50
10	2.16	100			2.16					2.16
		Budget by year ($m)			10.00	10.00	10.00	10.00	10.00	50.00

Source: Qiu, 2000

Staged construction

Sometimes a project needs to be constructed in stages. For instance a road section may be constructed initially with a gravel pavement then upgraded to emulsion seal and eventually asphalt pavement. Another common example is that at the first stage of construction the formation is constructed for an ultimate four-lane carriageway but with only two lanes paved at that stage (one lane in each direction) leaving the other two lanes to be paved at the second stage when justified by traffic volumes.

In practice the reason behind construction in stages is to supply roads (in terms of size and type) that are consistent with traffic volume and composition and so avoid wasting money on excess facilities. However there is a cost difference between single and multiple stages as well as differences in maintenance costs and vehicle operating costs.

It may be the case that the present value of the cost of completing a project in one stage is smaller than for multiple stages because staging activities involves added costs of administration, design and construction. In other cases the reverse may be true.

When a road development is staged by pavement type (often from gravel formation to emulsion seal then to asphalt pavement) the greater cost of high-quality pavement may sometimes be offset by savings in pavement maintenance and vehicle operating costs or vice versa. Another possible option is to construct a carriageway with fewer lanes but with higher congestion costs and possibly higher vehicle operating costs.

In summary staged construction reduces demand for funds in some years but is not necessarily a least-cost way of providing facilities in terms of total social costs. The least-cost method could be found by comparing the total social costs of different staging options. However identifying these options is likely to be a non-trivial task because the investigation involves many factors, such as construction, maintenance and vehicle operating costs, among which the relationships are complicated.

A simple practical procedure is to compare the present value of the cost of two-stage construction with that for completion in one stage assuming other things constant. This approach is taken in genetic algorithm modelling.

OPTIMIZING THE PROJECT SCHEDULE

The next chapter outlines the genetic algorithm model used to find the best investment schedule, in terms of the chosen evaluation criterion, within the constraints and management requirements discussed in this chapter.

REFERENCES AND FURTHER READING

Cost–Benefit Evaluation

Adler, M.D. and E.A. Posner (1999), 'Rethinking cost–benefit analysis', *Yale Law Journal,* **109** (2), 165-247.

Kanbur, R. (2003), 'Development economics and the compensation principle', *International Social Science Journal,* **55** (1), 27.

Neuburger, H. (1971), 'User benefit in the evaluation of transport and land use plans', *Journal of Transport Economics and Policy,* **5** (1), 52-75.

Willis, K.G., G.D. Garrod, and D.R. Harvey (1998), 'A review of cost–benefit analysis as applied to the evaluation of new road proposals in the UK', *Transportation Research D: Transport and Environment,* **3** (3), 141-156.

Discount Rate

Hartman, R. (1990), 'One thousand points of light seeking a number: a case study of CBO's search for a discount rate policy', *Journal of Environmental Economics and Management,* **18**, 3-7.

Lind, R. (1990), 'Reassessing the government's discount rate policy in light of new theory and data in a world economy with a high degree of capital mobility', *Journal of Environmental Economics and Management,* **18**, 8-28.

Luckbert, M.K. and W.L. Adamowicz (1993), 'Empirical measures of factors affecting social rates of discount', *Environmental and Resource Economics,* **3**, 1-21.

Marglin, S.A. (1963), 'The social rate of discount and the optimal rate of investment', *Quarterly Journal of Economics,* **77**, 95-11.

Price, C. (1993), *Time Discounting and Value,* Oxford: Blackwell.

Quirk, J. and K. Terasaw (1991), 'Choosing a government discount rate: an alternative approach', *Journal of Environmental Economics and Management,* **20**, 16-28.

Stiglitz, J.E. (1994), 'Discount rates: the rate of discount for benefit–cost analysis and the theory of the second-best', in Layard, R. and S. Glaister (eds), *Cost-Benefit Analysis,* 2nd edition, Cambridge: Cambridge University Press.

Benefit–Cost Ratio

Department of Finance (1991), *Handbook of Cost–benefit Analysis,* Canberra: Australian Government Publication Service.

Sugden, R. and A. Williams (1978), *The Principles of Practical Cost–Benefit Analysis,* New York: Oxford University Press.

Incremental Benefit–Cost Ratio

Farid, F., D.W. Johnston, M.A. Laverde and C.-J. Chen (1994), 'Application of incremental benefit-cost analysis for optimal budget allocation to maintenance, rehabilitation, and replacement of bridges', *Transportation Research Record 1442*, Washington, DC: Transportation Research Board, 88-99.

Han, R. (2002), *Genetic Algorithm to Optimise the Allocation of Road Expenditure Between Maintenance and Renewal*, PhD thesis, University of Western Australia.

Multi-criteria Evaluation

Greening, L.A. and S. Bernow (2004), 'Design of coordinated energy and environmental policies: use of multi-criteria decision-making', *Energy Policy*, **32**, 721-735.

Nijkamp, P., P. Rietveld and H. Voogd (1990), *Multicriteria Evaluation in Physical Planning*, Amsterdam: North-Holland.

Vreeker, R., P. Nijkamp and C. Ter Welle (2002), 'A multicriteria decision support methodology for evaluating airport expansion plans', *Transportation Research D: Transport and Environment*, **7** (1), 27-47.

Divisibility of Project Benefits

Qiu, M. (2000), *Optimising a Road Project Construction Timetable for Rural Roads*, PhD thesis, University of Western Australia.

The Financial Plan: Budgets in Individual Years

Brown, C.V. and P.M. Jackson (1990), *Public Sector Economics*, 4th edition, Oxford: Basil Blackwell.

Humphrey, T.F. (1981): 'Evaluation criteria and priority setting for sate highway programs', *National Cooperative Highway Research Program Synthesis of Highway Practice*, no. 84, Washington, DC: Transportation Research Board.

Meyer, J.R. and M.R. Straszheim (1971), 'Investment planning with capital budget constraints', in Meyer, J.R. (ed.), *Techniques of Transport Planning*, vol. 1, Washington, DC: Brookings Institution, Transport Research Program.

Wildavsky, A. (1964), *The Politics of the Budgetary Process*, Boston MA: Little, Brown.

Preferred Investment Profiles over Time

Meredith, J.R. and S.J. Mantel Jr. (1995), *Project Management – a Managerial Approach*. 3rd edition, New York: John Wiley & Sons.

4. Genetic Algorithm to Schedule Road Projects and Estimate Demand

This chapter presents the key issues and steps to be taken in solving a scheduling problem by genetic algorithm (GA) within the evaluation framework of Chapter 3. It ends with steps to shorten the computing task both by optimizing GA parameters and by using distributed computing for very large problems. In all cases, most of the computer time is taken by traffic assignments, one for each potential solution. The different assignment methods used in urban and rural studies are discussed in Chapters 5 and 6.

The robustness and efficiency of genetic algorithms in searching for solutions to problems has made them applicable to many problems that would otherwise be extremely difficult or impossible to solve. This is particularly true of the problem of optimizing a road project construction timetable. Genetic algorithm has offered the first realistic method of solving this non-linear combinatorial optimization problem which has both linear and non-linear constraints.

Two different types of genetic algorithm have been used. The first is applied to the core of the problem – project selection and scheduling. This is a discrete selection and sequence optimization problem. The second is an ancillary application to calibrate the parameters of the travel models which form an integral part of the search for the optimal sequence.

Genetic algorithm can be viewed as a template for solving problems based on an analogy with genetic inheritance and evolution. The problem to be solved is encoded into a string representing the pertinent variables. A string or 'chromosome' decodes to a 'fitness' value in the problem context. The principle of descent with modification is applied, with the fitter strings surviving and recombining with one another. Offspring have a chance of inheriting the best features as the population evolves and adapts. The initial population is usually randomly drawn while selection occurs with a probability based on fitness. Thus a population of chromosomes goes through a randomized but directed search among many possible solutions.

Because genetic algorithm is designed to mimic processes observed in natural evolution, the problem data is encoded by analogy on 'chromosomes'. The GA mimics natural selection whereby organisms with chromosomes carrying superior genes have more chance of producing successful offspring.

Mutations and recombinations of the genes on parental chromosomes may create quite different successor or offspring chromosomes. Key points on which genetic algorithm differs from other search methods can be summarized as follows:

- Each potential solution to a problem is encoded as a string of numbers and the string is treated as an entity rather than a collection of separate decision variables.
- A population of solutions to the same problem is evaluated at each generation (iteration) rather than just a single solution.
- At each generation, solutions are scattered over the solution space by various randomized operators. This gives a broad view of the space and a high degree of immunity to the danger of being trapped at a local optimum.
- The actual value of the objective function is used to guide the search rather than derivatives with respect to decision variables. This makes it possible to model a complex system without sacrificing realism or key aspects of the system. In a road study the objective function is the NPV of all projects included in a construction sequence, which is calculated with travel demand models and a procedure for economic evaluation of projects. The genetic algorithm operators interact with the net present value rather than with the process of calculating it.
- GA uses probabilistic transition rules in the search rather than deterministic rules like those in calculus-based or enumeration methods. One operator exchanges partial information between individuals in a GA population, another amends part of the information and the last decides which individuals are selected to reproduce offspring for the next round of search. The subsets of individuals to which these operators are applied is determined in probabilistic ways
- The process differs from random search because it systematically compares, combines and evaluates information as the search progresses.
- With its randomized procedures and fixed operators, genetic algorithm can explore many points in the solution space and exploits information embedded in each GA individual.

The first and main application of genetic algorithm considered here is to find the best sequence of road expenditures, but GA is also used to make initial approximations to the parameters of the combined non-urban travel demand and route assignment models discussed in Chapters 5 and 6. The possible occurrence of sub-optima in this case makes it highly desirable to use GA to estimate the parameters. They can be refined subsequently by a Newton or quadratic hill-climbing method but it has been found that the GA estimates differ little from the more precise ones. The genetic algorithm procedure for this type of estimation differs appreciably from project sequencing. It is outlined in this chapter after the sequencing sections.

PROJECT SEQUENCES: COMPUTATION PROCEDURE

An individual GA chromosome represents a feasible solution of a problem. For project selection and scheduling the values arrayed on a chromosome comprise the unique set of project identification numbers. The initial generation is a randomly generated pool or population of chromosomes, each being the projects arrayed in some sequence. These initial chromosome strings evolve by a simulation process, with genetic operations, to achieve better and better solutions as measured by the value of the objective function or fitness. Relatively good chromosomes have more chance to survive while worse ones gradually die off. The optimum or nearly optimum solution is found through the evolution of many generations.

Genetic Algorithm Representation of a Project Sequence

For project optimization either the project or the road segment on which there is a potential project is coded as an integer. The projects or road segments are represented by sequential integers from 1 to the number of potential projects or segments. An advantage of the ordered sequence representation that project scheduling shares with a number of other problems such as the 'travelling salesman problem' is that any rearrangement of the sequence is a feasible solution. Other classes of problem have to use penalty functions to keep the search more or less within a permissible region or simply drop any individuals that go outside it.

The process begins by randomly initializing a population of individuals in the first generation, that is by assigning a value or 'gene' to each position on every individual string. The values assigned are in the domain range with no repetitions. This is just like the cases illustrated by Tables 1.3 and 3.1 in previous chapters.

As an example an individual chromosome representing five road projects to be selected and scheduled might be randomized at the beginning as $(2, 3, 5, 1, 4)$. This would represent the construction sequence:

$$project_2 \rightarrow project_3 \rightarrow project_5 \rightarrow project_1 \rightarrow project_4$$

The information or solution embedded in each individual is then decoded and evaluated. The evaluated information (the value of the objective function) for an individual is called the fitness of the individual and the bigger (for a maximizing problem) or the smaller (for a minimizing problem) the value the fitter the individual. For instance the GA individual in the above example is translated into a construction timetable over a programme period and the corresponding net present value can be calculated and compared with those for individuals with other project sequences.

Then the search and improvement process begins with the application of the operators.

Genetic Operators

A genetic algorithm usually has three fundamental operators: reproduction, crossover and mutation.

Reproduction

Individual strings (chromosomes) are copied into the mating pool, those with higher objective function (fitness) values having a higher probability of being copied and thus contributing one or more offspring to the next generation. It is important to preserve genetic variability and concentrating only on the best individuals would not allow adequate exploration of the search space. Various reproduction methods have been tried but we have found binary tournament selection to be the most satisfactory.

In a so-called 'tournament' two chromosome strings are randomly chosen from the population and the better one is copied into the next generation for further genetic processing. This is repeated until the processing pool is filled to the predetermined population level. Some chromosomes of the old pool are left out while others have two or more copies in the new one. After a succession of generations the fitness of the individual chromosome strings in the pool tends to converge, with many fairly close to the optimum, but the components of the strings may still be dissimilar.

Crossover

This is a process by which members of a newly reproduced population are partially combined. It is done by exchanging genes between pairs of parent chromosomes. Crossover sometimes causes good genes to be inherited from two parents in such a way that better offspring are produced. Many crossover alternatives have been defined for sequence representation but partially-mapped crossover (PMX) has been found highly satisfactory. As an example these two parent chromosomes represent alternative sequences of ten projects:

$$p_1 = (1 \ 2 \ 3 \ 4 \ 5 \ 6 \ 7 \ 8 \ 9 \ 10)$$
$$p_2 = (2 \ 5 \ 9 \ 10 \ 6 \ 8 \ 4 \ 1 \ 7 \ 3)$$

PMX builds offspring by preserving the order and position of some of the genes in one parent and also preserving the order and position of many of the remaining genes from the other parent. The initial step is to randomly choose two cut-points for a series of swapping operations.

The first offspring is an exact copy of the first parent except that the genes between cut-points are replaced by the genes between cut-points in the second parent; the other offspring is created in the same way. The two offspring are completed by a series of swapping operations so that each gene appears only once in each.

For example two cut-points (marked by 'I') may be randomly located as follows:

p_1	1	2	3	4	5	6	7	8	9	10
p_2	2	5	9	10	6	8	4	1	7	3

Exchanging the elements between cut-points begins to build two offspring:

o_1	*	*	*	10	6	8	4	*	*	*
o_2	*	*	*	4	5	6	7	*	*	*

A number representing a project or road segment gene cannot appear more than once in a chromosome so the next step is to restore only those parent genes which cause no duplication:

o_1	1	2	3	10	6	8	4	*	9	*
o_2	2	*	9	4	5	6	7	1	*	3

Parent genes would cause duplication in the positions marked by * and they must be replaced. For example the first * in the offspring o_2 that was 5 in parent p_2 is replaced by the 6 of o_1 because it is in the corresponding position to the 5 in offspring o_2. But this would create duplication of the 6 already in o_2; so a further change is made.

For this second replacement the gene above 6 between the cuts in o_2 is used. This is 8 so that 8 is substituted for the *. All the other occurrences of * are replaced in a similar fashion by the appropriate genes. The resulting offspring after crossover are:

o_1	1	2	3	10	6	8	4	5	9	7
o_2	2	8	9	4	5	6	7	1	10	3

Mutation

This changes some elements of a chromosome and in project scheduling it is used to alter the order of a string. The changes are made randomly with some predetermined probability. Mutation is an insurance against premature loss of important solution possibilities. It helps to maintain diversity in a population of chromosomes and find new points in the search space to evaluate.

Reciprocal exchange is a convenient and effective mutation method for project scheduling. A chromosome is selected at random and then two of the genes in the string are chosen randomly to be exchanged. For example the two marked elements may be chance selections on the following randomly selected string:

$$1 \quad 2 \quad 3 \mid 4 \mid 5 \quad 6 \quad 7 \mid 8 \mid 9 \quad 10$$

The mutation operation exchanges the randomly chosen elements 4 and 8 to give:

$$1 \quad 2 \quad 3 \mid 8 \mid 5 \quad 6 \quad 7 \mid 4 \mid 9 \quad 10$$

Elitism

Elitism is a strategy used to ensure that the best solution in one generation survives into the next. It is used after crossover and mutation. A practical procedure is to replace the worst chromosome in the current population by the best chromosome in the previous generation. The elitism rate of this case is 1, a strategy which always hands over the best chromosome from generation to generation. An important consequence of applying the elitist strategy is that the objective function never decreases from generation to generation.

Population Size

The population size is the number of individual chromosomes in the reproduction pool. The length of chromosome (number of potential projects) and the operators are both factors in determining what the size should be. A small population means a sparse array of initial points and good solutions may not be found before the search converges on a poor local optimum – especially if the mutation rate is low. Such an outcome results from insufficient genetic diversity which is most important because the solution space is topographically rugged and not continuous.

At the other extreme there is a drawback to a large population. The early generations involve random searching which is expensive when the evaluation of a chromosome takes a long time as in road project selection. The greater the number of chromosomes, the greater the computing time needed for significant improvement.

Ensuring Appropriate Gene Exchange

A critical factor for the success of GA is the exchange of genetic material between strings. The conventional view is that crossover between the initially highly variable strings is more effective near the beginning of a run and that mutation becomes more effective later when the population has partly homogenized. If the mutation rate is low then crossover may cause the population to converge before the genes have been well mixed, resulting in premature convergence to a sub-optimal solution. On the other hand a high mutation rate may destroy good strings that have been found already but have not had a chance to reproduce. Compromise is needed and possibly an increasing mutation rate.

The crossover rate is the probability of a chromosome being selected to be a parent in a crossover. In a population containing 100 individuals with a crossover rate of 70 per cent one would expect approximately 35 pairs of chromosomes to be subjected to crossover in each generation. Many studies have indicated that it is effective to use a high rate (0.5 or greater). Such rates have been found suitable for project scheduling.

The mutation rate is the probability of a gene in a chromosome being replaced by another gene in the same chromosome and should be set to enhance exploration of the entire search space. Project scheduling work indicates that a high mutation rate is effective for this type of ordering problem. The mutation rate is the product of the probability that a chromosome is chosen and the probability that a gene is chosen to swap with another gene.

For example in a population of 100 individuals each with 200 gene elements and a mutation rate of 9 per cent (= 0.3×0.3), one would expect 1800 (= $100 \times 200 \times 0.09$) elements from 30 (= 100×0.3) chromosomes to be changed in each generation. Because GA operations are subject to random probabilities the number of changes might be more or less than the 1800 in a particular generation.

Search Termination

The search is terminated when initially set conditions or convergence criteria are satisfied. There are no rules for setting such conditions; it depends on the nature of the problem. Usual termination criteria are convergence within a given tolerance or completion of a set number of generations.

Convergence has two aspects, one relating to the objective function and the other to the individual chromosome. If the objective function of the best sequence is unchanged for a number of generations, even though many individual chromosomes are still being changed substantially by mutation and crossover, the search can be regarded as having converged to a solution. The other possibility is that all of the individual chromosomes have become the same, except for a few mutations, so that the objective function has little chance of changing from generation to generation.

Premature convergence to a local optimum is mainly controlled by mutation. When the mutation rate is small the procedure cannot explore the possibilities enough to jump out of a group of relatively fit individuals.

The alternative procedure that is often used is to terminate the search after an initially specified number of generations. The number of generations is large enough to achieve a good result without having a lot of unnecessary computation making no improvement. If it is clear that improvement is still continuing up to the end of the allotted number of generations then the length of run can be increased. For many problems 100 generations are sufficient.

Issues in Selecting Genetic Algorithm Parameters

The performance of a genetic algorithm depends on its parameter settings but there is no universal set to suit all cases. Consequently an effort should be made to specify parameters appropriately for each application. They include population size, number of generations, crossover rate and mutation rate.

The right parameters will strike a balance between 'exploration' and 'exploitation'. The randomized components of crossover and reproduction are exploratory and good coverage of the search space is achieved when the propensity to explore is driven by a large element of chance. However exploration slows down the search. On the other side a fitness function that captures the scale of the troughs and peaks in the problem space enhances the exploitation of sequences and gives high performance through appropriate combinations of crossover and reproduction. It may require experimentation to match parameters to the problem. Better exploration of the search region can be accomplished by increasing mutation rates as well as increasing population size and number of generations.

Selection of parameters is based mainly on the number of genes in a chromosome but also on computer resources, computing efficiency and convergence requirements. The possibility of optimizing parameters is discussed in a later section.

NUMERICAL OPTIMIZATION OF TRAVEL FUNCTIONS

When a travel demand function is as complex as those discussed in Chapters 5 and 6 it is possible that the estimation of the parameters may be entrapped in a local maximum. This means that convergence to the global maximum depends on the chance of choosing the right starting points for a conventional maximum likelihood search. It is difficult to determine a priori whether or not the log likelihood function L is globally concave with a single peak. Elements in the Hessian (the matrix of second derivatives) of L with respect to some of the parameters may be positive or negative.

The genetic algorithm used to approach the maximum of the log likelihood function has mutation, crossover and reproduction operators but they take different forms from those used for project scheduling.

Denote $P_t = \begin{bmatrix} \vartheta_1^t & \cdots & \vartheta_m^t & \cdots & \vartheta_p^t \end{bmatrix}$ as the GA population matrix at generation t. Each vector ϑ_m^t in matrix P_t represents an estimate of the demand model parameters at generation t. As an illustration, let $\alpha, \beta, \gamma, \xi, \theta$ be five parameter values. Let the objective function matrix at generation t be

$$L_t = \begin{bmatrix} L_1^t & \cdots & L_m^t & \cdots & L_p^t \end{bmatrix},$$

each element in this matrix being the value of the objective function for the corresponding solution.

Mutation Operators

The purpose of mutation is to change part of the information embedded in GA individuals to produce new individuals. The objective functions of some of these new individuals may be improved as the result of mutation. At generation t randomly select a GA individual from the population P_t of size p (the probability of selecting any individual being $1/p$), say:

$$\vartheta_m^t = \begin{bmatrix} \alpha_m^t & \beta_m^t & \gamma_m^t & \xi_m^t & \theta_m^t \end{bmatrix}.$$

An element (e.g. ξ_m^t) is selected from the vector at random (the probability of an element being selected is $1/5$). When a mutation operator is applied to the selected GA individual, ϑ_m^t becomes a new individual, that is:

$$\vartheta_m^t = \begin{bmatrix} \alpha_m^t & \beta_m^t & \gamma_m^t & \xi_m^t & \theta_m^t \end{bmatrix} \Rightarrow \vartheta_m^{t*} = \begin{bmatrix} \alpha_m^t & \beta_m^t & \gamma_m^t & \xi_m^{t*} & \theta_m^t \end{bmatrix}.$$

The value of ξ_m^{t*} depends on the type of mutation. All three of the following mutation operators have been used:

- Uniform mutation

  $\xi_m^{t\,*}$ is a random variable following a uniform distribution in range $[L_\xi,$ $R_\xi]$. The uniform mutation operator is applied to the GA population of size p, and the number of mutations in one generation is $p \times \text{probability}_{\text{uniform-mutation}}$.

- Boundary mutation

  $\xi_m^{t\,*}$ is equal to either the lower domain boundary L_ξ or the upper boundary R_ξ, each option having a probability of 0.5. The boundary mutation operator is iteratively applied to the GA population. The number of iterations is $p \times \text{probability}_{\text{boundary-mutation}}$.

- Non-uniform mutation

  If r is a random variable following a uniform distribution in the range $[0, 1]$ and T is the prescribed number of generations in the whole evolutionary process then

$$\xi_m^{t\,*} = \begin{cases} \xi_m^t + r\left(R_\xi - \xi_m^t\right)\left(1 - t/T\right)^2, & \text{if a random binary digit is 0,} \\ \xi_m^t - r\left(\xi_m^t - L_\xi\right)\left(1 - t/T\right)^2, & \text{if a random binary digit is 1.} \end{cases}$$

  The non-uniform mutation operator is applied to the GA population, the number of iterations being $p \times \text{probability}_{\text{non-uniform-mutation}}$.

Crossover Operators

As before, the purpose of the crossover operator is to partially swap information between two individuals to produce two new individuals. Each receives part of the information from the other and preserves part of its own original information. Objective functions may be improved as a result.

At generation t randomly select, with uniform probability, from population P_t two different GA individuals. For example individuals

$$\boldsymbol{\vartheta}_k^t = \begin{bmatrix} \alpha_k^t & \beta_k^t & \gamma_k^t & \xi_k^t & \theta_k^t \end{bmatrix}$$

$$\text{and} \quad \boldsymbol{\vartheta}_n^t = \begin{bmatrix} \alpha_n^t & \beta_n^t & \gamma_n^t & \xi_n^t & \theta_n^t \end{bmatrix}$$

are selected to partially swap information. Details of the process depend on the type of operator.

All three of the following crossover operators have been used in the studies reported in this book:

- Simple crossover
  Two crossing positions are randomly selected and information on the elements between them on the two GA individuals is partially exchanged. For example two positions including β and γ are chosen (that is the second and third elements of the two vectors) and the two GA individuals are transformed into two individuals with new values for β and γ:

$$\vartheta_k^t = \begin{bmatrix} \alpha_k^t & \beta_k^t & \gamma_k^t & \xi_k^t & \theta_k^t \end{bmatrix} \qquad \vartheta_k^{t*} = \begin{bmatrix} \alpha_k^t & \beta_k^{t*} & \gamma_k^{t*} & \xi_k^t & \theta_k^t \end{bmatrix}$$
$$\Rightarrow$$
$$\vartheta_n^t = \begin{bmatrix} \alpha_n^t & \beta_n^t & \gamma_n^t & \xi_n^t & \theta_n^t \end{bmatrix} \qquad \vartheta_n^{t*} = \begin{bmatrix} \alpha_n^t & \beta_n^{t*} & \gamma_n^{t*} & \xi_n^t & \theta_n^t \end{bmatrix}$$

where

$$\begin{cases} \beta_k^{t*} = a\beta_n^t + (1-a)\beta_k^t \\ \beta_n^{t*} = a\beta_k^t + (1-a)\beta_n^t \end{cases} , \qquad \begin{cases} \gamma_k^{t*} = a\gamma_n^t + (1-a)\gamma_k^t \\ \gamma_n^{t*} = a\gamma_k^t + (1-a)\gamma_n^t \end{cases}$$

  and a is a random variable uniformly distributed in the range $[0, 1]$.
  The operator is applied to the GA population and the number of crossover operations in one generation is $p \times \text{probability}_{\text{simple-crossover}}$.

- Single arithmetical crossover
  A single element (e.g. ξ) is selected at random and the values of this element in the two GA individuals are partially exchanged in such a way that

$$\vartheta_k^t = \begin{bmatrix} \alpha_k^t & \beta_k^t & \gamma_k^t & \xi_k^t & \theta_k^t \end{bmatrix} \qquad \vartheta_k^{t*} = \begin{bmatrix} \alpha_k^t & \beta_k^t & \gamma_k^t & \xi_k^{t*} & \theta_k^t \end{bmatrix}$$
$$\Rightarrow$$
$$\vartheta_n^t = \begin{bmatrix} \alpha_n^t & \beta_n^t & \gamma_n^t & \xi_n^t & \theta_n^t \end{bmatrix} \qquad \vartheta_n^{t*} = \begin{bmatrix} \alpha_n^t & \beta_n^t & \gamma_n^t & \xi_n^{t*} & \theta_n^t \end{bmatrix}$$

where

$$\begin{cases} \xi_k^{t*} = a\xi_n^t + (1-a)\xi_k^t \\ \xi_n^{t*} = a\xi_k^t + (1-a)\xi_n^t \end{cases} .$$

Parameter a is a random variable following a uniform distribution in one of the following ranges:

$$a \in \begin{cases} \left[\max(a_1, a_2), \min(a_3, a_4)\right], & \text{if } \xi_k^t > \xi_n^t, \\ [0, 0], & \text{if } \xi_k^t = \xi_n^t, \\ \left[\max(a_3, a_4), \min(a_1, a_2)\right], & \text{if } \xi_k^t < \xi_n^t, \end{cases}$$

and

$$\begin{cases} a_1 = \left(L_\xi - \xi_n^t\right)\left(\xi_k^t - \xi_n^t\right) \\ a_2 = \left(R_\xi - \xi_k^t\right)\left(\xi_n^t - \xi_k^t\right) \\ a_3 = \left(L_\xi - \xi_k^t\right)\left(\xi_n^t - \xi_k^t\right) \\ a_4 = \left(R_\xi - \xi_n^t\right)\left(\xi_k^t - \xi_n^t\right) \end{cases}$$

The operator is applied to the GA population, and the number of crossovers in one generation is $p \times$ probability$_{single\text{-}arithmetical\text{-}crossover}$.

- Whole arithmetical crossover
  This operator carries out linear transformations on each element in the two GA individuals in such a way that

$$\begin{cases} \vartheta_k^{t^*} = (1-a)\vartheta_k^t + a\vartheta_n^t, \\ \vartheta_n^{t^*} = (1-a)\vartheta_n^t + a\vartheta_k^t. \end{cases}$$

where a is a random variable following a uniform distribution in range [0,1]. The operator is applied to the GA population, and the number of whole crossovers is $p \times$ probability$_{whole\text{-}arithmetical\text{-}crossover}$.

Reproduction Operators

As in the project sequencing case, the function of a reproduction operator is to produce an offspring generation of individuals from the parent generation according to the principle that the fitter (better) an individual – in terms of the objective function – the more chance the individual has of being copied into the new generation. The operator is applied to a parent generation until the offspring generation has the same population size. Unlike mutation and crossover, reproduction does not produce new individuals but ensures that the population of offspring individuals are generally fitter (better) than those of the parent generation. This provides the basis for producing even fitter new individuals by further mutation and crossover.

As before a binary tournament reproduction operator is used. The operator randomly selects a pair of individuals from a parent population and makes a copy of the individual with the better objective function value in the offspring generation. An individual could be selected and replicated more than once. The elite scheme for preserving the best individual of a generation is also incorporated into the reproduction operator to make sure that the best individual has at least one copy in the next generation.

The best individual in an offspring generation after mutation and crossover have been applied is at least as good as the best in the parent generation, that is, $L_{best}^{t+1} \geq L_{best}^t$ in the case of maximizing the log likelihood function.

After successive generations, the process of selecting the best individual converges to a solution of the problem of estimating the travel function parameters.

OPTIMIZING GENETIC ALGORITHM PARAMETERS FOR A LONG PROJECT SEQUENCE

Genetic algorithm performance was simulated (Han, 2002) in preparation for the solution of the maintenance problem (Chapter 9) but the results have wider relevance. Because each chromosome for this problem has 319 elements representing road sections, a simple GA was specified with chromosomes of that length. The elements of a reference chromosome were specified as the integers in ascending order $(1,2,\ldots,318,319)$. The variable chromosomes with which it was compared had the same integers arranged in any order $(x_1,x_2,\ldots x_{319})$. The objective was to maximize fitness defined as the squared Euclidean distance between the variable chromosome and the reference chromosome:

$$\text{Fitness} = ED^2 = (x_1-1)^2 + (x_2-2)^2 +\ldots+ (x_{319}-319)^2$$

Obviously the solution is the furthermost point where the elements of the variable chromosome are the numbers in descending order $(319,318,\ldots,2,1)$. These give the maximum fitness value of 10 820 480. This is analytically trivial but finding the maximum with a non-analytical genetic algorithm search is difficult. The purpose of the test was to find values of the parameters, population size, crossover rate and mutation rates for both individuals and elements which made the GA as effective as possible in the search.

The parameter settings were explored under the constraint that the product of population and generation was always as near as possible to 240 000 (evaluations). A large number of generations was appropriate because the chromosome with 319 elements is very long and because of the need in a test like this to ensure that the solutions are close to the optimum. Results of 14 experiments are shown in Table 4.1, ranked by fitness value.

The first conclusion is that for this problem it is not necessary to use a large population. Populations from 42 to 226 all gave results close to the maximum. Many generations were required for the small populations to achieve the specified number of evaluations (approximately 240000). In a real GA search also it would be necessary to have a relatively large number of generations for a small population.

Crossover rates varied from 0.547 to 0.945. The results suggest that high crossover rates give better results but this has to be interpreted in relation to the mutation rate.

Table 4.1   Numerical convergence problem: solutions near the optimum

Pop. size	Number of generations	Crossover rate	Mutation rate			Fitness value
			Rate 1[a]	Rate 2[b]	Composite	
101	2376	0.945	0.336	0.872	0.293	10 820 048
101	2376	0.945	0.336	0.875	0.294	10 820 040
42	5714	0.845	0.336	0.872	0.293	10 819 898
100	2400	0.900	0.333	0.251	0.084	10 819 894
92	2609	0.871	0.336	0.857	0.288	10 819 848
126	1905	0.670	0.356	0.846	0.301	10 819 548
86	2791	0.679	0.342	0.586	0.200	10 819 418
54	4444	0.579	0.356	0.846	0.301	10 819 368
66	3636	0.628	0.336	0.784	0.263	10 819 360
77	3117	0.742	0.453	0.959	0.434	10 819 102
226	1062	0.644	0.248	0.715	0.177	10 818 738
74	3243	0.904	0.371	0.296	0.110	10 818 548
138	1739	0.733	0.474	0.784	0.372	10 818 380
170	1412	0.547	0.504	0.861	0.434	10 817 490

Notes:

[a] Mutation rate 1: the probability that a chromosome is selected for mutation.

[b] Mutation rate 2: the probability that a gene of the selected chromosome is chosen to be exchanged with another gene.

The composite mutation rate – the product of mutation rates 1 and 2 – ranged between 0.08 and 0.43. The results appear to indicate that rates as high as 0.43 may be somewhat less effective. A further test was done with mutation rates at the small composite value of 0.01 (0.2 x 0.5 for example). In seven runs at each of two settings the fitness values were at least 0.2 per cent below any in Table 4.1.

This may be the most significant result of the whole series of experiments. Composite mutation rates as low as 0.01 have been used in the past but these results indicate that they are too low. The experiments suggest that a composite rate of about 0.3 (such as 0.35 x 0.86) is likely to be effective but a composite rate of 0.4 may be almost as good.

These experiments indicate that the performance of genetic algorithm in a large problem is not very sensitive to the parameter settings other than the mutation rate. It is recommended that project scheduling problems with a large number of projects or road segments should have GA parameters set within the following ranges:

Population	100 to 200
Crossover rate	0.6 to 0.9
Composite mutation rate	0.1 to 0.5

Although the rural and urban studies (Chapters 7 and 8) with fewer chromosome elements were not the subject of such extensive numerical experiments, experience and tests indicated that the parameters above would also be applicable with far fewer elements than the 319 in the maintenance problem of Chapter 9.

Limiting the population size to reduce computing time may be necessary for very long strings but not for studies with fewer elements. The rural road investment study in Chapter 7 has 34 potential projects and used populations of 200 and 500. The urban study in Chapter 8 has 56 potential projects and used a population of 200.

DISTRIBUTED COMPUTING

To alleviate the burden of a large project scheduling problem it may be possible to distribute the load across a group of networked computers at night or on weekends (Han, 2002, 71-73). The chromosomes of each generation are distributed and evaluated simultaneously so that computing power is increased roughly in proportion to the number of computers available.

One computer is the 'master' responsible for running the GA. The others call for one chromosome at a time from a common network drive whenever they are free and send the results back to that drive when the evaluation is finished.

It is the fitness of each potential investment schedule that is sent back. When enough individuals have been received (equal to or exceeding the specified population size) the master computer executes the GA operations and produces the next generation of chromosomes to be separately evaluated by the supporting computers.

A potential hazard for distributed computing is that a computer may lose the connection with the network drive or be terminated by another user.

The result is a lost chromosome. To compensate for such occurrences and guarantee the full size of population at each generation, additional chromosomes are generated (say 30 per cent more). It is a good idea to make the number of excess chromosomes greater than the number of computers so that any power failure would still leave enough chromosomes for the GA to run a full population when all the computers restart.

Transferring chromosomes into files for writing and reading data in and from network disk drives takes much more time than exchanging information directly with the computer memory. However such time loss is negligible when compared with the time taken to evaluate fitness. A great advantage of this procedure is that the computers can stop and resume at any time without influencing the performance of the GA. The restarted procedure will continue from wherever it stopped.

TRAFFIC MODELLING

We noted early in this chapter that the computer time required to assign traffic far outweighs what is needed to perform the actual GA operations. Traffic modelling is a key part of finding the best investment schedule and is the topic of the next chapter.

REFERENCES AND FURTHER READING

Genetic Algorithm and Evolutionary Computing

Bäck, T., U. Hammel and H. Schwefel (1997), 'Evolutionary computation: comments on history and current state', *IEEE Transactions on Evolutionary Computation*, **1** (1), 3-17.

Goldberg, D.E. (1989), *Genetic Algorithms in Search, Optimization and Machine Learning*, Reading, US and Wokingham, UK: Addison-Wesley.

Holland, J.H. (1975), *Adaptation in Natural and Artificial Systems*, Ann Arbor, MI: University of Michigan Press.

Ma, W., R.L. Cheu and D-H. Lee (2004), 'Scheduling of lane closures using genetic algorithms with traffic assignments and distributed simulations', *Journal of Transportation Engineering*, **130** (3), 322-329

Michalewicz, Z. (1996), *Genetic Algorithms + Data Structures = Evolution Programs*, New York: Springer-Verlag.

Nunoo, C. and D. Mrawira (2004), 'Shuffled complex evolution algorithms in infrastructure works programming', *Journal of Computing in Civil Engineering*, **18** (3), 257-266

Genetic Algorithm Representation and Genetic Operators

Goldberg, D.E. and K. Deb (1991), 'A comparative analysis of selection schemes used in genetic algorithms', in Rawlins, G.J.E. (ed.), *Foundations of Genetic Algorithms*, San Mateo, CA: Morgan Kaufmann, 69-93.

Koza, J.R. (1991), 'A hierarchical approach to learning the boolean multiplexer function', in Rawlins, G.J.E. (ed.), *Foundations of Genetic Algorithms*, San Mateo, CA: Morgan Kaufmann, 171-192.

Lam, W.H.K. and Y.F. Yin (2001), 'Genetic algorithm-based approach for transportation optimisation problems', in Chambers, L. (ed.), *The Practical Handbook of Genetic Algorithms: Applications*, Boca Raton, FL: Chapman & Hall/CRC, 235-273.

Raich, A.M. and J. Ghaboussi (2001), 'Applying the implicit redundant representation genetic algorithm in an unstructured problem domain', in Chambers, L. (ed.), *The Practical Handbook of Genetic Algorithms: Applications*, 295-340.

Syswerda, G. (1991), 'Schedule optimisation using genetic algorithm, in Davis, L. (ed.), *Handbook of Genetic Algorithms*, New York: Van Nostrand Reinhold, 332-349.

Zhang, J., H.S.H. Chung, W.L. Lo, S.Y.R. Hui and A. Wu (2001), 'Decoupled optimization of power electronics circuits using genetic algorithms', in Chambers, L. (ed.), *The Practical Handbook of Genetic Algorithms: Applications*, Boca Raton, FL: Chapman & Hall/CRC, 135-166

GA Parameters, Gene Exchange and Search Termination

Alander, J.T. (1999), 'Population size, building blocks, fitness landscape and genetic algorithm search efficiency in combinatorial optimisation: an empirical study', in Chambers, L.D. (ed.), *Practical Handbook of Genetic Algorithms – Complex Coding Systems Volume III*, Boca Raton, FL: CRC Press LLC, 459-485.

Ankenbrandt, C.A. (1991), 'An extension to the theory of convergence and a proof of the time complexity of genetic algorithms', in Rawlins, G.J.E. (ed.), *Foundations of Genetic Algorithms*, San Mateo, CA: Morgan Kaufmann, pp. 53-68.

Davis, L. (1989), 'Adapting operator probabilities in genetic algorithms', *Proceedings of The Third International Conference on Genetic Algorithms*, San Mateo, CA: Morgan Kaufmann, 61-69.

Distributed Parallel Computing

Cantu-Paz, E. (1999), 'Implementing fast and flexible parallel genetic algorithms', in Chambers L.D. (ed.), *Practical Handbook of Genetic Algorithms – Complex Coding Systems Volume III*, Boca Raton, FL: CRC Press LLC, 66-83

Han, R. (2002), *Genetic Algorithm to Optimise the Allocation of Road Expenditure Between Maintenance and Renewal*, PhD thesis, University of Western Australia.

5. Modelling Traffic Responses to Road Improvements

From the very beginning of this book we have stressed that the key to selecting and scheduling the right sequence of projects is to take full account of interactions. The reliability and robustness of the genetic algorithm result depends on how well the combined impacts of the projects are estimated. Interaction is mainly through car drivers responding to road conditions and the network configuration. It was also noted in Chapter 4 that modelling these traffic responses takes most of the computer time required to find a genetic algorithm solution.

This chapter deals with approaches to traffic modelling and the broad issues involved. It also deals specifically with urban traffic assignment and the key role of traffic speed in distributing vehicles between routes within a city. It is followed in Chapter 6 with detailed treatment of non-urban traffic and the issues in specifying and estimating travel and assignment models.

In determining an optimum schedule of road projects the two main types of traffic are treated in different ways. The assessed personal travel by car generally contributes most of the benefits in the form of time savings and reduced vehicle operating costs. On some routes these may increase but reductions are expected to predominate. The other main type of traffic comprises trucks or large combination vehicles hauling freight. These cause most of the road damage that the maintenance projects and some of the major road projects are designed to offset or repair.

TRAVEL BEHAVIOUR AND TRAFFIC MODELLING

In this and the following chapter and in the chapters reporting specific regional studies, the personal travel models are of a generalized nature. One model covers urban traffic and another represents regional traffic. Certain types of truck traffic can also be generalized but some of it has special characteristics and must be modelled to take account of local factors. The following sections deal mainly with car traffic but they are followed by a treatment of generalized truck traffic modelling. The more specialized truck traffic is covered in the study of regional road maintenance in Chapter 9.

Car traffic models are designed to capture people's travel behaviour in response to road conditions, particularly the improvements that result from renovation or new construction. Traffic forecasts based on personal behaviour are needed to estimate the road expenditure benefits that are to be maximized through project scheduling. Forecasting the number of vehicles expected to travel on roads during future years is a vital stage in transport planning and the accuracy of demand forecasts directly influences the reliability of project decisions.

Each of the various road travel models has its own characteristics and requirements but the most general is the four-stage model discussed in the next section. The choice of model for a particular transport study depends on the application and the data available. Such studies investigate the relationship between travel demand and causal factors which include traveller characteristics, transport infrastructure conditions and transport policies. The importance of various influences and the details of analysis vary from one case to another.

These differences change the relevance of a particular modelling approach from application to application: a specific context calls for a particular approach. For example departure time has been recognized as a factor in travel choice; measures to alleviate road congestion (for example a real-time traffic information system or electronic tolling) influence when a commuter chooses to depart. So departure time becomes important when the effects of congestion-alleviating measures are analysed and it needs to be modelled explicitly.

Under these circumstances the four-step model would probably not work well because it treats departure time in an approximate way. Dynamic or activity-based modelling approaches are needed to take full account of the differences between traffic peak and off-peak periods as well as their duration. In a not very congested road network where the departure time is not a critical decision factor the four-step model is relevant and the use of daily traffic data may produce reasonable analytical results.

In order to estimate trips from traffic counts in a rural network, a population-based gravity model for passenger cars and a gravity model based on gross domestic product (GDP) for freight vehicles can be used to generate the origin–destination traffic. This is distributed to routes and links by a logit procedure.

Data required are link traffic counts, road lengths and classifications and populations. If freight traffic is to be modelled separately then regional gross domestic product is required.

FOUR-STAGE MODELLING

Traffic demand modelling is based on a set of assumptions, the most important ones being that travel behaviour is stable and predictable and that travel demand is related to zonal socio-economic characteristics. The purpose of modelling is to seek relationships among the various measurable factors and to calibrate these for the base year. They are then used to estimate future traffic patterns in keeping with socio-economic development plans and projections. An underlying assumption is that the modelled relationships will not change significantly in the future.

The four-step model is well developed and widely used. It is implemented in most commercially available transport planning software and is stipulated as the required method for traffic demand forecasting in the planning manuals of countries such as China and Japan. The four model stages, including trip generation, trip distribution, modal split and assignment, are usually applied in sequence and the output from one model is the input to the next.

Stage 1: Trip Generation

The purpose of the trip generation stage is to estimate the number of trips originating and terminating in different zones of the study area. These generation and attraction numbers are usually defined as functions of population, land use characteristics and socio-economic activities. At this stage of travel demand estimation, modelling may be at the aggregate level of the zone or at the disaggregate level of the household.

In either case there are alternative statistical methods of estimating the number of trips generated in each zone and these differ in degree of complexity. The easiest way is to predict future trip generation by applying simple growth rates, a method used in early transportation studies. Subsequent studies have sought relationships between trips and some independent variables including population and economic activity. Regression models can be used only in cases where at least partial origin and destination trip data are available. Furthermore regression can be applied for future trip generation only if the generation characteristics are assumed to remain stable with time; at least there are assumed to be no significant changes during the forecast period.

Stage 2: Trip Distribution

Models at this stage are derived to estimate the number of trips that will be made between each pair of zones – an origin–destination (OD) pair – given the aggregate trip numbers from all origins estimated at the previous stage.

These models are typically specified as functions of the production and attraction factors in the various zones and the travel costs between them.

The method that has been widely used to project OD traffic is the gravity model which is used to estimate the pattern of trips in terms of three factors: one associated with the zone in which a trip begins, one with the zone in which it ends and the third with the separation between the zones.

The term gravity stems from the assumption that the number of trips between an origin and a destination zone is directly proportional to the relative attraction of each zone and inversely proportional to some function of the spatial separation between them. The simplest form of the model is still analogous to Newton's gravitational law in which the power of the distance between the two centres of gravity is two.

The gravity model can be expressed in general terms as: $q_{rs} = A(r) \, B(s) \, f(c_{rs})$ where $A(r)$ is a factor related to the ability of zone r to generate trips and $B(s)$ is a factor related to the ability of zone s to attract trips. They are unspecified origin and destination 'weight functions' which may involve locational attributes and contain relevant dimensional constants. The term $f(c_{rs})$ is a measure of the effect of separation c_{rs} on the amount of travel from r to s. It is an unspecified 'distance deterrence function' possibly involving generalized measures of distance.

For prediction purposes, the gravity model may be expressed in different ways depending on the constraints. An unconstrained gravity model requires easily obtained information such as population and general economic activity (gross domestic product) by zone. The parameters may be calibrated by linear regression, non-linear regression or maximum likelihood; also information minimization and entropy maximization may be used.

Stage 3: Modal Split

Many models determine the proportion of trips on each transport mode between origins and destinations based on relative measures of attractiveness and competitiveness. This is often an important stage in an urban travel study. The split of freight between road, rail and sometimes waterway is important in non-urban transport but passenger mode split is often ignored. Mode split is outside the scope of this book which deals only with road traffic.

Stage 4: Traffic Assignment

The purpose of the traffic assignment part of the transport planning process is to provide an estimate of the amount of traffic that will use each link in a network under given conditions. This is generally done by allocating the estimated trips to routes through the network according to some hypothesis about the way in which people choose between them.

The input for the traffic assignment process is a complete description of the existing and proposed network and a matrix of interzonal trip movements obtained from the previous distribution stage. The output of the process is an estimate of the traffic volumes on each link of the network.

URBAN TRAFFIC

Urban traffic assignment differs radically from non-urban and is considered first. The origin–destination flows are assumed to have been estimated already.

The first task in assigning traffic to an urban network is to identify the shortest route or 'path' (in terms of travel time) between each of the many pairs of origins and destinations. The next step is to assign all of the traffic to these shortest routes. Figure 5.1 shows traffic assigned to the shortest (quickest) routes from A to B and so on. After the traffic has been assigned to only four of these, the links in the K–J corridor are becoming congested. In real life motorists would start to seek alternative routes and the modeller must mimic this behaviour.

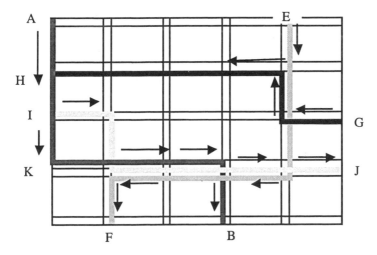

Figure 5.1   Initial assignment of traffic to shortest routes

Shortest-path problems can be specified in a number of different forms other than the obvious one of finding the shortest route between one node and another. These include finding the shortest path from a root node to all other nodes in the network and finding the shortest path between all pairs of nodes. The following brief comments refer to the widely used label-correcting algorithms. The efficiency of a shortest-path algorithm depends on the type of network, the range of arc lengths, the distribution of arc lengths across the network and the density of the network.

The 'label' of a node j is the shortest distance found so far from the source node to node j. The value depends on the length of each arc in the path and is taken to be the free-flow travel time. The algorithm selects arcs (i,j) such that $d(i)$ represents the shortest path from source to i but all labels are temporary until the final step when the shortest path has been found.

The important issue is the order in which to pick arcs for updates because this will determine how quickly the algorithm arrives at the solution. A list is maintained to keep track of the order in which nodes are to be scanned. The particular algorithm used in the study reported in Chapter 8 is of the threshold or partitioning type (a modified 'Thresh-X2'). It divides the nodes to be scanned into different lists according to some threshold value.

If the label of a node is less than or equal to the threshold value then it is scanned first. Thus the nodes are sorted according to label and examining the smaller-valued labels first results in fewer nodes being examined. Performing these operations is the most time-consuming part of urban traffic assignment so that it is important to use an efficient shortest-path algorithm.

Congestion in an Urban Network

At low traffic levels each user of an urban network can travel without having much effect on others but at higher levels even one additional vehicle causes delay to everyone. This means that as flow increases the external effect of each vehicle on other users of a link also increases. Link level costs are a function of flow, length of link, free-flow speed and road capacity. A commonly used function is the Bureau of Public Roads (BPR) travel time function:

$$tt_i = tt_{0i}(1 + b_i x_i^4) \qquad (5.1)$$

where tt_{0i} is the free-flow travel speed on link i, and b_i is a link constant which factors in the number of lanes and hourly lane capacity. This function is not asymptotic to the capacity of the road so that maintaining flow feasibility in traffic assignment needs considerably increased computing time. Davidson's function is asymptotic to the capacity Q_i of link i:

$$tt_i = tt_{oi}(1 + J\frac{x_i}{Q_i - x_i}) \qquad (5.2)$$

The *J* parameter reflects the delay on a particular road class. For instance freeways have a low value while secondary roads have a relatively high value. The function used in the urban study of Chapter 8 is an expanded form of equation (5.2).

Urban Traffic Assignment

The economically rational traveller chooses the route which minimizes his or her own perceived generalized cost. Although factors such as type of road, scenery, roadworks and habit affect the choice of route, travel time and money cost are taken to be the most important influences on this decision. The calculation of travel time is therefore an important component in the approximation of a generalized user cost.

The planner's ideal for urban traffic is embodied in Wardrop's second principle:

- The average journey time is a minimum.

If this principle were to hold then the traffic pattern would be system optimized. It would require an infeasible degree of cooperation between drivers who are largely unaware of the costs they impose upon other users of the road system and may not care about them.

It is more realistic to assume that drivers seek routes in accordance with Wardrop's first principle:

- The journey times on all routes actually used are equal and less than those which would be experienced by a single vehicle on any unused route.

This practical principle implies that drivers seek the routes which minimize their individual travel times. Such user optimization may be analysed as a snapshot in time, for instance the morning peak hour, so that an equilibrium flow pattern is determined for the network at that hour. The resulting model is called deterministic user equilibrium (DUE).

An even more realistic assumption is that drivers take account of a variety of external and personal factors and consequently distribute themselves across reasonable routes in a seemingly random fashion. This leads to the stochastic user equilibrium (SUE) model. Although this model has been found difficult to apply, Ernst (2003) has used it in a realistic but limited application. Stochastic network loading is the normal approach for uncongested inter-urban and rural routes; it is discussed in some detail later in this chapter and in Chapter 6.

A standard deterministic user equilibrium (DUE) model initially assigns traffic to shortest routes between origins and destinations but then congestion usually distributes the traffic between each origin–destination pair to multiple routes. The DUE model will adequately represent the traffic responses to upgrading or other network changes. The user-optimized equilibrium traffic flows are found as the solution to the following mathematical program:

$$\text{Minimize} \quad \sum_a \int_0^{f_a} c_a(x)dx \tag{5.3}$$

$$\text{Subject to} \quad \sum_{r \in R_{ij}} h_r = T_{ij} \forall i, j \tag{5.4}$$

$$h_r \geq 0 \forall r \in R$$

$$f_a = \sum_{r \in R} \delta_{ar} h_r \forall a \in L$$

where f_a is the flow of vehicles on link a and c_a is travel cost on link a. T_{ij} represents trips from origin i to destination j and h_r is the flow on route r. R includes all routes from origins to destinations and L includes all links on these routes. δ_{ar} is 1 if link a is on route r, 0 otherwise.

Equation (5.4) states that the sum of flows going over all routes from origin i to destination j must be equal to the demand given by T_{ij}. Traffic is loaded on to the least-cost routes, the effects of congestion on travel times are calculated and traffic is reassigned.

If traffic were simply assigned to the new least cost routes there would be cycling and the process would be unlikely to converge. This is overcome by the Frank-Wolfe algorithm which makes a series of efficient reassignments to reach the user equilibrium solution of Wardrop's second principle. Convergence generally takes a small number of iterations, even for a large urban network. The method has been a fairly good predictor of what will happen after a network is modified, as drivers do some experimenting and settle down to the new 'equilibrium'.

There are a number of well-known computer packages of this type and it is also possible to program a DUE model for a particular case, as was done for the optimization of urban road investment reported in Chapter 8.

TRIP MATRIX ESTIMATION

Having passed over it in the discussion of urban traffic we now return to the problem of estimating origin–destination (OD) traffic. A trip table is a matrix whose elements represent the number of trips made between various zones located within a road network. A 'true' origin–destination matrix is seldom available and methods commonly used to estimate it can be divided into three categories: direct sample estimation, model estimation and estimation from traffic flows.

Direct sample estimation by home interview survey or roadside interview to obtain trip data is costly and time consuming. Labour and budget constraints often make it difficult for planning agencies to conduct such surveys. Then changes in land-use and economic structure may soon make the resulting trip table outdated. For these reasons researchers have sought to develop methods for estimating the trip matrix from traffic counts that are inexpensive and regularly collected. The calibrated models can be updated easily from new count data.

Estimation from Link Counts

Approaches to estimation from link counts can be grouped into two categories: matrix estimation and parameter calibration. Matrix estimation relies on link traffic counts and reference OD matrices, which may be target, partial or outdated matrices. When parameters are to be calibrated it can be done by linear or non-linear regression, assuming a gravity-type flow pattern.

Zonal information such as population and economic activity is regularly published and easily collected. This provides a basis for estimating trip matrices and calibrating travel demand models. We present a parameter calibration technique for non-urban traffic and the actual estimation procedure is covered in Chapter 6. Because OD estimation from traffic counts covers three of the four modelling stages – trip generation, trip distribution and traffic assignment – the gravity and assignment models are combined into a single model.

Combining Distribution and Assignment Models

Two travel models have been jointly estimated to capture travellers' responses to changes in the rural and interurban road network. The first is a direct demand gravity model to predict traffic volumes between centres and the second is a choice model to distribute this traffic across reasonable alternative routes.

Trip generation

Car trip generation has been treated as a function of populations P while freight vehicle trip generations and attractions have been treated as a function of GDP. Passenger car trips T from r to s are represented by a gravity model:

$$T_{rs} = \alpha(P_r P_s)^\beta f(C_{rs})$$

where C_{rs} is user travel cost (distance or time) between r and s, and $f(C_{rs})$ is the impedance function. The parameter β is the trip demand elasticity with respect to the population product and α is a scale parameter.

The theoretically preferred representation of impedance function $f(C_{rs})$ is an exponential function with the logsum of travel costs over all reasonable routes connecting each pair of centres, that is $C_{rs} = \frac{1}{\theta} \ln \sum_k e^{\theta C_{rs}^k}$, then:

$$f(C_{rs}) = e^{\gamma C_{rs}} = \left(\sum_k e^{\theta C_{rs}^k} \right)^\phi$$

where C_{rs}^k is the travel cost (distance or time) by route k from r to s and $\phi = \gamma/\theta$. The θ in this formula is the one shown in logit model (5.6) on the next page. The value of ϕ is in the range $(0, 1)$. However application of this form to two rural and inter-urban cases gave a very small ϕ estimate, implying that trips are not significantly influenced by distance. Consequently minimum travel time was used in the impedance function:

$$f(C_{rs}) = C_{rs}^{\min \gamma}.$$

Route choice

Although many travellers on uncongested rural roads choose the shortest route, others choose longer routes for a variety of reasons. They may simply change route for the sake of variety. When the logit model is applied to a population of travellers the probability of choosing an alternative can be interpreted as the proportion who actually choose it:

$$p_{rs}^k = \frac{e^{\theta C_{rs}^k / C_{rs}^{\min}}}{\sum_{k \in K_{rs}} e^{\theta C_{rs}^k / C_{rs}^{\min}}} \tag{5.5}$$

Using the ratio of the travel time on a particular route (C_{rs}^k) to that on the minimum travel-time route (C_{rs}^{min}) makes the probability of route choice predicted by logit model (5.5) sensitive to total route distance. This point is discussed fully in Chapter 6, Appendix 6A.

Nevertheless some of the standard packages cannot readily accept the ratio formulation and it may be necessary to adopt the standard form of the logit shown in equation (5.6):

$$p_{rs}^k = \frac{e^{\theta C_{rs}^k}}{\displaystyle\sum_{k \in K_{rs}} e^{\theta C_{rs}^k}} \qquad (5.6)$$

If the ratio is used instead of the standard form then routes are enumerated for each origin–destination pair. Thus computing time is reduced by using the standard form (5.6) for the traffic assignment.

Combined model

The direct travel demand model and the multipath logit traffic assignment model are estimated jointly if the number of trips between origins and destinations is unknown. If the knowns are populations P, travel times on road links C, observed flows on a substantial number of links F, and the topology of the road network, then the direct demand and assignment models are combined for joint estimation as:

$$F_l = \sum_{\forall r \in O} \sum_{\forall s \in D} \sum_{\forall k \in K_{rs}} \frac{\delta_l^k \alpha (P_r P_s)^\beta C_{rs}^{min\ \gamma} e^{\theta C_{rs}^k / C_{rs}^{min}}}{\displaystyle\sum_{\forall k \in K_{rs}} e^{\theta C_{rs}^k / C_{rs}^{min}}} \qquad (5.7)$$

Model (5.7) differs from those used in cities, where congestion is important, in that it does not contain production and attraction constraints and it is derived as the best fit to the observed data. Applicable versions of this model are discussed in Chapter 6 and specific estimation methods are discussed in the Chapter 6 appendices.

DISAGGREGATE TRAVEL DEMAND ESTIMATION

The discussion so far has been in terms of the relationship between aggregate travel demand and related factors, the analysis unit being the population of trip makers. Other methods model the relationship between the travel behaviour of an individual (a single person, a household or an organization) and various causal factors. The responses of individuals to a change, expressed as probabilities of choosing alternatives from a travel choice set, are aggregated across the individuals to obtain the total travel demand.

The disaggregate travel model is based on random utility theory, with arguments in the indirect utility function including observed attributes of individuals, the alternatives in the choice set and a term for unobserved attributes. Different assumptions about the distribution of the unobserved term result in various disaggregate models, among which the logit has been widely used and the probit has been gaining popularity due to advances in estimation technique.

From a theoretical point of view, the disaggregate model has advantages in predicting individual travel behaviour. One of the benefits is that it can capture a person's responses to changes in trip attributes. The information about these responses is likely to be lost when the details are summarized for an aggregate model. Another advantage of the disaggregate method is that it explicitly models the dispersion of individuals over choice alternatives when facing the same observed conditions, the dispersion being due to unobserved attributes and the tastes of individuals. This enhances the accuracy of prediction especially when the more complex probit and heteroscedastic extreme value models are estimated.

Activity-Based Models

A further step into the detail of individual behaviour is activity-based modelling. Demand for travel is usually derived from the need to connect activities scattered at different locations and at different times. However trip-based models focus on travel per se with little or no regard to the activities which underly the decision to travel. Activity-based methods on the other hand explicitly model not only the trips but also activities associated with them, taking account of spatial and temporal linkages between activities and constraints.

In addition to enhancing the understanding of traveller behaviour, the development of activity-based modelling has been motivated by the need to assess transport policies such as electronic road pricing. These have impacts not only on travel generation, choice of destinations, modes and routes, but also on aspects of travel behaviour such as the choice of departure time. The activity approach treats travel as a multi-purpose and multi-stop process and involves direct study of people's activity patterns and how these patterns respond to changes in the human environment.

Data Limitations

The prerequisite for all types of trip and activity-based models is detailed information about individuals. This is not as easy to obtain as aggregate data and without adequate information a disaggregate transport model does not necessarily produce better results. Thus the use of models based on individual behaviour in transport studies tends to be limited by lack of details about the the traveller as well as insufficient fine detail about the transport system and the options which the traveller faces.

GENERALIZED MODELLING OF TRUCK TRAFFIC

As already noted, responsive models of truck traffic are essential for a proper assessment of road deterioration. The generalized model of truck traffic is based on the assumption that truck movements can be represented by a gravity model using zonal economic activity and haulage costs between zones and that route choice behaviour is represented by a logit model. This is similar to the non-urban personal travel model but population is replaced by economic activity.

A combined model based on economic activity and link traffic data requires simultaneous estimation of gravity and route choice models. The available data for each zone is gross domestic product (GDP). The gravity model is:

$$q_{rs} = \alpha (G_r G_s)^\beta f(C_{rs}) \tag{5.8}$$

where there are q_{rs} truck trips between origin r and destination s, G_r and G_s are the GDPs of r and s and C_{rs} is user travel cost (distance or time) between r and s. The parameter β is the trip demand elasticity with respect to the GDP product and α is a scale parameter. $f(C_{rs})$ is the impedance function.

Calibration of this generalized truck traffic model and the introduction of a logit choice function are discussed in Chapter 6. It has already been noted that much truck traffic has special characteristics and must be modelled to take account of local factors. Such traffic is considered in the specific context of regional road maintenance in Chapter 9.

CALIBRATION OF MODELS

Calibration of the inter-urban and rural car and truck models is the subject of Chapter 6. The main topic is how to formulate and estimate models but

Chapter 6 also presents a relatively simple version of the car model, using parameters that have already been estimated.

REFERENCES AND FURTHER READING

Urban Traffic Modelling

Burrell, J.E. (1976), 'Multiple route assignment: a comparison of two methods' in Florian, M. (ed.), *Lecture Notes in Economics and Mathematical System (118) – Traffic Equilibrium Methods*, Berlin: Springer-Verlag, 229-239.

Domencich, T.A. and D. McFadden (1975), *Urban Travel Demand – A Behavioural Analysis*, Amsterdam and New York: North-Holland and American Elsevier.

Ernst, W.F. (2003), *The Economic Rationale for Stochastic Urban Transport Models and Traffic Behaviour*, PhD thesis, University of Western Australia.

Karlqvist, A. and B. Marksjo, (1971), 'Statistical urban models', *Environment and Planning*, **10A**, 371-388

Mahmassani, H.M. (1997), 'Dynamics of commuter behaviour: recent research and continuing challenges', in Stopher, P. and M. Lee-Gosselin (eds), *Understanding Travel Behaviour in an Era of Change*, Oxford: Pergamon, 279-313.

Oppenheim, N. (1995). *Urban Travel Demand Modeling*, New York: John Wiley & Sons.

Salim, V.K. (1997), 'A comparison of shortest path algorithms in urban traffic assignment', *Mathematics and Computers in Simulation*, **43**, 545-551.

Sheffi, Y. (1985), *Urban Transportation Networks: Equilibrium Analysis with Mathematical Programming Methods*, Englewood Cliffs, NJ: Prentice-Hall.

Wardrop, J.G. (1952), 'Some theoretical aspects of road traffic research', *Proceedings of the Institute of Civil Engineers*, Part II, vol. 1, 325-378.

Trip Generation and Distribution

Bates, J. (2000), 'History of demand modelling', in Hensher, D.A. and K.J. Button (eds), *Handbook of Transport Modelling*, Amsterdam: Pergamon, 11-33.

Bell, M.G.H. (1995), 'Alternatives to Dial's logit assignment algorithm', *Transportation Research Part B*, **29B**, 287-295.

Ben-Akiva, M. and S.R. Lerman (1979), 'Disaggregate travel and mobility-choice models and measures of accessibility', in Hensher, D.A. and P.R. Stopher (eds), *Behavioural Travel Modelling*, London: Croom Helm, 654-679.

Ben-Akiva, M. and S.R. Lerman (1985), *Discrete Choice Analysis: Theory and Application to Travel Demand*, Cambridge, MA: MIT Press, 55-57.

Borgers A.W.J., F. Hofman and H.J.P. Timmermans (1997), 'Activity-based modelling: prospects', in Ettema, D. and H. Timmermans (eds), *Activity-Based Approach to Travel Analysis*, Oxford: Pergamon, 339-351.

Cascetta, E. (1984), 'Estimation of trip matrices from traffic counts and survey data: a generalised least squares estimator', *Transportation Research Part B*, **18B** (4/5), 289-299.

Cochrane, R.A. (1975), 'A possible economic basis for the gravity model', *Journal of Transportation Economics and Policy*, **9**, 34-49.

Fisk, C. (1977), 'Note on the maximum likelihood calibration of Dial's assignment method', *Transportation Research*, **11**, 67-68.

Fisk, C.S. and D.E. Boyce (1983), 'A note on trip matrix estimation from link traffic count data', *Transportation Research Part B*, **17B** (3), 245-250.

Gärling, T., R. Gillholm, J. Romanus and M. Selart (1997), 'Interdependent activity and travel choices: behavioural principles of integration of choice outcomes', in Ettema, D. and H. Timmermans (eds), *Activity-Based Approach to Travel Analysis*, Oxford: Pergamon, 135-149.

Hensher, D.A. (1996), *Establishing a Fare Elasticity Regime for Urban Passenger Transport: Non-Concession Commuters*, Institute of Transport Studies, Graduate School of Business, University of Sydney.

Hogberg, P. (1976), 'Estimation of parameters in models for traffic prediction: a non-linear regression approach', *Transportation Research*, **10**, 263-265.

Isard, W. (1998), 'Gravity and spatial interaction models', in Isard, W., I. Azis, M. Drennan, R. Miller, S. Saltzman, and E. Thorbecke (eds), *Methods of Interregional and Regional Analysis*, Aldershot: Ashgate Publishing Company, 243-279.

Kirby, H.R. (1974), 'Theoretical requirements for calibrating gravity models', *Transportation Research*, **8**, 97-104.

Liu, S. and J.D. Fricker, (1996), 'Estimation of a trip table and the θ parameter in a stochastic network', *Transportation Research Part A*, **30A** (4), 287-305

McFadden, D., and F. Reid (1975), 'Aggregate travel demand forecasting from disaggregate behavioural models', *Transportation Research Record 534*, Washington, DC: Transportation Research Board, 24-37

Nihan, N.L. and G.A. Davis, (1987), 'Recursive estimation of origin-destination matrices from input/output counts', *Transportation Research Part B*, **21B** (2), 149-163

Ortúzar, J. de D. and L.G. Willumsen (1994), *Modelling Transport*, 2nd edition, Chichester: John Wiley & Sons.

Patriksson, M. (1994), *The Traffic Assignment Problem – Models and Methods*, Utrecht: VSP.

Robillard, P. (1975), 'Estimating the O-D matrix from observed link volumes', *Transportation Research*, **9**, 123-128

Sen, A. and T.E. Smith (1995), *Gravity Models of Spatial Interaction Behaviour*, Berlin: Springer-Verlag.

Sherali, H.D., R. Sivanandan and A.G. Hobeika (1994). 'A linear programming approach for synthesizing origin–destination trip tables from link traffic volumes', *Transportation Research Part B*, **28B** (3), 213-233

Williams, H.C.W.L. and J. de D. Ortuzar (1982), 'Behavioural theories of dispersion and the mis-specification of travel demand models', *Transportation Research Part B*, **16B** (3), 167-219.

Wilson, A.G. (1967), 'A statistical theory of spatial distribution models', *Transportation Research*, **1**, 253-269

Wilson, A.G. (1974), *Urban and Regional Models in Geography and Planning*, London: John Wiley & Sons.

6. Estimating Rural and Inter-urban Traffic Models

In this chapter the broad issues introduced in Chapter 5 are brought down to the specifics of model estimation. It was noted there that the reliability and robustness of the project scheduling depends on how well the combined impacts of the projects are estimated. Interaction is mainly through car and truck drivers responding to road conditions and the network configuration. The first part of this chapter presents detailed issues in specification and estimation of non-urban travel and assignment models. Urban travel has already been covered in Chapter 5.

Models are presented here as an aid to those considering whether or how to undertake the task of applying genetic algorithm to select and schedule road projects. To do this some type of traffic model is essential and the ones discussed here are designed to cope with situations where the data sources are limited to little more than a moderate number of traffic counts. If there are better data resources, such as travel surveys, then it would be advisable to use a formulation which exploits them to the full.

Any modelling method can be incorporated into the GA optimization. Model builders may well use different specifications not only because they have better data sources but also because they disagree with our formulation or prefer some other approach. Specification of cost variables in both the gravity and logit route choice models are areas where differences of approach may reasonably be expected.

Whereas car traffic contributes most of the benefits in the form of time savings and reduced vehicle operating costs, trucks cause virtually all of the road deterioration. Consequently truck trips need to be modelled too. Some truck traffic can be represented by a generalized model but much of it has special characteristics and must be modelled to take account of local factors. Estimation of a generalized truck model is presented later in this chapter but more specialized truck traffic is covered in the study of regional roads in Chapter 9 and was also taken into account in the study reported in Chapter 7.

The next section outlines a procedure for estimating model parameters. An important theoretical aspect of the model form is discussed in Appendix 6A and Appendix 6B shows a hypothetical application of a slightly simplified model while Appendix 6C presents complete model estimates and considers cases where estimation can be done in a spreadsheet, possibly aided by genetic algorithm. Appendix 6D deals with the identification of reasonable routes and Appendix 6E discusses the choice of distribution for maximum likelihood estimation.

MODELLING DEMAND AND ASSIGNMENT TOGETHER

The traffic model for an uncongested network should reflect the fact that a traveller does not necessarily take the shortest route. This means that a stochastic network loading model is used to make the traffic assignments. If the only source of travel data is provided by traffic counts then a combination of direct demand and logit traffic assignment models offers an effective way of predicting network traffic for any configuration and road conditions.

As discussed in Chapter 5 a gravity formulation is used to model the number of trips between origins and destinations while the logit models the distribution of trips among the various possible routes. Where there is little or no origin–destination trip data, the combined model can be estimated from traffic counts and readily available population data.

Direct Demand

A direct demand gravity model for cars and other light vehicles is based on the trip generation model of Chapter 5 and takes the general form for trips between r and s:

$$T_{rs} = \alpha (P_r P_s)^\beta C_{rs}^\gamma$$

If destinations such as tourist resorts are expected to generate relatively more trips than other centres, then a multiplier of population can be used to account for the higher trip rates, the model being expanded to:

$$T_{rs} = \alpha \left[(1 + \varphi_r \xi) P_r (1 + \varphi_s \xi) P_s \right]^\beta C_{rs}^\gamma \tag{6.1}$$

where C_{rs} is the cost between r and s, often based on travel time, α is a scale parameter, β is the demand elasticity with respect to population, γ is the demand elasticity with respect travel cost (or time), ξ is a population multiplier for tourist-destination centroids, and φ_r, φ_s are dummy variables (1 for tourist destination, 0 otherwise). Parameters α, β, γ and ζ are to be estimated.

Model (6.1) shows the power form C_{rs}^{γ}. Alternative ways of dealing with cost C_{rs} are:

- Exponential: $\exp(\gamma \, C_{rs})$.
- Log sum across routes: $C_{rs} = \dfrac{1}{\theta} \ln \sum_{k} e^{\theta C_{rs}^{k}}$ where θ is a route distribution parameter and C_{rs}^{k} is travel cost from r to s by route k.
- Minimum cost: $C_{rs} = \min\limits_{k \in K_{rs}}(C_{rs}^{k}) = C_{rs}^{\min}$.

As explained in Chapter 5, the preferred form is the logsum but in estimating the joint gravity and route distribution model in two specific cases this formulation gave results implying that trips were not significantly influenced by distance. Consequently the minimum cost form was adopted in these cases. It implied that travellers selecting a destination assess distance along the shortest route even though some choose to take longer routes after the destination choice is made. This measure is naive but it requires minimal calculation.

When the number of trips between each pair of centroids is not known, model (6.1) cannot be estimated directly and needs to be estimated in conjunction with the traffic assignment model.

Multipath Traffic Assignment

Although many travellers on uncongested rural roads go directly to their destinations by the shortest paths, others choose longer routes for various reasons. They may simply change route for the sake of variety. The logit model of route choice is used to represent all such behaviour. When it is applied to a population of travellers the probability of choosing an alternative can be interpreted as the proportion who choose it:

$$p_{rs}^{k} = \frac{e^{\theta C_{rs}^{k}/C_{rs}^{\min}}}{\sum\limits_{k \in K_{rs}} e^{\theta C_{rs}^{k}/C_{rs}^{\min}}} \qquad (6.2)$$

In this model θ is a negative taste parameter to be estimated. The traffic on each route is calculated as:

$$T_{rs}^{k} = T_{rs} p_{rs}^{k}.$$

Using the ratio of the travel time on a particular route (C_{rs}^k) to that on the minimum travel-time route ($C_{rs}^{\min}$) makes the probability of route choice predicted by logit model (6.2) sensitive to the total distance. If the costs were not in ratio form, the denominator ($C_{rs}^{\min}$) being omitted, then the probabilities of route choice would be determined only by travel-time differences. This means that the route shares predicted by the model would be constant for a constant difference in travel-time, regardless of the length of trip. This is counter-intuitive because it is to be expected that the time difference will have less effect as the routes become longer.

Appendix 6A compares the ratio form of the logit with the simple logit and with probit alternatives.

As noted in Chapter 5, a computer package may require the simple standard form of logit to represent route choice. It is less restrictive than the ratio form with respect to the specification of reasonable routes. This model is equation (5.6), which is repeated here:

$$p_{rs}^k = \frac{e^{\theta C_{rs}^k}}{\sum_{k \in K_{rs}} e^{\theta C_{rs}^k}}$$

Joint Estimation of Direct Demand and Assignment Models

The concept of a combined model was introduced in Chapter 5. Direct demand and multipath assignment models must be estimated jointly if the numbers of trips between origins and destinations are unknown. The following procedure is based on the assumption that the knowns are populations P, travel time C on each road link, observed flows F on a substantial number of links, any recognized tourist destinations (dummy variables φ), and the topology of the road network.

For joint estimation, the direct demand and assignment models are combined as:

$$T_{rs}^k = \frac{\alpha \left[(1 + \varphi_r \xi) P_r (1 + \varphi_s \xi) P_s \right]^\beta C_{rs}^{\min \, \gamma} e^{\theta C_{rs}^k / C_{rs}^{\min}}}{\sum_{k \in K_{rs}} e^{\theta C_{rs}^k / C_{rs}^{\min}}} \tag{6.3}$$

It may be specified that route k comprises road links which take a traveller further away from the trip origin and closer to the destination (Dial's double-pass rule) but this may be relaxed to the single-pass rule discussed later.

The relationship between routes and links is expressed by a link-route incidence matrix whose elements are defined as:

$$\delta_l^k = \begin{cases} 1, & \text{if link } l \text{ is on route } k \\ 0, & \text{otherwise.} \end{cases}$$

This matrix is used to sum travel time C over the links forming route k,

$$C_{rs}^k = \sum_{\forall l \in L} C_l \delta_l^k ,$$

and to sum over all trips between origins O and destinations D in order to estimate flow on link l:

$$F_l = \sum_{\forall r \in O} \sum_{\forall s \in D} \sum_{\forall k \in K_{rs}} T_{rs}^k \delta_l^k \tag{6.4}$$

A practical example of this operation is shown in Appendix 6B, Table 6.3.

Equation (6.4) is expanded by substituting (6.3) for T_{rs}^k to give the estimating model:

$$F_l = \sum_{\forall r \in O} \sum_{\forall s \in D} \sum_{\forall k \in K_{rs}} \frac{\delta_l^k \alpha [(1 + \varphi_r \xi) P_r (1 + \varphi_s \xi) P_s]^\beta C_{rs}^{\min \gamma} e^{\theta C_{rs}^k / C_{rs}^{\min}}}{\sum_{\forall k \in K_{rs}} e^{\theta C_{rs}^k / C_{rs}^{\min}}} \tag{6.5}$$

Results obtained with this model are shown in Appendix 6C, Table 6.4.

If tourist destinations are not important then estimating model (6.5) is simplified to (5.7) as presented in Chapter 5:

$$F_l = \sum_{\forall r \in O} \sum_{\forall s \in D} \sum_{\forall k \in K_{rs}} \frac{\delta_l^k \alpha (P_r P_s)^\beta C_{rs}^{\min \gamma} e^{\theta C_{rs}^k / C_{rs}^{\min}}}{\sum_{\forall k \in K_{rs}} e^{\theta C_{rs}^k / C_{rs}^{\min}}}$$

Determining Reasonable Routes

Whether Dial's STOCH algorithm or complete enumeration (Appendix 6D) is used for traffic assignment, the basic assumption is that only reasonable routes connecting each origin–destination (OD) pair are used. The critical step is to identify these reasonable or efficient routes. Different definitions lead to different procedures: 'double-pass' and 'single-pass'.

In the double-pass procedure a reasonable route is one which includes only links that take the traveller further away from the origin and closer to the destination. The simpler single-pass procedure discards the condition that the links bring the traveller closer to the destination. A route is defined to be efficient if it includes only links that do not take the traveller back toward the origin. This definition gives a greater number of reasonable routes between a given OD pair than the double-pass definition, so that trips will be spread over more links.

Despite the greater number of reasonable routes the single-pass procedure gives a computational benefit. It simultaneously assigns all trips originating at a given node to all efficient paths in a single execution of the assignment algorithm whereas the double-pass procedure needs to assign trips for each OD pair.

If the ratio form of the logit model is used – as in equations (6.2), (6.3) and (6.5) – then the double-pass procedure may be preferred. If the simple logit model is employed then it is usual to adopt the single-pass procedure.

A GENERALIZED TRUCK TRAFFIC MODEL

The generalized model of truck traffic has two components similar to the car passenger model. The first is a gravity model based on zonal economic activity and haulage distance between zones. Population is replaced by economic activity G.

Route choice is represented by a probabilistic logit model which takes into account errors of judgement or selection of non-minimum routes. In the maintenance study reported in Chapter 9, the simple non-ratio form of the logit has been used, leading to the combined model:

$$F_l = \sum_{\forall r \in O} \sum_{\forall s \in D} \sum_{\forall k \in K_{rs}} \frac{\delta_l^k \alpha \left(G_r G_s\right)^\beta C_{rs}^{\min \; \gamma} e^{\theta C_{rs}^k}}{\displaystyle\sum_{\forall k \in K_{rs}} e^{\theta C_{rs}^k}} \tag{6.6}$$

The variables and parameters in (6.6) are similar to those in (6.5) and (5.7) except that G_r and G_s represent local economic activity (gross domestic product) in zones r and s and the θ is estimated for the simple non-ratio logit.

Estimation of model (6.6) involves the same issues and methods as are discussed for the passenger model in Appendix 6C and 6E. The results of estimating it for the Southern Wheatbelt of Western Australia and connecting zones are stated in Table 6.1. The R^2 for the final result is 0.817.

Table 6.1   Estimated freight vehicle trip and route choice parameters

Parameter	Genetic algorithm estimate	Quadratic hill-climbing (from the GA results)	
		Estimate	Standard error
α Scalar	6.48	6.489	1.1959
First derivative	18.3	0.0000	
β GDP product elasticity	0.57	0.549	0.0095
First derivative	1172	0.0000	
γ Distance elasticity	−1.504	−1.457	0.0306
First derivative	705	0.0000	
θ Route dispersion (non-ratio logit)	−0.072	−0.0633	0.0030
First derivative	1321	0.0000	

Note: Based on distances measured in kilometres. The θ value is sensitive to the units of measure.

Source: Han, 2002

Local truck traffic is additional to the generalized inter-zonal traffic modelled by equation (6.6) – as reported in Table 6.1 – and is considered in the specific regional road context in Chapter 9.

ESTIMATION AND DATA

Calibration of the models is discussed in Appendix 6C and also in Appendix 6E. Because this is not strictly convex optimization a gradient method may merely find a local optimum. To ensure convergence on the global optimum, genetic algorithm can be used for an initial search. The result found in that search then becomes the starting point for the application of Newton's method and quadratic hill-climbing. Table 6.1 (above) and Appendix 6C Table 6.4 provide examples.

It may be found possible to estimate the parameters of a joint model for a moderate sized network by using Excel Solver to minimize the sum of squared deviations from observed traffic counts. As the network becomes larger there is a risk of sub-optimizing with this method too and it may be advisable to use genetic algorithm to achieve partial convergence before switching to the Solver. There is further discussion of this approach in

Appendix 6C. The estimates made in this way will give predictions of traffic that are very similar to those made by the more rigorous methods.

However if standard errors of the estimates are required then a gradient method of maximum likelihood estimation with an explicit distribution must be used, as outlined in Appendix 6E. For simple least squares, the specification of the probability distribution of the link flows can be ignored but specification of the distribution is necessary for maximum likelihood estimation.

Traffic count information is collected in various ways. Permanent stations record traffic counts continuously for 24 hours a day through the whole year whereas records are shorter at non-permanent stations and there may also be ad hoc counts for very short periods at some other locations.

The results from all methods are usually recorded as annual average daily traffic (AADT). It has been found that satisfactory model estimates can be obtained even when there are counts for less than half of the road links in the network.

Truck traffic estimates are often based on occasional classification counts but reliable estimates are sometimes obtained by detection devices which identify axle configurations.

TRAFFIC MODELS IN GA INVESTMENT OPTIMIZATION

Detailed issues in model estimation and application are considered in the appendices to this chapter (6A, 6B, 6C, 6D and 6E). Formulation of the traffic models has set the stage for them to be included in a full genetic algorithm (GA) road investment optimization, as in the regional road investment problem of Chapter 7 and the road maintenance problem of Chapter 9.

Because it is not feasible to show the programming and computational details of these substantial applications, a relatively small but realistic case has been developed for spreadsheet application. This is presented in Chapter 10 which shows how a traffic demand model is incorporated into a genetic algorithm application. It uses the traffic model that is introduced in Appendix 6B.

Chapter 8 presents the method of finding the best sequence from a number of potential urban road projects. In this case the deterministic user equlibrium (DUE) method, as discussed in Chapter 5, is used to assign the traffic.

APPENDIX 6A   THE TRAVEL COST RATIO COMPARED WITH OTHER CHOICE SPECIFICATIONS

The following material is based on Qiu (2000). It has been noted already that if the costs in logit model (6.2) were not in ratio form then the route choice probabilities would be determined only by travel-time differences so that predicted route shares would be constant for a constant difference in travel-time, regardless of the length of trip.

The use of travel-time difference, instead of the ratio, implies that the error variance is constant across alternative routes k between r and s. This means that the unobserved terms ε_{rs}^k in the utility function,

$$U_{rs}^k = \theta C_{rs}^k + \varepsilon_{rs}^k \qquad (6.7)$$

follow a Gumbel distribution with a scale parameter μ_{rs}. This parameter is inseparable from the taste parameter θ and unidentifiable. When μ_{rs} is set equal to 1,

$$\mathrm{var}(\varepsilon_{rs}^k) = \sigma_{rs}^{k^2} = \frac{\pi^2}{6\mu_{rs}^2} = \frac{\pi^2}{6}.$$

This is a constant variance. In reality the variance of the unobserved term is more likely to be associated with travel time – the longer the travel route the greater the variance. Utilities (U_{rs}^k) represented by formula (6.7) are ordinal and division by a positive constant $C_{rs}^{\min}$ does not change the ranking of the preferences of the travellers:

$$U_{rs}^k = \theta \frac{C_{rs}^k}{C_{rs}^{\min}} + \frac{\varepsilon_{rs}^k}{C_{rs}^{\min}}, \qquad (k \in K_{rs}).$$

It can be shown that, on reasonable assumptions, this leads to model (6.2):

$$p_{rs}^k = \frac{e^{\theta C_{rs}^k / C_{rs}^{\min}}}{\sum_{k \in K_{rs}} e^{\theta C_{rs}^k / C_{rs}^{\min}}}.$$

A simple road network with two nodes connected by two links is used to compare the price ratio logit model with the simplified logit model and two probit models. The difference in travel time between the two routes is one unit of time, that is, $C_2 - C_1 = 1$. For convenience, the taste parameter θ in the utility function is set equal to –1, and it is assumed that the two routes are independent, that is $\text{cov}(\varepsilon_1, \varepsilon_2) = 0$.

The relative sensitivity of the price ratio logit model (6.2) and three alternatives are illustrated in Figure 6.1. It shows the relationships between the travel time ratio (C_1/C_2) and the probability of choosing the shorter route (p_1) predicted by the four models.

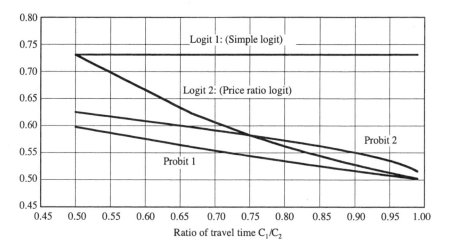

Source: Qiu, 2000

Figure 6.1   Alternative models: probability of choosing the shorter of two routes as a function of the ratio of travel times

These results have been based on the following specifications of the four models – two logit and two probit. The choice probability of the shorter route (Route 1),

$$p_1 = \Pr(\varepsilon_2 - \varepsilon_1 \leq C_2 - C_1)$$

and the related variance, as predicted by each of the alternative models, are shown as follows:

• Logit model 1: This is the simple logit model.

$$p_1 = \frac{e^{-C_1}}{e^{-C_1} + e^{-C_2}}, \qquad \text{var}(\varepsilon_1 - \varepsilon_2) = \frac{\pi^2}{3}$$

- Logit model 2: This is the price ratio logit model.

$$p_1 = \frac{e^{-C_1/C_1}}{e^{-C_1/C_1} + e^{-C_2/C_1}}, \qquad \mathrm{var}(\varepsilon_1 - \varepsilon_2) = \frac{C_1 + C_2}{C_1}\frac{\pi^2}{6}$$

- Probit model 1: The variances of ε_1 and ε_2 are proportional to the square of travel time. In this case, a scaling factor $\pi^2/3$ brings the variance of the probit to the same level as that of the logit model.

$$p_1 = \Phi\left[\frac{C_2 - C_1}{\mathrm{var}(\varepsilon_2 - \varepsilon_1)}\right], \qquad \mathrm{var}(\varepsilon_1 - \varepsilon_2) = \left(C_1^2 + C_2^2\right)\frac{\pi^2}{3}$$

- Probit model 2: The variances of ε_1 and ε_2 are proportional to travel time.

$$p_1 = \Phi\left[\frac{C_2 - C_1}{\mathrm{var}(\varepsilon_2 - \varepsilon_1)}\right], \qquad \mathrm{var}(\varepsilon_1 - \varepsilon_2) = \frac{C_1 + C_2}{C_1}\frac{\pi^2}{6}$$

Figure 6.1 indicates that the choice probability of Route 1 predicted by the simple logit model 1 is a constant irrespective of the length of travel time on the two routes. The probit models give realistic predictions for the choice probability.

However the important conclusion is that the easily managed price ratio logit model 2 is sensitive and gives very similar results to the probit models. This is particularly true when the time taken on the shorter route is at least 70 per cent of the time on the longer, as would be usual.

APPENDIX 6B   AN APPLIED NON-URBAN CAR MODEL

The structure of the combined direct demand and logit assignment model of non-urban car travel has already been discussed. The procedure for its estimation and the estimates obtained are presented in Appendix 6C. The example presented here is a slightly simplified version which is picked up again in the spreadsheet GA application of Chapter 10. It might even be possible to scale it for applied work to suit local conditions in other contexts and so be sufficient for selection and scheduling. It would satisfy the need for sensitivity to changes in road configuration or condition.

If the traffic between centres is not known then the first step is to estimate it with the direct demand gravity model. The following specification uses the minimum time cost between centres for the reason explained earlier: it was found in two applications that this gave consistent results.

$$T_{rs} = \alpha \left(P_r P_s \right)^{0.49} \left(C_{rs}^{\min} \right)^{-1.7} \tag{6.8}$$

T_{rs} is the number of trips daily between r and s, P_r, P_s are the populations, $C_{rs}^{\min}$ is the minimum travel time, in hours, between r and s, and α is a scale parameter.

The size of the scalar α depends upon local factors, including car ownership and the availability of alternative transport modes. The range for daily two-way traffic is likely to be between 0.2 and 1.5.

The second step is to identify the reasonable routes between each pair of centres which do not involve backtracking. If there are many centres and links then Appendix 6D indicates a method for identifying the reasonable routes. Alternatively Dial's STOCH method may be used. Again the relationship of routes to road links is expressed by the incidence matrix whose elements are:

$$\delta_l^k = \begin{cases} 1, & \text{if link } l \text{ is on route } k \\ 0, & \text{otherwise.} \end{cases}$$

The cost of using route k, C_{rs}^k, expressed in hours, is the sum of link costs. The next step is to estimate the logit probability p_{rs}^k, that route k will be used between r and s:

$$p_{rs}^k = \frac{e^{-15.0\left(C_{rs}^k / C_{rs}^{\min} \right)}}{\sum_{k \in K_{rs}} e^{-15.0\left(C_{rs}^k / C_{rs}^{\min} \right)}} \tag{6.9}$$

A simple transfer of the choice parameter estimate is not feasible if the computer package requires the standard form of the logit shown in equation (5.6) of Chapter 5. The θ in that formulation has a different basis from the constant value given in equation (6.9) and it is affected by the measurement units.

Nevertheless it may be reasonable to arbitrarily select a value for θ because the resulting aggregated link loads have been found to be only moderately sensitive to it. When the separation between centres is measured in hours a θ as large in absolute value as -5 may be reasonable (or $\theta = -0.1$ if the separation units are in kilometres). The larger the absolute value of θ the smaller the proportion of motorists assigned to routes other than the shortest.

As before a local application of the combined models will still require calibration of the parameter a in equation (6.8).

A Hypothetical Example

The hypothetical uncongested network shown in Figure 6.2 links six population centres A to F. The average driving time in hours is shown for each link; populations are in brackets.

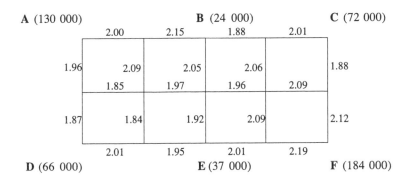

Figure 6.2   Hypothetical network linking six centres

From the data shown in Figure 6.2 the gravity model (6.8) with $\alpha = 0.53$ gives the estimated daily two-way traffic between the origin and destination centres that is shown in Table 6.2. All reasonable routes between each city pair are identified; the number of such routes varies from one to 15. The driving time for each route is found by summing over links and the shortest route is identified.

The link loadings are found by applying the logit model to the origin–destination traffic of Table 6.2 to obtain the route traffic. The driving times calculated for all reasonable routes provide the input data for the logit assignment model (6.9) to distribute trips between alternative routes linking each city pair:

$$p_{rs}^k = \frac{e^{-15.0\left(C_{rs}^k / C_{rs}^{\min}\right)}}{\sum_{k \in K_{rs}} e^{-15.0\left(C_{rs}^k / C_{rs}^{\min}\right)}} \cdot$$

Here, p_{rs}^k is the proportion of trips between r and s along route k. In each case p_{rs}^k is applied to the estimated total daily city pair trips shown in the fifth column of Table 6.2. Resulting route traffic numbers are shown in column 3 of Table 6.3.

Table 6.2   *Gravity model estimates of daily two-way origin–destination traffic for the example in Figure 6.2*

Centres linked	Shortest travel time, hrs	Population P_r	Population P_s	Estimated daily trips	Reasonable routes
A – B	4.15	130 000	24 000	2117	1
A – C	8.04	130 000	72 000	1178	1
A – D	3.83	130 000	66 000	3983	1
A – E	7.60	130 000	37 000	936	6
A – F	11.80	130 000	184 000	972	15
B – C	3.89	24 000	72 000	1769	1
B – D	7.74	24 000	66 000	526	6
B – E	3.97	24 000	37 000	1233	1
B – F	7.89	24 000	184 000	842	6
C – D	11.62	72 000	66 000	452	15
C – E	7.85	72 000	37 000	663	6
C – F	4.00	72 000	184 000	4577	1
D – E	3.96	66 000	37 000	2033	1
D – F	8.16	66 000	184 000	1305	1
E – F	4.20	37 000	184 000	3040	1

Finally the route traffic is summed with equation (6.4) to obtain link traffic. This is done by multiplying the column of route traffic (Table 6.3) by the column of the incidence matrix (the last 22 columns of Table 6.3) for each link and summing (using the SumProduct function).

The results are the link sums at the foot of Table 6.3. These are also shown alongside links in Figure 6.3.

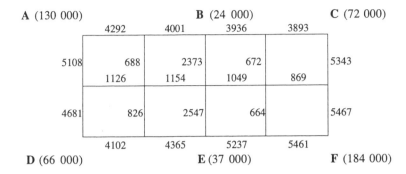

Figure 6.3   Hypothetical network: link loads calculated by logit model from the origin–destination traffic in Table 6.2

When the link shown as a heavy line adjoining F in Figure 6.4 is upgraded so that the travel time is reduced from 2.19 to 2.00 hours, a complicated series of traffic changes results. Because a logit formulation is used, the increases in traffic using the upgraded link occur on multiple paths between F and the centres A, B, D and E. The traffic changes include the generation, calculated by gravity model (6.8), of 249 new trips between E and F, 54 between D and F and 27 between A and F, a total of 329 generated trips. Trips between the other centres are unchanged.

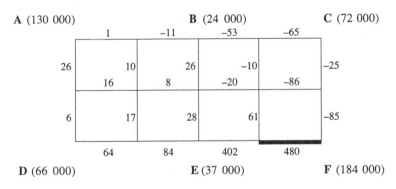

Figure 6.4   Traffic change results of upgrading link adjoining city F

Changes in link loads can be deceptive. The decreases on the two links between C and F are due to the diversion of some of the A–F and B–F traffic to routes which include the upgraded link (Figure 6.4). There is no decrease in origin–destination travel between C and F.

Table 6.3   Links loaded by applying the incidence matrix to route trips

Route	Drive Time	Trips	Link Number																				
			1	2	3	4	5	6	7	8	9	10	11	12	13	14	15	16	17	18	19	20	21	22
AB	4.15	2117	1	1																				
AC	8.04	1178	1	1	1	1																		
AD	3.83	3983					1									1								
AE1	8.12	86	1	1							1									1				
AE2	7.98	113	1						1	1										1				
AE3	7.88	138	1						1									1	1					
AE4	7.70	196					1	1		1										1				
AE5	7.60	239					1	1										1	1					
AE6	7.79	164					1									1	1			1				
AF1	12.04	73	1	1	1	1									1									1
AF2	12.30	52	1	1	1								1	1										1
AF3	12.37	48	1	1	1								1									1	1	
AF4	12.37	48	1	1							1	1		1										1
AF5	12.44	44	1	1								1	1									1	1	
AF6	12.32	51	1	1							1									1	1		1	
AF7	12.23	57	1						1	1		1		1										1
AF8	12.30	52	1						1	1		1										1	1	
AF9	12.18	61	1						1	1										1	1		1	
AF10	12.08	69	1							1									1	1		1	1	
AF11	11.95	81					1	1		1		1		1										1
AF12	12.02	74					1	1		1		1										1	1	
AF13	11.90	87					1	1		1										1	1		1	
AF14	11.80	98					1	1										1	1			1	1	
AF15	11.99	77					1									1	1			1		1		
BC	3.89	1769			1	1																		
BD1	7.93	86									1					1		1	1					
BD2	7.87	96							1	1						1	1	1						
BD3	8.09	63		1				1								1	1							
BD4	7.74	124					1		1	1					1									
BD5	7.96	81		1				1	1						1									
BD6	7.98	78	1	1			1								1									
BE	3.97	1233									1								1					
BF1	7.89	226			1	1									1									1
BF2	8.15	138			1								1	1										1
BF3	8.22	120			1								1									1	1	
BF4	8.22	120									1	1		1										1
BF5	8.29	105									1	1										1	1	
BF6	8.17	132									1									1	1		1	
CD1	12.16	20												1		1		1		1			1	1
CD2	12.03	24											1	1		1		1		1	1			
CD3	12.13	21				1							1			1		1		1	1			
CD4	11.81	31									1		1	1		1		1	1					
CD5	11.91	28				1						1	1			1		1	1					
CD6	11.82	31			1	1					1					1		1	1					
CD7	11.75	34							1			1		1	1	1	1							
CD8	11.85	30				1			1			1	1			1	1							
CD9	11.76	34			1	1			1	1						1	1							
CD10	11.98	25		1	1	1			1							1	1							
CD11	11.62	40					1		1		1		1	1	1									
CD12	11.72	35				1	1		1		1	1			1									
CD13	11.63	40		1	1		1		1	1					1									
CD14	11.85	30		1	1	1		1	1						1									
CD15	11.87	29	1	1	1	1	1								1									
CE1	8.20	75													1							1		1	1
CE2	8.07	96											1	1								1	1		
CE3	8.17	80				1							1									1	1		
CE4	7.85	147									1		1	1						1					
CE5	7.95	121				1					1	1								1					
CE6	7.86	144		1	1						1									1					
CF	4.00	4577													1									1
DE	3.96	2033															1		1					
DF	8.16	1305															1		1		1		1	
EF	4.20	3040																			1		1	
	Link Total		4292	4001	3936	3893	5108	1126	688	1154	2373	1049	672	869	5343	4681	4102	826	4365	2547	5237	664	5461	5467

APPENDIX 6C   ESTIMATION OF THE DIRECT DEMAND AND ASSIGNMENT FUNCTION

The genetic algorithm procedure for function estimation was outlined in Chapter 4. The example is the Chapter 7 road network in the Pilbara and adjoining areas in the north of Western Australia. With simplified connections to the rest of Australia, the network has 83 road links and 68 nodes of which 36 are centroids, including six recognized tourist destinations. There was information on observed link flows on 33 links in the network, census populations for the 36 centroids and travel times on all 83 road links.

Model (6.5) was estimated in two steps. The first used genetic algorithm to search for a point near the optimum solution and the second applied quadratic hill-climbing to this candidate solution in a final search for the optimum. Here we are concerned primarily with the first step.

Three runs or experiments had 200, 400 and 500 generations, with 500 individuals in each GA population. Results are shown in Table 6.4 and the changes in the objective function of the best GA individual at each generation are shown in Figure 6.5.

Table 6.4   Estimation of travel and route choice parameters

	Genetic algorithm estimates			Quadratic hill-climbing	
Parameter	Expt 1	Expt 2	Expt 3	Estimate	Std Error
α Scalar	0.3769	0.0417	0.0422	0.0418	0.00002
First derivative	−3.5883	4.82689	4.21727	0.01212	
β Popn elasticity	0.3033	0.4332	0.4315	0.4330	0.0015
First derivative	−4.4770	7.1049	8.5824	0.0186	
γ Time/cost elast.	−1.8020	−1.8299	−1.8482	−1.8300	0.0338
First derivative	0.0866	−1.5542	4.5870	−0.0097	
ξ Tourist attractor	6.9644	4.5625	5.5435	4.5625	1.8343
First derivative	−0.0158	0.0112	0.0035	0.0220	
θ Route dispersion (price ratio logit)	−16.6750	−14.9824	−14.8021	−14.9895	3.2834
First derivative	0.0004	−0.0007	0.0004	−0.0590	
Log-likelihood	−192.033	−186.133	−186.288	−183.522	

Source: Qiu, 2000

Experiment 1 was trapped in an inferior solution and so was discarded. This indicates that it is essential to do multiple experiments.

Figure 6.5 shows that GA rapidly improves the objective function in early generations but the improvements become marginal in later generations. Thus GA can efficiently locate the vicinity of the global optimum in the solution space but no more. Several of the first derivatives of the objective function with respect to the estimated parameters deviate substantially from zero, indicating that none of the GA solutions is at the optimum (Table 6.4).

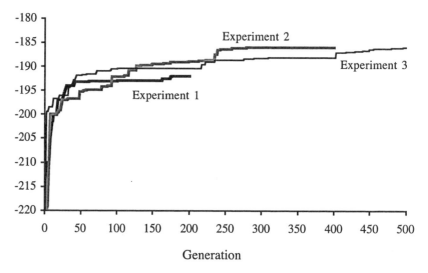

Source: Qiu, 2000

Figure 6.5   Changing log-likelihood objective function of the best GA individual: estimation of travel and route choice parameters

Nevertheless the estimates obtained with GA differ little from the final result obtained by applying quadratic hill-climbing to the starting points obtained by GA experiments 2 and 3 (converging to a common solution) as shown in Table 6.4. Theoretical aspects of maximum likelihood specification and estimation are introduced in Appendix 6E.

Estimation with Solver in Simple Cases

In some cases, the parameters of the combined gravity and assignment model can be estimated by using the same spreadsheet layout as in the simple traffic estimation and allocation of Appendix 6B. In that case, the parameters α, β, γ

and θ were set to arbitrary starting values and Excel Solver was used to find values which minimized the sum of squared deviations from the observed traffic counts. In the Solver, α and β were constrained to positive values, γ between 0 and –3, and θ between –1 and –30.

A first test was to use the final link loads in Table 6.3 (and Figure 6.3) as input data, along with the populations and travel times. From these, Solver found the initial parameter values almost exactly. When random variations in the range –100 to +100 were added to the link loads, Solver generally gave parameter estimates close to the original values but occasionally it tended to hang at a θ value of –20 or less.

With a much larger network and no knowledge of parameter values, it would be advisable to do an initial search with genetic algorithm. This would give reasonable assurance of convergence on the optimum and not a sub-optimum. There are commercial GA packages, such as Evolver, which work within a spreadsheet (workbook); the same suggested layout can be used. The estimation is completed by switching to Solver.

In the test example, a GA fairly quickly converged on parameter values close to the correct ones, except that the θ value was about –12, instead of –15. From these values Solver quickly converged on the optimum.

APPENDIX 6D   IDENTIFYING REASONABLE ROUTES

It is computationally economical to use Dial's STOCH algorithm to avoid identifying routes; this algorithm allocates traffic progressively from each node. However economy of computing power is no longer as important as in the past. An alternative to using Dial's STOCH method is to enumerate routes with an easily understood branching method. It has been demonstrated that, using the same definition of 'reasonable route', both methods give the same result.

Full route enumeration is computationally intensive because a substantial network gives many thousands of routes, but a modern desk computer can readily handle the task. In an actual rural network with 125 nodes and 194 links, there were calculated to be more than 185 thousand reasonable one-way routes between nodes, the distribution being as shown in Figure 6.6.

A procedure for enumerating reasonable routes from an origin is:

- Compute the minimum travel cost from the node r (origin) to all other nodes. Determine the node label $r(i)$ for each node i. Sort all the nodes in ascending order according to $r(i)$.
- Consider each node in ascending value of $r(i)$, enumerate all connecting nodes in which $r(j) > r(i)$ until there is no further connecting node label

less than or equal to the node label; this is a possible route and is recorded. Enumerate all routes.

- For an OD pair r and s, among all the possible routes starting from origin r, search the node code of destination s. A route is found if it is not the same as any previously identified one.

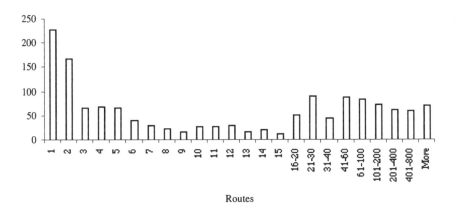

Routes

Source: Han, 2002

Figure 6.6   Distribution of reasonable routes between 125 nodes on 194 links in a rural network

APPENDIX 6E   THE DISTRIBUTION FOR MAXIMUM LIKELIHOOD ESTIMATION

The following introductory note is based on Han (2002) and is intended to indicate the nature of full maximum likelihood estimation and some of the decisions to be made. Maximum likelihood is used because the least squares estimator may lose the property of statistical efficiency for non-linear models although it remains unbiased.

A maximum likelihood estimator gives the values of the parameters for which the observed sample is most likely to have occurred. Under fairly general assumptions it is consistent, asymptotically normal and asymptotically efficient, so that the asymptotic variance of the estimates is given by the Cramer-Rao bound. The probability of obtaining the value of an actual link flow f_i is expressed in terms of the estimated value F_i by $\phi(f_i, F_i)$. The maximum likelihood procedure is formulated as follows.

Let N denote the number of the links on which there are observed traffic counts. The compound probability of obtaining the base-year link flows f_i is

then $\Phi = \prod_{i=1}^{N} \phi(f_i, F_i)$. The log-likelihood is defined as $L = \ln\Phi = \sum_{i=1}^{N} \ln\phi(f_i, F_i)$.

Since the logarithm is a monotonic function, the values that maximize Φ are the same as those that maximize $\ln\Phi$. The necessary condition for maximizing L is $\dfrac{\partial L(\hat{X})}{\partial \hat{X}} = 0$ where $\hat{X}$ is the estimated matrix of parameters, that is $\hat{X} = (\alpha, \beta, \gamma, \theta, \xi)$.

When maximum likelihood is the objective function for model calibration, it is necessary to assume a sampling distribution. The Normal and Poisson distributions are appropriate alternatives for traffic counts.

The Normal Distribution Option

If the values of traffic flow f_i at a count station are assumed to have a Normal distribution with mean F_i and an unknown variance σ^2, $f_i \sim N(F_i, \sigma^2)$, then the probability density function of the traffic flow on a link f_i is:

$$\phi(f_i, F_i) = \frac{1}{\sigma\sqrt{2\pi}} \exp\left[-\frac{(F_i - f_i)^2}{2\sigma^2}\right]$$

The log-likelihood is: $L = -\dfrac{N}{2}\ln\sigma^2 - \dfrac{N}{2}\ln(2\pi) - \dfrac{1}{2}\sum_{i=1}^{N}\dfrac{(F_i - f_i)^2}{\sigma^2}$.

When the constant part is deleted, the objective function becomes:

$$\max \quad L = -\frac{N}{2}\ln\sigma^2 - \frac{1}{2}\sum_{i=1}^{N}\frac{(F_i - f_i)^2}{\sigma^2} \qquad \text{s.t. } F_i \geq 0, \quad i = 1,\dots,N$$

where N is the number of links for which observed traffic counts are available and σ is the standard deviation of link traffic flow.

A drawback of the normal distribution for traffic counts is that it permits negative values, but a large number of trips on each observed link may make it reasonable to assume this distribution. A serious objection is that this option implies that the standard deviation σ is the same for all observed links (homoscedasticity) which is unrealistic. If the normal distribution is assumed then the maximum likelihood method leads to the same requirements as least squares. A more realistic alternative is to assume heteroscedasticity, with standard deviation proportional to the mean. That is $\sigma_i^2 = \kappa^2 F_i^2$ where κ is

Cost–Benefit Analysis and Evolutionary Computing

the coefficient of variation, giving: $\phi(f_i, F_i) = \dfrac{1}{\kappa F_i \sqrt{2\pi}} \exp\left[-\dfrac{(F_i - f_i)^2}{2\kappa^2 F_i^2}\right]$.

In this case, the objective function is: $\max L = -N\ln(\kappa F_i) - \dfrac{1}{2}\sum_{i=1}^{N}\dfrac{(F_i - f_i)^2}{(\kappa F_i)^2}$.

The Poisson Distribution Option

The Poisson distribution is applicable to random arrivals in any given length of time and has been found to realistically represent day-to-day variations in the number of vehicles on a road. As the time period is lengthened and the number of vehicles becomes large, the Poisson approaches a Normal distribution. A discrete random variable f, following a Poisson distribution with mean $F > 0$, has a variance which is also equal to F. In other words the standard deviation is equal to the square root of the mean.

If the traffic counts are assumed to be Poisson distributed with mean F_i then the probability of counting f_i vehicles on link i is:

$$\phi(f_i, F_i) = \frac{(F_i)^{f_i} \exp(-F_i)}{f_i!}$$

and the log-likelihood estimator is: $L = \sum_{i=1}^{N}(f_i \ln F_i - F_i) - \sum_{i=1}^{N}\ln f_i!$

The last part is constant, so the objective is:

$$\max L = \sum_{i=1}^{N}(f_i \ln F_i - F_i)$$

where f_i is the observed traffic count and F_i is the estimated value.

Calibration

In large applications of this kind of not strictly convex optimization, a gradient method may fail to reach the global optimum when used alone and may merely find a local optimum. As indicated in Appendix 6C genetic algorithm can be used as the initial search procedure with the result obtained becoming the starting point for the final application of Newton's method to search for the optimal solution. Because GA explores points throughout the solution space, using it as the first stage in the solution procedure gives a high degree of assurance that the result is not a sub-optimum.

Calibration of the combined gravity and logit model requires the derivatives with respect to each of the parameters. Some of these are complex but a package such as Mathematica can be used to help in their derivation. The most difficult are the first and second order partial derivatives with respect to θ, $\partial F_i / \partial \theta$ and $\partial^2 F_i / \partial \theta^2$.

In difficult cases Newton's method may fail to converge when applied to the genetic algorithm result because the second derivatives matrix (the Hessian) is not negative definite. If this happens then the solution is to apply quadratic hill-climbing. The procedure is outlined in Greene (1993).

REFERENCES AND FURTHER READING

Demand and Multipath Assignment

Bell, M.G.H. (1995), 'Alternatives to Dial's logit assignment algorithm', *Transportation Research Part B*, **29B**, 287-295.

Daganzo, C.F. and Y. Sheffi (1977), 'On stochastic models of traffic assignment', *Transportation Science*, **11** (3), 253-274.

Dial, R.B. (1971), 'A probabilistic multipath traffic assignment model which obviates path enumeration', *Transportation Research*, **5**, 83-111.

Florian, M. and B. Fox (1976), 'On the probabilistic origin of Dial's multipath traffic assignment model', *Transportation Research*, **10**, 339-341.

Han, R.L. (2002), *Genetic Algorithm to Optimise the Allocation of Road Expenditure Between Maintenance and Renewal*, PhD thesis, University of Western Australia.

Ortúzar, J. de D. and L.G. Willumsen (1994), *Modelling Transport*, 2nd edition, Chichester: John Wiley & Sons.

Qiu, M. (2000), *Optimising a Road Project Construction Timetable for Rural Roads*, PhD thesis, University of Western Australia.

Calibration of Models

Ben-Akiva, M. and S.R. Lerman (1985), *Discrete Choice Analysis: Theory and Application to Travel Demand*, Cambridge MA: MIT Press.

Cameron, A.C. and P.K. Trivedi (1998), *Regression Analysis of Count Data*, Cambridge: Cambridge University Press

Goldfeld, S.M., R.E. Quandt, and H.F. Trotter, (1966), 'Maximization by quadratic hill-climbing', *Econometrica*, **34** (3), 541-551.

Gray, R.H. and A.K. Sen (1983), 'Estimating gravity model parameters: a simplified approach based on the odds ratio', *Transportation Research Part B*, **17B** (2), 117-131.

Greene, W.H. (1993), *Econometric Analysis*, 2nd edition, Englewood Cliffs, NJ: Prentice-Hall.

Han, R. (2000), 'Calibration of parameters for a combined gravity and traffic assignment model', in *Progress in Optimisation: Contribution from Australia*, New York: Kluwer Academic Publishers, 287-303.

Kirby, H.R. (1974), 'Theoretical requirements for calibrating gravity models', *Transportation Research*, **8**, 97-104.

Qiu, M. (1995), 'Simultaneous calibration of gravity and logit models of road traffic by a genetic algorithm', in *Proceedings of 1995 International Conference on Evolutionary Computing*, Piscataway, NJ: IEEE Service Centre, 162-165.

Taplin, J.H.E. and M. Qiu (1997), 'Car trip attraction and route choice in Australia', *Annals of Tourism Research*, **24** (3), 624-637.

7. Application to Regional Road Projects

As discussed in Chapter 1, the selection and sequencing of road projects was previously an insoluble problem. Because it is important to achieve a reasonable solution to joint selection and timetabling needs, responsible authorities have developed various approximate heuristic methods which help to avoid the worst errors of faulty scheduling (Chapter 2). However such methods would be ineffective in even the most straightforward case reviewed in this book, the case of 34 potential road projects scattered widely over a regional road network. There are 34 factorial (approximately 2.95×10^{38}) possible sequences to be considered.

The specific regional road investment problem with 34 potential projects was solved with a genetic algorithm specifically coded for the task. However problems with this number of potential projects may be soluble in a spreadsheet workbook so long as the number of links and routes in the network is not too large. This topic is discussed in Chapter 10. A possible way of keeping a problem within spreadsheet dimensions is to limit the study to a partial network with no more than 20 population centres. This would be appreciably smaller than the whole regional network modelled in this study.

This chapter outlines the way in which genetic algorithm has been used to select and schedule the 34 regional projects (Qiu, 2000, 163-211). The budget constraints limited the number selected and only 19 could be wholly or partially included in the optimal schedule. The projects included construction of new links, upgrading existing ones and road widening. Some of the upgrading proposals were for the same links at different project stages. Brief details of each project, including summary description, predecessor project if any, cost, benefit divisibility and preferred investment profile, are shown in Appendix 7A.

STUDY AREA AND PROJECTS

The region embraces the Pilbara and adjoining areas in the north of Western Australia. The general location is shown in Figure 7.1. Mining is the main industry in the region but there is also extensive grazing and tourist activity. Iron ore is carried to ports by rail but some other minerals are hauled by road.

Network data were provided by Main Roads WA, the road authority that collaborated in the study. The model took account of traffic between 610 origin–destination pairs, including a few remote zone centres like Sydney, 5700 kilometres away.

Main Roads WA had identified 34 regional road projects in a planning process involving industry, the community and local governments. They included construction of new links and upgrading existing ones, some projects being proposed for the same links as different project stages. Not only were annual budget constraints imposed but also there were limits to yearly expenditure on individual projects and preferred investment profiles for some. Details are shown in Appendix 7A. This includes information on whether there is a preceding (predecessor) project and whether the benefits are divisible in the manner discussed in Chapter 3.

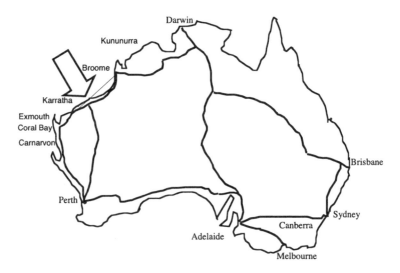

Figure 7.1   General location of regional study projects

DATA FOR CALCULATING NET PRESENT VALUE

The following information and models were used to calculate the net present value of each candidate road construction timetable generated by the genetic algorithm:

- Base network – information in the road network inventory used to establish the base case. This included the link lengths and vehicle speeds used to derive travel time on the links.

- Proposed projects – information on proposed projects included the construction timetable, input from the genetic algorithm, and whether benefits were divisible or indivisible. Construction costs, budgets in individual years, limits to annual expenditure on particular projects, preferred investment profiles over years for individual projects, and projects constructed in stages were embedded in the construction timetable generated by the genetic algorithm.
- New road network in the project case – the project construction timetable is used to derive the new road network from the base network. The progressive investment in projects in the programme period changes the physical condition of the network from the project case.
- Populations and recognized tourist destinations – existing and forecast populations at the travel origins and destinations were used in the estimation of passenger vehicle traffic between origins and destinations. Significant tourist destinations were identified for the estimation.
- Direct travel demand model – to estimate passenger vehicle origin–destination traffic.
- Heavy vehicle origin–destination traffic – separately compiled.
- Traffic assignment models – the multipath traffic assignment model loaded the passenger vehicle origin–destination traffic on to the network. In this particular study, an all-or-nothing model was used to assign the heavy vehicle origin–destination traffic volumes to the network.
- Cost–benefit parameters – the value of time, vehicle operating cost, road maintenance cost by road classifications and the discount rate were used to calculate the total net present value. Vehicle operating costs vary with speed. For example this cost was 24 cents per kilometre for a car at 110 km/h and 49.3 cents per kilometre for a truck at the same speed.
- Net present value formula – to calculate total NPV for projects in a construction timetable. The NPV for each GA individual (a candidate project construction timetable) was fed back to the genetic algorithm as the value of that individual's objective function.

TRAFFIC GENERATION AND ASSIGNMENT

People's decisions on when and where to travel and by what route are the main determinants of the benefits of a road investment programme. They are what make the evaluation of projects so highly interactive. Each change in road conditions due to upgrading or new construction will divert trips between routes and links across much of the network. And a series of road investments through time may result in traffic shifting to a link for a few years and then a shifting away as another route is made more attractive.

The counterparts of the motorists' decisions in modelling terms are generation and assignment of traffic. The combined effect of the decision to travel and the route to use must be translated into the incidence of traffic on links. Thus model (6.5) was used to estimate traffic F on each link in the study network:

$$F_l = \sum_{\forall r \in O} \sum_{\forall s \in D} \sum_{\forall k \in K_{rs}} \frac{\delta_l^k \alpha[(1+\varphi_r \xi)P_r(1+\varphi_s \xi)P_s]^\beta C_{rs}^{\min \, \gamma} e^{\theta C_{rs}^k / C_{rs}^{\min}}}{\sum\limits_{\forall k \in K_{rs}} e^{\theta C_{rs}^k / C_{rs}^{\min}}}$$

The link–route incidence term δ_l^k and the summation over all travel routes and road links gives the estimated link flow on link l. The parameters and their estimated values are given in Table 7.1 which summarizes Table 6.4 in Chapter 6 Appendix C.

Table 7.1   Estimated travel and route choice parameters

Parameter		Estimate	Standard Error
α	Scalar	0.0418	0.00002
β	Population elasticity	0.4330	0.0015
γ	Time/cost elasticity	−1.8300	0.0338
ξ	Tourist attractor	4.5625	1.8343
θ	Route dispersion	−14.9895	3.2834

COMPUTATION

The genetic algorithm was formulated along the lines presented in Chapter 4 with each string of potential projects having 34 elements. The GA procedure used binary tournament selection, partially mapped crossover (PMX) and mutation. Values for the parameters used in various runs of the genetic algorithm are shown in Table 7.2.

The order-based integer vector was transformed into an investment schedule of amounts to be expended on individual projects during the programme years. Annual budgets, limits to yearly expenditure on individual projects, preferred investment profiles and any requirement to construct in stages were imposed in this transformation process.

Table 7.2   Parameters for the regional road project genetic algorithm

Parameter	Value
Individual 'chromosomes' in the GA population	200, 500
Number of generations	100
Probability of partially mapped crossover	0.6
Probability of mutation	0.5

Convergence of Solutions

The progressive improvements in the objective functions of the two best solutions through the genetic algorithm generations are shown in Figures 7.2 and 7.3 and a summary of the convergence of the ten best is shown in Figure 7.4. The convergence patterns for all genetic algorithm runs can be classified into three groups:

• In the first group it takes appreciably less than 100 generations for the best individual to reach the maximum value through gradual steps. Because the search space has been thoroughly explored, the solution giving the maximum objective function value is likely to be close to the global optimum. Figure 7.2 provides an example.

• In the second group the objective function for the best individual makes gradual improvements and this trend continues to the end of the 100 generations. The search space has been thoroughly explored but more generations might improve the result. Figure 7.3 provides an example.

• In the third group the objective function for the best individual reaches its maximum at a very early generation, and no further improvement is made. One individual found early in the evolution process is so superior that it inhibits the exploration of the search space. In other words the genetic algorithm finds premature solutions that may be far from optimal. Examples of these cases have not been shown.

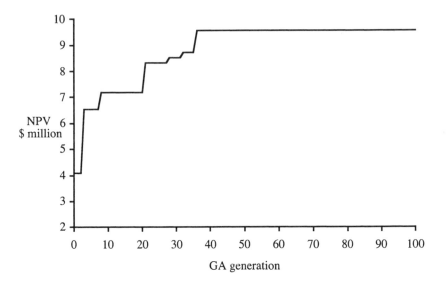

Figure 7.2   The objective function (NPV) of the best GA individual converges fairly rapidly (Experiment 1)

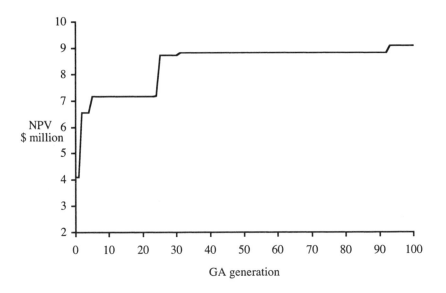

Figure 7.3   Slow convergence of the objective function value (NPV) of the best GA individual (Experiment 2)

Although the individual cases are not easily distinguished, Figure 7.4 shows that the objective functions for the best GA individuals in the various runs do not converge to a common value. The smallest NPV among these te¬ good results is 13 per cent less than the largest.

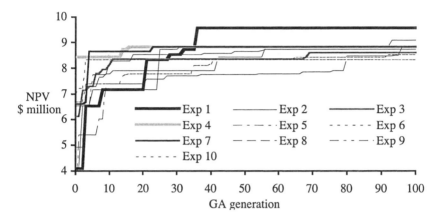

Figure 7.4   Convergence of the objective function values (NPV) of the best GA individuals in ten experiments (computing runs)

SOLUTIONS

Each project sequence can be divided into annual expenditure schedules as the construction authority would view them, with some being spread across adjoining years. One solution represents a collection of information on the various aspects of the projects included. Underlying the timetable are the complicated relationships between projects that have been discussed in earlier chapters.

The Ten Best Project Sequences

Although the entire ordered string of projects is presented in Table 7.3, only those that could be completed within budget (in bold) are to be implemented. All projects remain in the string but those that are not implemented have no influence on the solution or the calculated net present value. In some cases the final project is only partially completed in year 10, the final construction year of the analysis.

The projects in bold – to be wholly or partly implemented within the program period – contribute to the objective function. In some cases an

122   *Cost–Benefit Analysis and Evolutionary Computing*

outlier in bold is a 'predecessor' project to be implemented as part of its more highly ranked 'successor'.

The solution ranked first is probably nearly optimal. The other highly ranked GA individuals differ considerably in sequence as well as in objective function values.

The benefit from a road project to be implemented in a network depends on the other projects in the sequence and the benefits (and benefit–cost ratios) for individual projects are unknown. The marginal benefit–cost ratio of an individual project could be calculated by deleting it from the optimal schedule, recalculating total benefits of the remaining project group and expressing the lost benefits as a ratio to the cost saved on the particular project.

Table 7.3   The ten best project sequences

NPV ($)	Road project construction order
9 566 049	**8** **23 22** **6** **18** **7** **14** **25** **28** **31** **33** **9** **21** **2** **27** **13** **10 5 20 34** 29 12 **26** 19 11 17 32 4 3 30 24 16 **1** 15
9 083 365	**15** **34** **8** **21** **1** **10** **18** **23** **4** **24** **17** **3** **5** **31** **19** **14** **26 22 2 33 16 32 28** 9 20 11 **29 25** 30 7 12 13 6 27
8 825 857	**1** **21** **8** **4** **17** **24** **27** **33** **19** **5** **12** **16** **34** **3** **22** **29** **18 14** **6** **15 23 28** **9** **7** 10 20 2 25 13 31 30 32 26 11
8 825 826	**17** **23** **16** **8** **21** **2** **20** **31** **30** **4** **12** **10** **5** **34** **3** **32** **22 33 14 26** 29 24 19 27 18 6 13 9 1 28 7 11 25 15
8 824 625	**30** **2** **8** **16 22 32** **4** **5** **20 24 31** **7** **26** **27** **21** **28** **17** **19 33** **3** **11 15** **6** **13 34 1** **23** 29 25 14 10 9 12 18
8 824 545	**8** **22** **2** **33 12** **4** **19** **5** **34 28 25** **6** **27 26 23** **11** **20** **15 17 31** **3** 29 **9** **1 21 16** **30 13** **24** 18 10 7 14 32
8 824 536	**8** **22** **2** **33** **12** **4** **19** **5** **34** **28** **11** **6** **27** **26** **23** **25** **20 15 17** **31** **3** 29 **9** **1** **21** **16** **30** **13** **24** 18 **10** 7 14 32
8 728 765	**21** **8** **1** **12** **20** **2** **18** **4** **15** **25** **31** **10** **7** **9** **3** **16** **34** **5** **27 29 30 26** **24 17 33 13** 32 14 22 19 **23** 11 6 28
8 615 099	**22** **8** **23** **24** **33** **2** **21** **6** **12** **13** **5** **26** **17** **18** **15** **30** **19** 14 **16** **28** **31 11** 9 7 20 27 29 **10** **1** **25** 32 4 3 34
8 542 897	**12 17** **30** **8** **22** **4** **7** **23** **1** **3** **33** **10** **32** **28** **31** **19** **9** **20** **6** **15** **34** **2 27 26 21 11 24** 29 14 18 **16** 5 25 13

Notes:
- The projects in bold are those that contribute to the objective function and are to be wholly or partly implemented within the programme period.
- In some cases an outlier in bold is a 'predecessor' project to be implemented as part of its more highly ranked 'successor'.

The Best Sequence Transformed into Annual Investments

Table 7.4 shows the effect of the computation procedure in mapping the best project sequence (first solution in Table 7.3) into annual expenditures.

Table 7.4   The best project sequence transformed to annual investments

									Annual Total	
Year 1	Project	**8**	**2 3**	**2 2**						
	$m	10.60	5.28	11.12					27.00	
Year 2	Project	**2 2**	**6**	**1 8**						
	$m	13.50	3.85	9.65					27.00	
Year 3	Project	**2 2**	**6**	**1 8**						
	$m	13.50	3.85	9.65					27.00	
Year 4	Project	**2 2**	**1 8**	**7**	**1 4**	**2 5**				
	$m	7.28	1.20	4.90	11.40	2.22			27.00	
Year 5	Project	**1 4**	**2 5**	**2 8**						
	$m	11.40	9.80	5.80					27.00	
Year 6	Project	**1 4**	**2 5**	**2 8**	**3 1**					
	$m	13.50	6.19	7.06	0.25				27.00	
Year 7	Project	**1 4**	**3 1**	**3 3**	**9**	**2**	**1 3**	**1 0**		
	$m	1.70	3.84	5.80	2.50	6.30	5.49	1.37	27.00	
Year 8	Project	**3 1**	**1 0**	**5**	**2 0**	**3 4**	**2 9**			
	$m	2.11	0.79	6.54	7.80	1.00	8.76[a]		18.24	27.0[b]
Year 9	Project	**2 9**	**2 6**							
	$m	13.50[a]	13.50						13.50	27.0[b]
Year 10	Project	**2 9**	**2 6**							
	$m	13.50[a]	13.50						13.50	27.0[b]

Notes:

[a] To use up the budget in the last three years, nominal amounts have been allocated to benefit indivisible projects which cannot be completed within the programme period.

[b] The total includes the nominal amounts invested in the incomplete benefit indivisible projects.

If funds are insufficient to complete a project in a year then further amounts are allocated to it in subsequent years. If a benefit indivisible project cannot be completed within a ten-year programme period then nominal rather than actual amounts of investment are allocated to it during the programme period. This leads to total investment in later years of the programme (the eighth, ninth and tenth) being less than the annual budget of $27 million.

This treatment of such benefit indivisible projects is justified on two grounds:

1. The firmness of the schedule of road projects decreases with time as funding projections and travel demand forecasts become less reliable.
2. Road project programming is a rolling process to be repeated every year or every few years. In the next programming round the benefit indivisible projects that cannot be completed in the current programme period will have an extended time span for completion and the nominal amounts of investment in the projects will become actual amounts in the new programme period.

Sometimes a project is spread over more than two successive years to meet a financial constraint. This may be an absolute limit on annual expenditure on an individual project, such as project 22, or the effect of a preferred investment profile, as in the case of project 14 (which is also constrained by the absolute limit in its third construction year). Spreading over two years may also be due to a specific financial constraint, such as the preferred investment profile imposed on project 6.

The Best Solution Expressed as a Construction Schedule

Details of the implementation plan for the best solution are shown in Table 7.5. Staged construction has a substantial effect. Cases where a predecessor project has been absorbed by its successor because the successor is higher in the GA ranking, are:

Predecessor project no.	Successor project no.
1	2
12	13
21	22
27	28

Although project 1 is low in the ranking, the combination of 1 and 2 ranks high enough to be implemented in year 7. Absorption of predecessor by successor, as in this case, has been taken into account in the assessment of network effects and benefits for every GA individual in every generation. An example of two stages being constructed separately is provided by predecessor project 25 followed by successor project 26, with a gap of two years intervening.

Projects 3, 14, 16 and 29 are to construct formed roads; 21, 31 and 32 are upgrades from unformed to formed road; 1, 6, 9, 10, 12, 17, 22, 23, 24, 25, 27 and 30 are to construct or upgrade to gravel road; and projects 2, 4, 5, 7, 8, 11, 13, 18, 19, 20, 26 and 28 are upgrades from gravel to sealed road. More details are given in Table 7.6 (Appendix 7A).

Table 7.5   The best solution formulated as a construction timetable

	Project specification				Investment in road projects by year ($m)										Total
Prj	Cost ($m)	Pred proj	Bene-fits[b]	Preferred profile %	1	2	3	4	5	6	7	8	9	10	($m)
1	0.0[a]		Div	100											0.00
2	6.30	1	Div	100							6.30				6.30
3	10.20		Indiv	30 30 40											0.00
4	15.26		Div	100											0.00
5	6.54		Div	100								6.54			6.54
6	7.70		Indiv	50 50		3.85	3.85								7.70
7	4.90		Div	100				4.90							4.90
8	10.60		Div	100	10.6										10.6
9	2.50		Indiv	100							2.50				2.50
10	2.16		Div	100							1.37	0.79			2.16
11	5.04	10	Div	100											0.00
12	0.0[a]		Div	100											0.00
13	5.49	12	Div	100							5.49				5.49
14	38.00		Indiv	30 30 40				11.4	11.4	13.5	1.70				38.0
15	5.30		Indiv	100											0.00
16	0.0[a]		Indiv	50 50											0.00
17	14.85	16	Indiv	50 50											0.00
18	20.50		Div	100		9.65	9.65	1.20							20.5
19	4.80		Div	100											0.00
20	7.80		Div	100								7.80			7.80
21	0.0[a]		Div	50 50											0.00
22	45.40	21	Div	50 50	11.1	13.5	13.5	7.28							45.4
23	5.28		Div	100	5.28										5.28
24	8.73	23	Div	100											0.00
25	18.21		Div	33 33 34					2.22	9.80	6.19				18.2
26	42.50	25	Div	33 33 34									13.5	13.5	27.0
27	0.0[a]		Div	100											0.00
28	12.86	27	Div	100						5.80	7.06				12.9
29	43.00		Indiv	30 30 40											0.00
30	7.20		Div	33 33 34											0.00
31	6.20		Div	33 33 34						0.25	3.84	2.11			6.20
32	5.30		Div	50 50											0.00
33	5.80		Div	100							5.80				5.80
34	1.00		Div	100								1.00			1.00

Notes:

[a] If a predecessor project is ranked lower than its successor then construction of the successor also includes the predecessor, so that the cost of the predecessor becomes zero.

[b] 'Div' means divisible and 'Indiv' means indivisible benefits.

INTERDEPENDENCE OF PROJECT BENEFITS

Three phenomena are observed in the genetic algorithm results:

1. Some significantly different solutions have objective function values that are close to each other.
2. In some cases two solutions are similar to each other and the values for the objective functions are also similar.
3. In some cases two similar solutions have significantly different objective function values, one being large and the other small or negative.

These occurrences are associated with the interdependence of road project benefits and they carry real dangers for those interpreting the results. It is important to identify the relationships between the solutions. The ability of a genetic algorithm to find a good solution is affected by the shape of the search space. If the better GA individuals consistently cluster together in the search space then it is likely that there is a single peak in that vicinity. Otherwise the search space may have multiple peaks.

Difference Measured by Euclidean Distance

Comprehending the differences between project timetables is difficult because each has 340 elements or dimensions (34 projects over 10 years). Plotting objective function values against space dimensions is not an option and Euclidean distance is used as a summary measure across dimensions. It is the same measure as was used in Chapter 4 to measure fitness in the experiment to optimize GA parameters.

In this case the proportion of each project constructed annually is used. The measure of Euclidean distance between chromosome vectors,

$X = (x_1, \quad x_2, \quad \cdots \quad x_n)$ and $Y = (y_1, \quad y_2, \quad \cdots \quad y_n)$, is written as:

$$\sqrt{\sum_{i=1}^{n}(y_i - x_i)^2}.$$

Because each of the 340 elements is a proportion (a domain range of [0,1]), the maximum possible Euclidean distance between two solutions is:

$$\sqrt{340} = 18.44.$$

To make a comparison, the best ten individuals at the last generation of each separate run of the genetic algorithm were pooled across the ten experiments to give a set of 100 fair to good solutions. Euclidean distances were calculated between the best solution and the other 99 (Figure 7.5). Even those which also have very high objective function values differ substantially from the best solution.

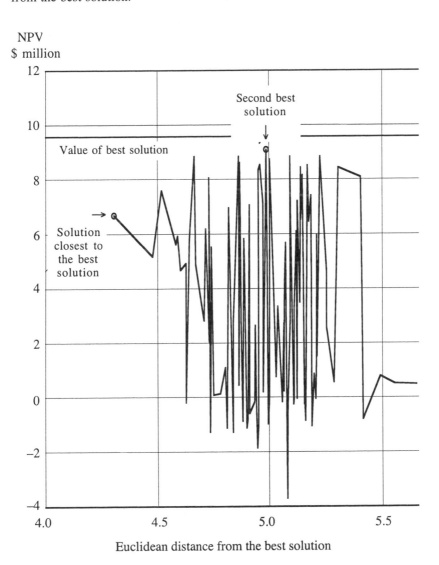

NPV
$ million

Figure 7.5   Distribution of objective function (NPV) against Euclidean distance from the best to the 99 fair to good GA solutions

Different Timetables but Almost Equally Large NPV

The practical point of Figure 7.5 is to show that a number of solutions that are appreciably different, in terms of projects selected and order of construction, can give almost equal economic pay-offs. For example six of the projects in the best solution do not even occur in the second best, nine of the projects in the second best do not occur in the best and those projects which are in both are scheduled at considerably different times. And yet the NPVs summarizing costs and road user benefits of these two solutions differ by only 5 per cent.

This phenomenon of having multiple almost equally good solutions to a road project selection and scheduling problem gives decision makers a good deal of freedom in choosing a sound programme. Being responsible for allocating scarce resources to road projects, they are interested not only in narrowly defined efficiency of resource allocation but also in wider impacts such as environment protection and development of the local economy.

From a group of solutions that are almost equally good with respect to the calculated benefits a decision-maker can choose the one that is also most effective on other criteria. In other words they can choose a solution that is as good as others in terms of narrowly defined allocation efficiency but better when environmental, developmental and other impacts are take into account.

However there is another important implication. A solution that is apparently similar to an excellent one can deviate in small but crucial aspects which make the outcome extremely poor. One solution similar to the second best (Euclidean distance from it of 3.03) has a negative NPV (–$1 million) whereas the NPV of the second best is over $9 million.

The implication is that a decision maker may reasonably choose between the good solutions but should not modify the one chosen in any way. Any modification might well turn it into a bad construction programme. The reason for this sensitivity is the high degree of interactiveness between the elements of the programme. At the behavioural level it means that apparently small changes can cause motorists to change their route choices substantially to suit their needs and so change the total outcome radically.

APPLYING GENETIC ALGORITHM IN THE MORE COMPLEX URBAN CASE

The next chapter deals with an urban application which is more complex in two ways. It has more potential projects and it has to deal with morning and evening peaks and the off-peak period. Unlike the regional case it follows the usual convention of using deterministic user equilibrium (DUE) for the traffic assignments.

APPENDIX 7A   THE PROPOSED RURAL PROJECTS

Table 7.6 Details of proposed rural road projects

Proj	Description[a]	Preceding project	Cost by stages ($m)[b]		Benefit divisibility[c]		Preferred invest profile by year (% of cost)		
			One stage	Two stages	One stage	Two stages			
1	Unformed road to gravel road	–		2.10	–	Div	100		
2	Gravel road to sealed	1	6.30	4.90	Div	Div	100		
3	Construct a formed road		10.20		Indiv		30	30	40
4	Gravel road to sealed		15.26		Div		100		
5	Gravel road to sealed		6.54		Div		100		
6	Construct a gravel road		7.70		Indiv		50	50	
7	Gravel road to sealed		4.90		Div		100		
8	Gravel road to sealed		10.60		Div		100		
9	Construct a gravel road		2.50		Indiv		100		
10	Unformed road to gravel road		–	2.16	–	Div	100		
11	Gravel road to sealed	10	6.48	5.04	Div	Div	100		
12	Unformed road to gravel road		–	1.83	–	Div	100		
13	Gravel road to sealed	12	5.49	4.27	Div	Div	100		
14	Construct a formed road		38.00		Indiv		30	30	40
15	Construct an unformed road		5.30		Indiv		100		
16	Construct a formed road		–	8.25	–	Indiv	50	50	
17	Formed road to gravel road	16	14.85	8.25	Indiv	Div	50	50	
18	Gravel road to sealed		20.50		Div		100		
19	Gravel road to sealed		4.80		Div		100		
20	Gravel road to sealed		7.80		Div		100		
21	Unformed road to formed road		–	20.18	–	Div	50	50	
22	Formed road to gravel road	21	45.40	30.27	Div	Div	50	50	
23	Unformed road to formed road		–	5.28	–	Div	100		
24	Formed road to gravel road	23	14.56	8.73	Div	Div	100		
25	Formed road to gravel road		–	18.21	-	Div	33	33	34
26	Gravel road to sealed	25	54.64	42.50	Div	Div	33	33	34
27	Formed road to gravel road		–	4.29	–	Div	100		
28	Gravel road to sealed	27	12.86	10.00	Div	Div	100		
29	Construct a formed road		43.00		Indiv		30	30	40
30	Formed road to gravel road		7.20		Div		33	33	34
31	Unformed road to formed road		6.20		Div		33	33	34
32	Unformed road to formed road		5.30		Div		50	50	
33	Pavement seal from 6.2m to 7.0m		5.80		Div		100		
34	Single sealed lane to 2 sealed		1.00		Div		100		

Notes:

[a] An 'unformed road' is the first stage in development; a 'formed road' is constructed with local material and has improved drainage. A 'gravel road' has suitable material; a 'sealed road' has the gravel pavement built up to full thickness and is compacted and sealed.

[b] If a pair of predecessor and successor projects are constructed in one stage then construction of the successor includes the part that would otherwise be constructed as predecessor. The cost of the predecessor project becomes zero, as indicated by '–'.

[c] 'Div' stands for benefit divisible, and 'Indiv' for benefit indivisible.

REFERENCES AND FURTHER READING

Qiu, M. (1997), 'Prioritising and scheduling road projects by genetic algorithm', *Mathematics and Computers in Simulation*, **43**, 569-574.

Qiu, M. (2000), *Optimising a Road Project Construction Timetable for Rural Roads*, PhD thesis, University of Western Australia.

8. Application to Urban Projects

The urban application (Salim, 2000, 117-152) used genetic algorithm to select and sequence projects on or associated with a freeway running north from Perth, Western Australia (Figure 8.1).

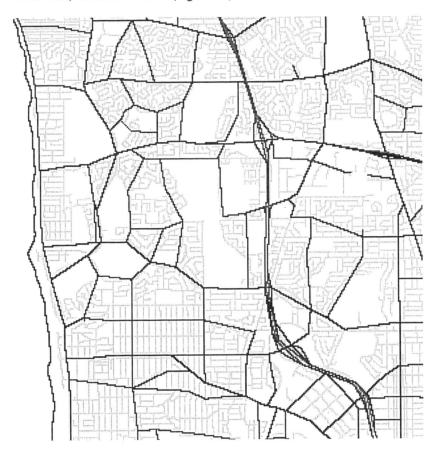

Source: Main Roads, Western Australia

Figure 8.1   Part of urban study network: northern corridor of Perth

NETWORK AND PROJECTS

Network and project data were provided by Main Roads WA which was the road authority collaborating in the study. The study network has 782 nodes, and 2335 links. To cover traffic changes during the day (Figure 8.2) the model combined separate analyses for the morning peak period with 11928 origin-destination (OD) pairs, the afternoon peak with 11635 OD pairs and the hours outside the two peak periods with 9853 OD pairs.

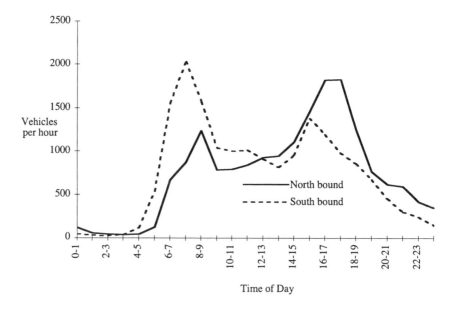

Source: Sapkota, 2004, 174

Figure 8.2   Hourly traffic: freeway 22 km north of Perth CBD (Section 7)

Ten composite projects were proposed, three being new highway construction and seven being upgrading or widening. The ten projects were split into 56 sub-projects (SPs). On and off ramps were separated from the associated links and from each other; also links were split according to direction of traffic flow. To some extent this extreme decomposition of projects was done in order to check the effectiveness of the GA.

Splitting the projects has the effect of increasing the size of the solution space. This meant that the study provided a check on the sensitivity of schedules to directional effects and on the capacity of the GA algorithm to logically combine sub-projects. Furthermore this splitting of projects demonstrated the ability of the data encoding to incorporate different levels of evaluation as set by the decision maker.

TRAFFIC ASSIGNMENT

As noted in Chapter 5, modelling urban traffic and assigning it to routes differs radically from non-urban traffic modelling. The basis of urban modelling is identifying the shortest route or 'path' (in terms of travel time) between each of the many pairs of origins and destinations. The efficiency of a shortest-path algorithm depends on the type of network, the range of arc (link) lengths, the distribution of arc lengths across the network and the density of the network.

The economically rational traveller chooses the route which minimizes his or her own perceived generalized cost and the calculation of travel time is an important part of this cost. Because we need to mimic traveller choices as nearly as possible the outcome is unlikely to satisfy Wardrop's second principle or planning ideal that the average journey time is a minimum. The realistic assumption is that drivers seek routes consistently with Wardrop's first principle that the journey time on all routes actually used are equal and less than those which would be experienced by a single vehicle on any unused route.

This is clearly an approximation because drivers may take account of other factors such as type of road or scenery and adjust their route choices accordingly. Nevertheless it is reasonable to assume that the overwhelming majority of drivers seek the routes which minimize their individual travel times. Such behaviour may be analysed for a particular time period such as the morning or evening peak, so that an equilibrium flow pattern is determined for the network at that hour. The resulting deterministic user equilibrium (DUE) model is the type used in this study.

As discussed in Chapter 5, a DUE model assigns traffic to shortest routes and relies on congestion to distribute traffic across multiple routes. It will adequately represent the traffic responses to upgrading or other network changes. Traffic is loaded on to the least-cost routes, the effects of congestion on travel times are calculated and traffic is reassigned.

The process is modelled with the Frank-Wolfe convex combinations quadratic programming algorithm which ensures convergence by making a series of efficient reassignments to reach the user equilibrium solution of Wardrop's first principle. Convergence took a small number of iterations for this fairly large network. There are a number of well-known computer packages of this type but the DUE model was specifically programmed for this study.

Data and Assumptions

The trip data within the study area and the traffic at crossing points from external zones were provided by the road authority. The set of potential projects were designed to improve network capacity and comprised both road widening and upgrading as well as new roads. The following assumptions were made:

- Future origin–destination trip rates increase by a constant annual growth factor.
- Traffic consists of privately owned motor vehicles.

Travel Time Function

As traffic flow increases the external effect of each vehicle on other users of a link also increases. Link level costs are a function of flow, length of link, free-flow speed and road capacity. The function used in this study had been developed from the Bureau of Public Roads (BPR) travel time function:

$$tt_i = tt_{0i}(1 + b_i x_i^4)$$

where tt_{0i} is the free flow travel speed on link i, and b_i is a link constant which factors in the number of lanes on the road and hourly per lane capacity of the road. To make the function asymptotic to the capacity of the road Q_i it has previously been modified to Davidson's function:

$$tt_i = tt_{oi}(1 + J\frac{x_i}{Q_i - x_i})$$

The travel-time function actually used in the urban study is an expanded form due to Akcelik (1991). It reflects the physical and control characteristics of the roads so that policy impacts can be predicted or analysed. The specification satisfies the assumed properties of the travel time function in user equilibrium:

$$tt = tt_0\left\{1 + 0.25r_f\left[(s-1) + \sqrt{(s-1)^2 + \left(\frac{8J_A}{Qtt_0r_f}\right)s}\right]\right\}$$

where tt is travel time, tt_0 is free flow travel time, s is degree of saturation ($s = x_a/Q$, where Q is the capacity and x_a the flow on arc a), J_A is a delay parameter which reflects the road class (Table 8.1), r_f is the ratio of flow period to free flow travel time, $r_f = T_f / tt_0$.

The function allows for intersection delays to be reflected in the delay parameter, J_A. As an example the upgrade of a road from an interrupted arterial to a freeway, by eliminating signals and road widening, may be modelled by changing both the delay parameter and the capacity Q (Table 8.1). The greater the number of parameters in the travel-time function the greater the cost of calibration. Approximate values may be used but it is necessary to keep in mind the trade-off between cost and accuracy.

Table 8.1   Values for capacity and the delay parameter by road class

Road Class	Description	Capacity Q (vehicles/hr/lane)	Delay Parameter J_A
1	Freeway	2000	0.1
2	Arterial (uninterrrupted)	1800	0.2
3	Arterial (interrupted)	1200	0.4
4	Secondary (interrupted)	900	0.8
5	Secondary (high friction)	600	1.6

Performance Measures

Traffic assignment is used to capture the congestion effects and the changing link flows (and hence travel-time savings) as the network changes. Therefore the inputs to the GA objective function are the standard outputs of the traffic assignment:

$$\text{Vehicle-kilometres travelled } VKT = \sum_{a=1}^{A} x_a l_a$$

$$\text{Vehicle-hours of travel} \quad VHT = \sum_{a=1}^{A} x_a t_a(x_a)$$

where l_a is the length of arc a, x_a is the flow of traffic on arc a, and $t_a(x_a)$ is the travel time function on arc a. Vehicle operating and travel-time costs are used in evaluating road user costs. These are calculated for the morning and afternoon peaks and the off-peak, so that the sensitivity of projects to directional flow may be detected:

Travel-time costs for period k, $TTC_k = \gamma_k VHT_k F_k$

Vehicle operating costs for period k, $VOC_k = \varphi VKT_k F$

where F_k is the annual expansion factor for period k, γ_k is the value of time in period k and φ is a constant parameter denoting vehicle operating costs per kilometre. The expansion factor F_k converts time and operating cost savings hourly to an annual figure.

FORMULATION OF THE OPTIMIZING PROBLEM

The number vector of projects implemented in year t is given by:

$$y_t = \left(y_{t_1}, y_{t_2}, \ldots, y_{t_{nt}} \right)$$

where $0 \leq y_{t_i} \leq 1$ for $i = 1, \ldots, n_t$ and y_{t_i} denotes the fraction of a project that is completed in terms of the cost of that particular project.

The performance of the road system is measured by vehicle operating costs (VOC) and travel-time costs (TTC). The lower the costs the better the performance of the system. Cost in terms of traffic flows x_a in year t is an unknown function of the elements in the vector y_t. Costs are discounted to the base year at the rate D. Total cost for time period π is written as:

$$TC_\pi(x, t, y_t) = \sum_t \frac{VOC_\pi(x,t,y_t) + TTC_\pi(x,t,y_t)}{(1+D)^t} \qquad (8.1)$$

The base or 'do nothing' case is the same but with every y_t being the null vector. It is therefore a constant in the optimizing process, total base cost being:

$$BC_\pi(x, t) = \sum_t \frac{VOC_\pi(x,t) + TTC_\pi(x,t)}{(1+D)^t} \qquad (8.2)$$

The objective is to maximize net present value, which is the difference between the base and project cases, by varying the project vector y_t. The objective function is a non-linear function of the flows x_a.

$$Max\ NPV = \sum_{\pi} \left(BC_{\pi}(x,\ t) - TC_{\pi}(x,\ t,\ y_{t}) \right) \qquad (8.3)$$

This maximizing problem is subject to annual budget constraints.

GENETIC ALGORITHM COMPUTATION

The genetic algorithm formulation was along the lines presented in Chapter 4 with each string of potential projects having 56 elements. The population of individual strings was 200, the crossover rate 0.7 and the mutation rate 0.1.

The genetic algorithm was used to generate road investment timetables for years zero to ten which constitutes a planning period of 11 years. Network traffic was analysed for each of these years and again at 15, 20, 25 and 30 years from the base year.

The combined result of modelling three traffic periods daily over 15 evaluation years for 100 generations with 200 GA individuals was a total of 900 000 traffic assignments. With the computer then in use an assignment took about four seconds but this would now be greatly reduced. Results would probably have been satisfactory if the population of GA individuals had been limited to 100 or even less.

Total costs were calculated for each year on the basis of the traffic analysis and estimated by linear interpolation for the intervening years. A discount rate of 4 per cent was used in the optimizing process. As the time needed for another genetic algorithm run to arrive at a solution for 7 per cent would have been too expensive, the 4 per cent solution was simply re-evaluated at 7 per cent.

Convergence

The convergence of the genetic algorithm can be seen in Figure 8.3 showing a plot of the evolution of the best individual in each generation. The NPV of the optimum road investment schedule is $1642 million.

The improvement between generations had become very small from generation 79 to 80. The objective function (fitness) of the best individual at generation 79 was 99.64 per cent of the best individual at generation 80. At the final generation, 108 individuals were found to have a fitness value approximately equal to the best.

Hence the population was becoming homogeneous in fitness value even though the solution details were different. In formal genetic algorithm language that means the 'phenotypes' were almost the same but the 'genotypes' were different.

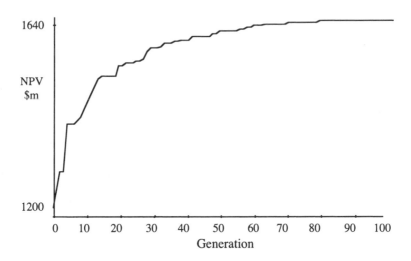

Figure 8.3   Objective function (NPV) of the best GA individual

RESULTS

The details of the projects to be implemented in the best GA solution (individual) are presented in Table 8.2. Each number in the body of the table shows the proportion of the project to be implemented during that year.

There are many indications that the genetic algorithm has logically scheduled sub-projects, for example, placing together at the beginning the widening sub-projects 39 to 56 on the arterial roads which run north–south parallel to the freeway. This indicates that these projects generate large benefits.

The results as a whole show that directional effects are important, southbound (toward Perth CBD) and westbound traffic being favoured. Sub-projects favouring southbound morning peak traffic, particularly large SPs 2 and 4 and smaller SPs 20, 18 and 8, are to be implemented well before the matching northbound sub-projects. SPs 14 and 16 favour westbound traffic and are to be implemented well before the matching eastbound sub-projects.

The road network is seen to evolve rationally through time as the projects are implemented. Composite project 9 on the arterial road to the east of the freeway, project 10 on the arterial road to the west and sections of the intersecting arterial road that do not cross the freeway (project 6) are most important as they are scheduled to be completed in year 0. For the remainder of year 0 some small project sections of the freeway are implemented as allowed by the budget.

There is an element of intelligent forward planning evident in this, as construction of the ramps given by SPs 5, 18 and 20 is scheduled ahead of the associated freeway sections due to the budget availability at that time. The last projects to be completed are the eastbound portions of projects 7 and 8 on the intersecting arterial and the northbound section of project 2 (SP 3).

Table 8.2 *Optimum construction timetable*

Prj	SP	Cost $M	Description	km	Drn	Percentage to be constructed by year										
						0	1	2	3	4	5	6	7	8	9	10
1	1	45.37	New frwy link	3.04	N											
1	2	45.37	New frwy link	3.04	S						29	56	14			
1	19	0.23	New on-ramp	0.40	N											
1	20	0.23	New off-ramp	0.40	S	100										
2	3	84.59	New frwy link	3.40	N								22	30	30	18
2	4	84.59	New frwy link	3.40	S			26	30	30	14					
2	5	0.38	New off-ramp	0.40	N											
2	18	0.38	New on-ramp	0.40	S	100										
3	6	18.89	New frwy link	1.50	S											
3	7	18.89	New frwy link	1.50	N											17
3	8	0.40	New off-ramp	0.40	S	100										
3	9	0.40	New on-ramp	0.40	N		100									
			Widen freeway													
4	21	0.43	Section 1	0.72	S		100									
4	22	1.15	Section 2	1.18	S		100									
4	23	0.43	Section 3	0.72	S		100									
4	24	0.45	Section 4	0.74	N											
4	25	1.44	Section 5	1.32	N		100									
4	26	0.45	Section 6	0.74	N		100									
5	27	0.08	Section 7	0.36	S		100									
5	28	2.20	Section 8	1.92	S		100									
5	29	0.31	Section 9	0.72	S	100										
5	30	0.33	Section 10	0.74	N											
5	31	2.11	Section 11	1.88	N			100								
5	32	0.05	Section 12	0.40	N	100										
			Widen intersecting arterial													
6	10	0.94	Section 1	0.41	W	100										
6	11	0.94	Section 2	0.41	E	100										
6	12	0.89	Section 3	0.40	W											
6	13	0.89	Section 4	0.40	E											
6	33	0.90	Section 5	1.09	W	100										
6	34	0.90	Section 6	1.09	E	100										
7	14	4.54	Section 7	1.75	W		100									
7	15	4.54	Section 8	1.75	E											100
8	16	2.63	Section 9	1.67	W		100									
8	17	2.63	Section 10	1.67	E											100

Table 8.2   Optimum construction timetable (continued)

Prj	SP	Cost $M	Description	km	Drn	Percentage to be constructed by year										
						0	1	2	3	4	5	6	7	8	9	10
			Widen parallel arterial east													
8	35	1.76	Section 1	0.21	S											
8	36	1.76	Section 2	0.21	N											
9	37	5.69	Section 3	2.89	S		75	25								
9	38	5.69	Section 4	2.89	N		100									
9	39	0.11	Section 5	0.41	S	100										
9	40	0.11	Section 6	0.41	N	100										
9	41	1.47	Section 7	1.47	S	100										
9	42	1.47	Section 8	1.47	N	100										
9	43	1.34	Section 9	1.40	S	100										
9	44	1.34	Section 10	1.40	N	100										
9	45	0.25	Section 11	0.60	S	100										
9	46	0.25	Section 12	0.60	N	100										
9	47	1.79	Section 13	1.62	S	100										
9	48	1.79	Section 14	1.62	N	100										
9	49	0.50	Section 15	0.86	S	100										
9	50	0.50	Section 16	0.86	N	100										
9	51	0.29	Section 17	0.65	S	100										
9	52	0.29	Section 18	0.65	N	100										
			Widen parallel arterial west													
10	53	3.29	Section 1	1.45	S	100										
10	54	3.29	Section 2	1.45	N	100										
10	55	2.60	Section 3	1.29	S	11	89									
10	56	2.60	Section 4	1.29	N	100										

Total project expenditure, $M: 26 26 26 26 26 26 26 26 26 26 26

It is apparent that projects 2 and 3 are relatively low in priority as the competing projects 9 and 10 have been completed earlier.

When the results were presented to the engineers concerned, they found them rational and acceptable. Decomposing composite projects into component sub-projects was novel to them and they agreed that optimizing the construction sequence at this finely specified level was an improvement on existing practice.

Benefits and the Discount Rate

The net present value (NPV) at the optimum of $1642 million at a discount rate of 4 per cent is the cumulative base cost minus the cumulative total cost over the evaluation period. This can be visualized as the difference between the area under the base case total cost curve and the area under the project case curve in Figure 8.4.

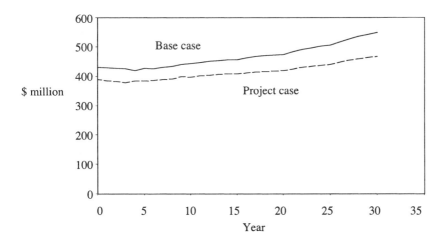

Figure 8.4   Annual base and project costs discounted at 4 per cent

Figure 8.4 indicates that the discounted costs are increasing at a greater rate in the base case than in the project case, which implies that benefits will continue to grow as the evaluation period is extended.

The fact that benefits are growing with time means that estimation of the residual benefit becomes arbitrary and depends upon when we specify that the evaluation period ends. If a discount rate of 7 per cent is used and the network is re-evaluated with the same schedule of projects then not only is the fitness reduced to $1052 million but also the benefits decrease with time. This eliminates the potential explosion of benefits as the evaluation period is extended.

Planning Context

Within a planning process, evaluation has a cyclic rather than linear nature. In practice the genetic algorithm would be used in an iterative manner, new data being included in the search process as it becomes available. After the initial round has been implemented, subsequent runs of the GA incorporating new project information may be seeded with a small proportion of high-performing strings from populations obtained in the previous runs, in order to hasten convergence.

The computational cost is not as heavy after the initial round of investments if this method is used. It is advisable not to replace the entire population with good strings, but only a fraction of it, so that a diversity of genetic material is carried into subsequent generations. Furthermore a diverse range of high-performing strings (that is strings of diverse genotype but comparable performance) should be chosen so that multiple peaks in the search space may be more effectively explored.

As discussed in Chapter 7 with respect to non-urban projects, an added benefit of using GA is that a pool of potential investment timetables is generated for the planner to consider. A number of possible solutions are available at the end of a run and their deviations from the optimum with respect to system criteria are known. These provide a set of feasible solutions which may be reviewed in relation to relevant factors that were not included in the GA optimization.

The final generation of the urban study provided 108 GA individuals with investment programmes almost as good as the best. Many of these were similar to the best solution but some offered significantly different sequences. The planner is able to take account of a variety of factors in choosing between such alternatives. The moderate reduction in calculated pay-off can be weighed against other benefits.

REFERENCES AND FURTHER READING

Akcelik, R. (1991), 'Travel time functions for transport planning purposes: Davidson's function, its time-dependent form and an alternative travel time function', *Australian Road Research*, **21**, 49-59.

Florian, M. and S. Nguyen (1976), 'An application and validation of equilibrium trip assignment methods', *Transportation Science*, **10**, 374-390.

Salim, V.K. (1997), 'A comparison of shortest path algorithms in urban traffic assignment', *Mathematics and Computers in Simulation*, **43**, 545-551.

Salim, V.K. (2000), *Genetic Algorithms for the Evaluation and Scheduling of Urban Road Projects in Optimal Network Design*, PhD thesis, University of Western Australia.

Sapkota, V.A. (2004), *Welfare Implications of Nonidentical Time Valuations Under Constrained Road Pricing Policies: Empirical Studies with Corridor and Urban-Wide Networks*, PhD thesis, University of Western Australia.

9. Optimizing Road Maintenance

It was noted in Chapter 1 that roads in many countries have expanded to such an extent that controlling or reversing the deterioration of the whole network has become the main task for road authorities. Maintenance is sometimes seen as primarily reactive but the example in this chapter shows that forward planning and optimization are at least as beneficial for maintenance as for major projects. The difference is that the planning must be in terms of many small road sections or segments – 319 in this case. But planning by segments means that the time since the last treatment must be incorporated in the solution procedure.

Finding an optimal maintenance plan depends not only on reliable forecasts of road deterioration under various conditions but also on correct projection of the degree to which maintenance treatments will delay the decline of or restore the road condition. Whereas models to project the effects of overlay were found to be reliable, the available road roughness models did not adequately deal with the effects of other maintenance measures. This weakness would have undermined the optimization process and a separate study was necessary to enhance the incremental roughness model so that it takes proper account of maintenance. That study is reported in Appendix 9A. The whole of this chapter is based on Han (2000; 2002,147-182).

The important issues in maintenance scheduling are not merely selecting the right order to restore road sections but also the level or degree of restoration to be applied. Selecting the best order of treatment for many short road segments is itself a major computational task but it is complicated by the fact that the ordering must be done jointly with the determination of the type of treatment.

The treatment is determined by a heuristic that takes account of the state of the road segment at the particular maintenance date; this in turn is calculated by a road deterioration function into which traffic by years is a major input. The practical result was that maintenance optimization was the heaviest task undertaken by genetic algorithm. At the outset we wondered whether the gain would be sufficient to justify such heavy computing but it turned out that the optimized schedule was much superior to one based on reasonable judgement.

This application used genetic algorithm to select from all road segments in the southern wheatbelt of Western Australia those which should be scheduled for maintenance. Network and project data were provided by Main Roads, Western Australia. Both maintenance and widening are required to keep roads in the region up to an acceptable service level. The maintenance activities include routine maintenance, reseal, thin overlay and thick overlay.

Routine maintenance is performed according to immediate need but other kinds of maintenance as well as widening are treated as discrete projects. The actual treatment was determined in relation to the position of the segment in the sequence determined by the GA. The result was an optimal maintenance timetable.

ROAD DETERIORATION AND ROUGHNESS

In order to optimize road maintenance schedules it was necessary to develop a new model of road deterioration which took full account of the restoration effects of all forms of maintenance. It is based on the World Bank's HDM3 incremental roughness model. The new model outlined in Appendix 9A forecasts roughness as a function of age, traffic, strength and maintenance, under given environmental conditions.

Rutting, cracking, patching and potholing are important in many of the countries to which the HDM models are applied and consequently are inputs to those models, but are less important in relatively well-maintained networks such as in the wheatbelt of Western Australia. These surface defects have been dropped because good maintenance practice in the study area prevents ruts, cracks and potholes from developing so far as to critically affect roughness. They were replaced by variables constructed from maintenance records.

In the new model, the modified structure number in the traffic-related term is replaced by falling weight deflection. The model estimates imply that the age–environment variable explains about 52.5 per cent of the roughness changes that would have occurred without maintenance, while traffic explains about 47.5 per cent. This result indicates a much greater contribution of traffic to deterioration than has been found in a number of previous studies, partly because the relatively thin pavements in the study area are easily damaged by heavy trucks and also because maintenance effects are specified separately.

The calibrated incremental model has been applied for roughness prediction under various conditions and was the main basis for determining the optimal maintenance schedule under annual budget constraints. However this newly developed incremental model deals only with routine maintenance and reseal. For thin and thick overlays, which are also major highway maintenance treatments, existing models were used to predict roughness and strength changes.

PROBLEM AND PROJECT SPECIFICATION

The highways and main roads in the region were split into segments about 5 kilometres long, each being viewed as a candidate for maintenance or renewal, depending on forecasts of traffic demand and road condition. There were 319 of these segments. During the ten-year planning period all segments were modelled as competing for project expenditure but from year 11 to year 40 only routine maintenance was included. The problem was to determine where and when maintenance and renewal projects would be carried out to maximize net present value within annual budgets of \$14.1 million in year 1 and increasing linearly to \$15.0 million in year 10.

Traffic Modelling

There were three components to the traffic modelling for this study: car passenger traffic, general truck traffic and local traffic. The car and general truck traffic were modelled as in Chapters 5 and 6; only the local truck traffic modelling was specific to the maintenance study. The procedure is explained in Appendix 9C.

Applying a Maintenance Heuristic

The meaning of a code number or gene in a GA chromosome differed from the studies presented in Chapters 7 and 8. It did not represent a project but gave an instruction for the numbered road segment to be checked. In this check a heuristic method was used to determine what maintenance treatment should be selected at a particular time. Incorporation of the heuristic made it relatively easy to determine periodic maintenance and renewal projects and so optimize the complex mix of maintenance and renewal in time and space. It also simplified the coding of the genetic algorithm.

The algorithm first predicts the roughness of each segment, updates the consequent vehicle operating and time costs, forecasts travel demand and then assigns the traffic on the basis of the new road user costs. The maintenance treatment is selected according to the predicted road conditions and the time when each segment is to be maintained. The maintenance treatment is based on the criteria set out in Table 9.1. The process is repeated for each gene representing a road segment in rank order from the first to the last.

Table 9.1   Criteria warranting various maintenance treatments

Criteria	Treatment*
If $2.5 < R \leq 3$	Reseal
If $R > 3$ & $W \geq W_{standard}$ & DEF < 0.7	Thin overlay (25mm)
If $R > 3$ & $W \geq W_{standard}$ & DEF ≥ 0.7	Thick overlay (45mm)
If $R > 3$ & $W < W_{standard}$	Widening (+ overlay)

Notes:
R   Roughness, measured by the International Roughness Index, i.e. accumulated vertical
        suspension motion divided by distance travelled (metres/km).
W   Width in metres. $W_{standard}$ depends on road class.
DEF   Falling weight deflection (millimetres)
 *   The interval between major treatments is at least ten years.

OBJECTIVE FUNCTION AND BENEFIT CALCULATIONS

The objective function is the net present value (NPV) of costs and benefits based on equation (3.6) in Chapter 3. Link-based volumes and costs in that equation made Dial's STOCH algorithm applicable because it is designed to assign flows based on links, instead of paths. It includes calculation of travel costs, link likelihoods and link weights. An efficient single-pass algorithm was used in this study (see Chapter 6).

To estimate benefits on a network the following four assignments are required each year according to equation (3.6):

- base-case traffic on the base-case network
- project-case traffic on the base-case network
- base-case traffic on the project-case network
- project-case traffic on the project-case network.

Dial's single-pass method is formulated in the following four programming steps:

- searching for the shortest paths
- calculating link likelihoods
- calculating link weights
- assigning traffic.

Searching for the shortest paths takes more than half of the computing time of these four steps.

As far as the benefit calculation is concerned, all potential project combinations have the same base case so that the demand and costs of the base case are estimated only once. The intermediate base case outputs are calculated initially and saved as hard-disk data files. These data files are extracted to the computer memory for direct use once the optimizing program starts to run.

Assignment of the project-case traffic to the base-case network is achieved by extracting and applying the saved link likelihoods and weights of the base case, instead of going through the four steps of Dial's single-pass method. Assignment of the base-case traffic to the project-case network is done by utilizing the calculated link likelihoods and weights for the project case and the saved base-case demands.

In summary the base-case data to be saved and extracted as needed include calculated travel demands, travel costs, link likelihoods, link weights and the node order for traffic assignment. The computing time for the four assignments is reduced by the extraction of the saved base-case data and so is equivalent to just a little more than the time for one assignment.

STEPS IN THE OPTIMIZATION

Each GA chromosome is composed of an ordered sequence of integers from 1 to 319 representing the road segments. Projects are implemented year by year to exhaust each annual budget and a project that can only be partially completed in one year continues in the next. The interval between major treatments (reseal or overlay) must be more than ten years.

The procedure used to optimize the GA parameters, outlined in Chapter 4, led to the selection of a population of 100, a crossover rate of 0.7 and a mutation rate of 0.09 (= 0.3 x 0.3). As explained in Chapter 4, the two components of the mutation rate are the probability that a chromosome will be selected for mutation and the probability that a gene of the selected chromosome will be chosen to be exchanged with another gene.

An important consequence of using the quasi-optimizing heuristic to select the maintenance treatment is that each chromosome is mapped into a reasonable maintenance programme. This is in contrast to the scheduling studies of Chapters 7 and 8 where a major project was defined in advance and implemented according to the GA sequence, regardless of the appropriateness of that action at that stage of the programme. One of the unknowns at the beginning of the maintenance study was whether the heuristic would result in so many good programmes that the GA would be unable to converge on one or two outstanding solutions.

Procedure

Calculating the objective function from a GA ordering of the set of integers, representing links to be treated, is not straightforward. The procedure for each GA chromosome is as follows.

First
The chromosome is mapped into an implementation timetable and the following steps are taken:

1. Predict road roughness for each segment and update the consequent link costs, including vehicle operating and time costs.
2. Forecast travel demands including passenger cars and freight vehicles between each OD pair on the basis of population and economic activity (GDP) forecasts and then assign traffic to obtain volumes on each link according to updated link costs.
3. By reference to the criteria shown in Table 9.1, determine what kind of treatment is to be carried out according to the predicted road conditions and the time when each segment is to be maintained. This is done for each road segment (gene) in rank order from the first to the last.
4. Calculate the costs of the projects to be implemented.
5. Implement projects year by year to use up each annual budget. If a year's funds are not enough to complete the last project then part of it is implemented and the remainder is done in the following year.
6. If all road segments have been checked through to the end by some year i then repeat steps 3 and 4 from the first gene of the chromosome. However it is necessary to impose the constraint that the interval between two major maintenance treatments (reseal or overlay) must be greater than 10 years.
7. Repeat steps 1 to 6 until the timetable for the planning period from year 1 to year 10 is complete.

For years 11 to 40, steps 1 and 2 are the same but steps 3 to 6 are replaced by one step: estimating the quantity and cost of routine maintenance for each segment in terms of the predicted roughness.

Second
Estimate annual benefits by comparing the project case with the base case year by year.

Third
Calculate the objective function, the (discounted) net present value of all benefits.

These steps were followed in the maintenance study and were repeated for each member of the population of 100 GA chromosomes in each generation. The full evaluation for at least 500 generations was repeated ten times from the beginning to give reasonable assurance that the optimal or near optimal result had been found. There were annual traffic assignments for years 1 to 10 and for every fifth year in years 11 to 40. In one GA run lasting 2400 generations, this amounted to a total of $(10 + 6) \times 2400 \times 100 \ (= 3.84$ million) traffic assignments. Thus allocating traffic in response to the various sets and sequences of road conditions was a heavy burden in computing time and dominated the entire computation process.

Convergence

Figure 9.1 shows a plot of the evolution of the best individual in each of the first 800 generations of the run (experiment) that produced the best result. The fact that the best of the 100 solutions in each of the first 50 generations would give a negative net present value (NPV) answers the question posed at the end of the last section. Although the heuristic summarized in Table 9.1 makes the best of any sequence, it is not sufficient to ensure a sound maintenance programme. Starting from a (best) solution with an NPV of −$18 million, 800 GA generations were sufficient to find a good maintenance programme.

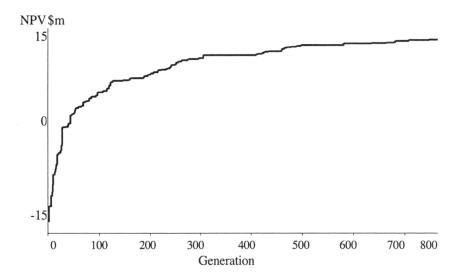

Figure 9.1   NPV ($ million) of the best solution: first 800 GA generations

A test of many more generations gave only a slight improvement. However the results indicate that it would always be advisable to do at least three runs of 500 to 800 generations for a very large problem like this one. This is in contrast to the regional road project study of Chapter 7 where the much smaller number of potential projects (34) made 100 generations adequate.

RESULTS

Nine solutions to the maintenance problem had net present values between $10.5 million and $12.8 million, the second best being only 0.2 per cent less than the best. Table 9.2 shows the best solution in the optimal sequence found by the GA. It is expressed as a project timetable showing each segment in each year over the entire network during the ten-year planning period. Part of the last project (widening segment 306) in the eleventh year is also included. Road segments are in a sequence list and years run across columns.

Treatment codes used in Table 9.2 are: 0 = routine maintenance, 1 = reseal, 2 = thin overlay, 3 = thick overlay, 4 = widening. The location of a road segment can be found by reading the link end nodes in Table 9.9 (Appendix 9B) and then identifying these two nodes on the map shown in Figure 9.2.

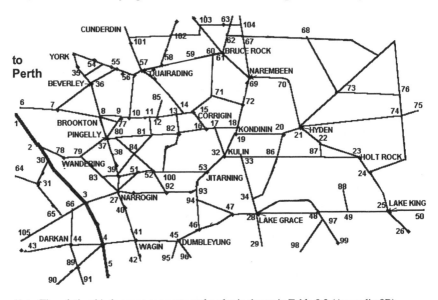

Note: The relationship between segments and nodes is shown in Table 9.9 (Appendix 9B)

Figure 9.2   Road network of the study area showing numbered nodes

Table 9.2 Treatments in best solution (segments* listed in GA result order)

Seg.	Year	Seg.	Year		Seg.	Year			Seg.	Year				Seg.	Year				Seg.	Year	
	1		1	2		2	3	4		4	5	6	7		7	8	9	10		10	11
260	1	162	4	0	276	1	0	0	207	0	0	0	0	1	4	0	0	0	19	4	0
82	1	156	1	0	38	4	0	0	217	0	0	0	0	81	0	0	0	0	88	4	0
52	0	63	0	0	243	0	0	0	62	0	0	0	0	12	3	0	0	0	291	1	0
272	1	271	0	0	186	0	0	0	264	1	0	0	0	13	0	0	0	0	196	1	0
294	1	154	0	0	319	1	0	0	97	0	0	0	0	274	4	0	0	0	44	4	0
145	0	55	0	0	208	0	0	0	209	0	0	0	0	16	4	0	0	0	308	1	0
230	0	316	0	0	114	0	0	0	120	4	0	0	0	2	2	0	0	0	51	1	0
168	1	219	0	0	103	0	0	0	255	1	0	0	0	290	1	0	0	0	39	0	0
228	1	91	0	0	69	4	4	0	301	2	0	0	0	267	0	0	0	0	306	4	4
283	1	315	0	0	151	0	4	0	256	4	0	0	0	4	2	0	0	0	205	0	0
130	0	99	0	0	167	0	1	0	163	4	4	0	0	161	4	0	0	0	113	0	0
247	0	312	0	0	42	0	0	0	195	0	1	0	0	164	2	0	0	0	238	0	0
261	0	221	1	0	36	0	0	0	298	0	1	0	0	122	4	0	0	0	153	0	0
73	4	98	0	0	239	0	0	0	251	0	0	0	0	242	1	0	0	0	175	0	0
43	0	76	0	0	54	0	0	0	278	0	4	0	0	27	1	1	0	0	269	0	0
229	0	212	0	0	56	0	0	0	302	0	1	0	0	203	0	4	0	0	197	0	0
121	0	213	0	0	284	0	4	0	141	0	0	0	0	72	0	4	0	0	37	0	0
299	1	216	1	0	157	0	4	0	57	0	0	0	0	18	0	4	0	0	112	0	0
210	0	78	4	4	288	0	0	0	304	0	1	0	0	245	0	0	0	0	53	0	0
60	0	64	0	0	199	0	1	0	200	0	4	0	0	77	0	3	0	0	75	0	0
165	1	144	0	0	84	0	4	0	71	0	4	0	0	110	0	1	0	0	126	0	0
177	1	295	0	1	222	0	1	0	21	0	4	0	0	178	0	4	0	0	266	0	0
241	0	282	0	1	140	0	0	0	146	0	0	0	0	293	0	1	0	0	280	0	0
180	1	257	0	1	223	0	1	0	124	0	1	0	0	6	0	2	0	0	118	0	0
79	1	106	0	1	159	0	4	0	67	0	4	0	0	14	0	4	0	0	227	0	0
133	0	233	0	0	47	0	4	0	104	0	0	0	0	166	0	1	0	0	128	0	0
237	0	204	0	4	270	0	1	0	250	0	0	0	0	317	0	0	0	0	318	0	0
74	1	131	0	1	61	0	0	0	26	0	0	0	0	262	0	1	0	0	281	0	0
169	1	32	0	0	83	0	4	4	129	0	0	0	0	211	0	1	0	0	149	0	0
310	0	101	0	0	66	0	0	1	232	0	1	0	0	17	0	4	0	0	65	0	0
313	4	87	0	4	102	0	0	0	11	0	4	0	0	29	0	3	3	0	135	0	0
45	4	96	0	0	300	0	0	1	100	0	0	0	0	139	0	0	4	0	187	0	0
160	1	148	0	0	226	0	0	1	89	0	4	0	0	109	0	0	4	0	90	0	0
273	1	259	0	4	8	0	0	0	119	0	1	0	0	15	0	0	4	0	182	0	0
31	0	246	0	0	170	0	0	1	191	0	1	0	0	142	0	0	1	0	143	0	0
107	0	184	0	0	314	0	0	1	279	0	4	0	0	231	0	0	0	0	80	0	0
183	1	136	0	0	220	0	0	1	202	0	4	4	0	7	0	0	2	0	215	0	0
137	0	174	0	2	311	0	0	0	172	0	0	1	0	68	0	0	4	0	188	0	0
70	4	201	0	0	258	0	0	1	303	0	0	0	0	35	0	0	0	0	309	0	0
305	0	224	0	0	254	0	0	1	249	0	0	0	0	292	0	0	1	0	252	0	0
225	0	190	0	1	34	0	0	0	46	0	0	4	0	115	0	0	1	0	40	0	0
265	0	10	0	0	236	0	0	0	22	0	0	3	0	277	0	0	4	0	49	0	0
248	0	263	0	0	253	0	0	1	286	0	0	1	0	33	0	0	3	0	194	0	0
244	0	150	0	1	285	0	0	1	3	0	0	2	0	125	0	0	4	4	138	0	0
296	0	147	0	0	132	0	0	1	173	0	0	2	0	28	0	0	0	2	268	0	0
41	0	218	0	0	117	0	0	0	111	0	0	0	0	9	0	0	0	0	193	0	0
95	0	240	0	0	234	0	0	0	94	0	0	0	0	181	0	0	0	1	179	0	0
92	0	134	0	0	297	0	0	1	171	0	0	2	0	116	0	0	0	0	50	0	0
108	0	93	0	0	287	0	0	0	20	0	0	4	0	158	0	0	0	4	176	0	0
155	1	86	0	4	185	0	0	1	275	0	0	1	0	25	0	0	0	2			
235	0	192	0	1	307	0	0	4	23	0	0	1	0	5	0	0	0	1			
127	0	289	0	0	105	0	0	4	85	0	0	4	0	24	0	0	0	2			
206	1	189	0	1	123	0	0	4	48	0	0	4	4	198	0	0	0	1			
214	0	59	0	0	152	0	0	1	58	0	0	0	0	30	0	0	0	3			

Notes:
0 = routine maintenance, 1 = reseal, 2 = thin overlay, 3 = thick overlay, 4 = widening
* Appendix 9B gives relationships of segments to nodes, which are shown in Figure 9.2

The apparently random inclusion of segments needing no treatment other than routine maintenance (a treatment code of 0 in Table 9.2) occurs because the routine cost is not charged to the budget for the optimization. All segments are given such treatment every year unless there is a reseal, overlay or widening. Although their positions are irrelevant to the optimizing process, the segments given routine maintenance only have participated in crossover and mutation and it is noted that the genetic algorithm has segregated 40 of them to the end of the list.

Differences and Similarities between Solutions

The best and second best solutions differed substantially in programme details although the general composition of types of treatment is similar (Table 9.3). The fact that they are different in detail means that the senior engineer concerned has a choice of programmes. However among the remaining solutions there some that are very similar to one or other of the two best but with significantly lower net present values.

Table 9.3   Number of maintenance treatments by year (other than routine)

Year:	1	2	3	4	5	6	7	8	9	10	Total number of treatments	Share of spending %
Best solution												
Reseal	22	12	5	17	8	4	3	6	3	7	87	9.7
Thin overlay		1		1		3	3	1	1	3	13	11.2
Thick overlay					1	1	2	2	1		7	7.5
Widen	6	6	8	6	10	5	6	6	6	6	65	71.6
Second best												
Reseal	16	9	17	9	7	4	7	6	3	5	83	9.6
Thin overlay			3	1		1	3	1	2	2	13	10.3
Thick overlay				2				2	2		6	6.7
Widen	7	8	6	7	6	8	6	7	5	5	65	73.5

This reveals an important implication for practical expenditure scheduling. If a treatment for a segment at a certain time that would achieve a relatively high economic benefit is shifted to another time for some reason then the benefit may decrease significantly. Should the timing of a set of treatments need to be adjusted to meet any other objectives then caution should be exercised to avoid a substantial loss of benefits. These findings are similar to those discussed in Chapter 7 with respect to the problem of selecting and scheduling regional projects.

When maps of treatments over ten years were plotted for the solutions it was found that the treatments for the whole period in the two best solutions were very similar. They converged on much the same result but with differences in timing. Despite the substantial deviations between the years in which treatments are applied, these two have almost the same net present values. In these two cases different solutions simply mean that a specific treatment is implemented on a segment in different years.

The third-best solution viewed over the whole ten-year period is also very similar to the best two but the NPV is 4.3 per cent less. In this case the timing of the work does have an appreciable effect. There is also a striking similarity between the tenth GA solution and the best but in this case the differences in project timing affect benefits substantially. The result is that the NPV is only 44.6 per cent of the best.

The problem for the decision maker is that ten-year similarities between the two or three excellent solutions do not provide a good guide for practical management. Most of the rest of the ten GA solutions show much the same or even greater similarity. They are all beneficial solutions with positive NPVs but substantially inferior to the best two. Thus finding the best selection of projects for the whole period and arranging them in any convenient sequence might seem reasonable but would be far from optimal.

The next section gives specific examples to illustrate the problem.

Sensitivity to the Order of Treatment

In order to show the dangers of relying on engineering judgement to determine the order in which they should be treated, two pairs of segments have been chosen to have their positions in the sequence exchanged (Table 9.4). These examples illustrate the difficulties that arise even when the segments are widely separated.

The first exchange is to replace Segment 25 which is scheduled for thin overlay in year 10 (last column of Table 9.2) by Segment 268 which is not listed for treatment. If they are exchanged in the GA chromosome of the best solution then the heuristic would select widening for Segment 268 in year 10. The result would be a reduction in the NPV of the whole programme by

10.7 per cent (Table 9.4). This effect is due partly to the fact that the expensive widening would displace the resealing and/or overlaying of several segments in year 10 and to the fact that the traffic on Segment 25 is much higher than on Segment 268.

Table 9.4   Effect of exchanging the sequence positions of selected pairs of road segments

	Case 1		Case 2	
Segment number	25	268	277	280
Length, km	5	5	5	5
Width, metres	9.48	4.13	6.20	6.80
Roughness, metres/km	1.934	3.297	2.460	3.162
Traffic, AADT	1456	190	297	320
NPV of Whole Programme, $ million				
Original sequence positions	12.768		12.768	
Positions exchanged	11.407		12.260	

Selecting the right order for the second pair, segments 277 and 280, by engineering judgement is even harder. If Segment 277 which is scheduled for widening in year 9 (last column of Table 9.2) is replaced by unscheduled Segment 280 then the heuristic would select widening for Segment 280. The greater roughness and slightly higher traffic of 280 might lead an engineer to choose it. The roughness of Segment 280 would be greatly reduced but nevertheless the NPV over the whole network would decrease by 4.0 per cent (Table 9.4). Thus a segment in worse condition should not always be treated earlier.

These simple tests give some insight into the way in which this study has solved the problem of a variety of cases of pavement distress throughout a network competing for limited funds and thus made possible the optimization of maintenance and renewal projects together.

Marginal Benefit–Cost Ratio

It was noted in Chapter 3 that incremental cost–benefit analysis provides a rigorous way of testing whether the last budget increment for a complex maintenance programme is warranted. The truly marginal benefit is the benefit achieved by the last dollar which is a embodied in the 'last' project. This project is to widen Segment 306 at a cost of $0.0512 million in year 10 and also $0.7388 million in year 11.

The marginal evaluation considers removing this project and saving the associated outlays. The amount eliminated from the last year's budget is $0.0448 million, being the difference between $0.0512 million and the required routine maintenance cost of $0.0064 million. In addition the $0.7388 million in year 11 for this project is not required and accordingly the maintenance costs are also changed automatically. The same procedure has been followed to calculate the marginal benefit–cost ratio for the second-last project. The amounts are all discounted to the base year. Results of the marginal cost–benefit analyses for the last and second-last projects are shown in Table 9.5.

Table 9.5   Marginal cost–benefit analysis of the last and second-last projects (7% discount rate)

	Cost $million (discounted)	Benefit $million (discounted)	B/C ratio
Best solution	84.2055	96.9738	1.152
Best solution without last project	83.8439	96.7230	1.154
Marginal effect of the last project	0.3616*	0.2508	0.694
Best soln without last and second last	83.7695	96.6668	1.154
Marginal effect of second last project	0.07435	0.05625	0.757

Note:
* The sum of the discounted values of expenditures in years 10 and 11 on the last project

If the last project were dropped then the discounted cost reduction of $0.3616 million would result in the marginal benefit reduction of $0.2508 million (discounted). Thus the marginal benefit–cost ratio is 0.694, which can be interpreted as each dollar spent on the last project achieving a benefit of $0.694, ignoring any benefits other than vehicle operating costs and time savings. Similarly, the marginal benefit–cost ratio of 0.757 for the second-last project shows that each dollar spent on this project, if it were the last, would achieve a benefit of $0.757.

Both marginal benefit–cost ratios indicate that the proposed maintenance budgets for the Southern Wheatbelt were of approximately the right magnitude, but possibly a little too large. There might be other benefits which would justify the inclusion of the last two projects.

Traffic Responses to Road Conditions

If there is no change in link costs then traffic estimated by the combined gravity and logit direct demand model will always increase, or at least not decrease, with growth in population and economic activity. However link costs change with alterations in road conditions, such as roughness or widening, and these cost changes result in the generation of more traffic and redistribution of traffic between routes. To give an illustration of such dynamic changes in traffic in the best solution, the traffic on six links during the planning period is plotted in Figure 9.3.

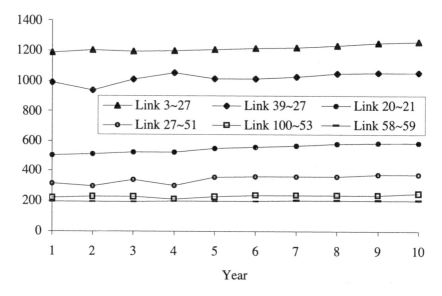

Note: The link numbers correspond to node numbers in Figure 9.2 and the links shown in the figure above comprise segments (Tables 9.2 and 9.9) as follows:

    Link 3~27   = 120+121+122+123+124+125
    Link 39~27   = 172+173+174
    Link 20~21   = 86+87+88+89
    Link 27~51   = 253+254+255+256+257
    Link 100~53 = 262+263+264+265+266+267+268+269
    Link 58~59   = 290+291+292+293+294

Figure 9.3   Daily traffic (AADT) on six links during the planning period

The presentation is in terms of links because traffic is counted on the basis that one link comprises several segments. The links are identified by node numbers in Figure 9.2 and these are related to segments in Table 9.9 (Appendix 9B) where details of lengths and widths are also shown.

Figure 9.3 indicates that traffic on Link 39~27 would decrease in year 2 and increase significantly in years 3 and 4. One reason is that the average roughness of this link would increase to 3.30 m/km in year 2 and decrease to 2.83 m/km in year 3. The roughness decrease is due to a thin overlay on Segment 174 in year 2 (second column of Table 9.2). Other traffic fluctuations can also be attributed to maintenance treatments. In contrast there has been little impact on links 20~21 and 58~59 even though they have received treatments.

Road Roughness Outcomes

Development of the roughness prediction model is explained in Appendix 9A. To illustrate the progression of roughness in the planning period, for the best solution, five segments have been selected. The year-by-year maintenance treatments for each of the five segments are shown in Table 9.6 (based on Table 9.2).

Table 9.6   Annual maintenance treatments on five selected road segments

Year	Segment number				
	127 (in Link 28~29)	**297** (in Link 59~60)	**6** (in Link 1~2)	**22** (in Link 3~4)	**200** (in Link 4~41)
1	Routine	Routine	Routine	Routine	Routine
2	Routine	Routine	Routine	Routine	Routine
3	Routine	Routine	Routine	Routine	Routine
4	Routine	**Reseal**	Routine	Routine	Routine
5	Routine	Routine	Routine	Routine	**Widen** (& thick overlay)
6	Routine	Routine	Routine	**Thick overlay**	Routine
7	Routine	Routine	Routine	Routine	Routine
8	Routine	Routine	**Thin overlay**	Routine	Routine
9	Routine	Routine	Routine	Routine	Routine
10	Routine	Routine	Routine	Routine	Routine

The major treatments shown in Table 9.6 cause the falls in roughness illustrated in Figure 9.4 after which the progressive deterioration – increasing roughness – sets in again. The rates of increase in roughness of the five segments differ because the traffic volumes and strengths are different. Segments 6 and 22 are on the only highway in the study area and Segment 200 is on an important connecting link to the highway.

Each of the major treatments, thin or thick overlay and widening (with thick overlay), results in a substantial reduction in roughness. Routine maintenance is not sufficient to prevent increasing roughness and a reseal gives only a temporary respite.

Most of the optimized expenditure on widening narrow roads would not reduce roughness substantially over the whole network but would achieve a high level of benefits. However roughness is not the only issue because the widened roads would improve the entire service level. Taking a long view it is clear that the emphasis on widening narrow pavements in the optimized programme represents a phase in development. Subsequent expenditure would arrest and even reverse the deterioration in roughness.

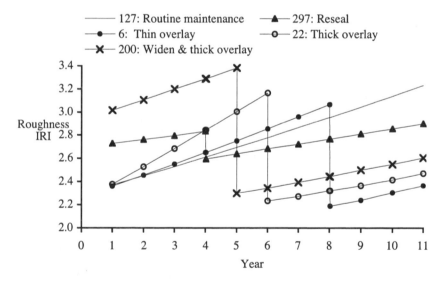

Note: The segments (also shown in Table 9.6) are located as follows:
Segment 127 in Link 28~29
Segment 297 in Link 59~60
Segment 6 in Link 1~2
Segment 22 in Link 3~4
Segment 200 in Link 4~41

Figure 9.4   Roughness progression (IRI, vertical metres per km) on five segments showing the results of the treatments in Table 9.6

APPENDIX 9A DEVELOPMENT OF A RESPONSIVE ROAD DETERIORATION MODEL

It was noted at the beginning of this chapter that the weakness of available road roughness models in not dealing adequately with maintenance could have undermined the optimization process. This appendix presents the results of a separate study (Han, 2000 and 2002) which extended and re-estimated the incremental roughness model in order to make it responsive to maintenance.

In broad terms the factors influencing roughness progression are traffic loading, environmental effects, maintenance, pavement characteristics and quality of the initial construction, as well as pavement age. Construction quality has rarely been specified in models since is not easy to measure. It is important to recognize that the combined environmental and traffic-loading effects on roughness may be masked by maintenance carried out to offset them and the model will be inaccurate if maintenance is not properly represented.

Since 1970 road authorities and researchers have developed various roughness prediction models to meet the requirements of their own management systems. These models express roughness as a function of some or all of four important explanatory variables: age, traffic, environment and maintenance. Many models do not cover all four, and a number include only age and traffic. Some have only one explanatory variable, age. There has been limited success in specifying a maintenance variable in a deterioration model because road maintenance history is not easily obtained.

The HDM Incremental Roughness Model

The best known road assessment model is the Highway Design and Maintenance Standards Model which was developed by the World Bank for the evaluation of road projects in developing countries. Its road deterioration sub-model is widely applied by researchers and road authorities. This sub-model estimates the combined effects of traffic, environment and age on the condition of the road; it has both incremental and aggregate forms.

The incremental model estimates the changes in roughness due to deterioration over a time period. Roughness progression is predicted as the sum of three components:

1. Structural deformation related to roughness, equivalent standard axle load, and structural number.
2. Surface condition, related to changes in cracking, potholing, patching and rut depth variation.
3. An age–environment related roughness term.

Increased roughness ΔR_t (m/km IRI) over time Δt is expressed as:

$$\Delta R_t = \alpha e^{\beta t}(1 + SNC)^\gamma \Delta NE4 + \beta R_t \Delta t + rut, \; crack, \; patch \; and \; pothole \; terms$$

where t is pavement age (years) since last overlay or reconstruction,

SNC is the structural number for pavement strength,

$\Delta NE4$ is the change in equivalent standard axles (ESAs) in period Δt (million ESAs/lane),

R_t is road roughness (m/km IRI) at the beginning of period Δt,

β is an age-environmental coefficient to be calibrated,

α, γ are other parameters to be calibrated.

The aggregate form of the HDM model takes account of pavement age in estimating roughness at a particular time. The relationships incorporated in the road deterioration models are structured on concepts of pavement behaviour and have been quantified from an extensive database. These mechanistic-empirical models are intended to be transferable because of the principles used to guide the general form and combination of parameters in the relationships. This intention has been borne out by the applications of the models in a wide range of countries. When they are used in countries other than Brazil where they were developed, the parameters should be recalibrated to suit local conditions.

Modification of the Models

The HDM incremental model for roughness progression contains sub-models for initiation and progression of cracking, patching, potholing and rutting. These distress sub-models are not needed if good maintenance practice prevents such distresses from developing so far as to critically affect roughness. That an adequate level of maintenance can retard and prevent deterioration has been confirmed by experienced maintenance engineers.

Thus it seems reasonable to put maintenance factors directly into the model rather than include terms for surface defects and patching. Consequently routine and periodic maintenance replaces rutting, cracking, potholing and patching in the modified incremental model. In addition the strength variable is represented by falling weight deflection instead of the modified structure number; the justification of this substitution is discussed later. After these two modifications, the increase in roughness ΔR_t (m/km IRI) over an increment of years Δt can be expressed as:

$$\Delta R_t = \alpha e^{\beta t} DEF^\gamma \Delta NE4 + (\beta \Delta t + \theta \; \text{Reseal} + \delta \; \Delta RM) R_t \qquad (9.1)$$

where *DEF* is falling weight deflection (not curvature) in millimetres

Reseal is the number of reseals during the period Δt

ΔRM is routine maintenance during Δt (square metres of patching per lane-km)

$\alpha, \gamma, \theta, \delta$ are parameters to be calibrated and other terms are as before.

Pavement age is defined as years since the last overlay, reconstruction or new construction. If the inventory data does not include items for overlay and reconstruction then pavement ages must be calculated from construction.

Effective and commonly used measures for assessing pavement/subgrade strength include the modified structural number and surface deflection. The modified structure number (MSN) is a comprehensive indicator commonly calculated from the contribution to pavement strength of each pavement layer and subgrade dependent on its California bearing ratio (CBR) value. The formulation in HDM3 is:

$$MSN = \sum_{i=1}^{n} a_i h_i / 25.4 + 3.51\log_{10} CBR - 0.85(\log_{10} CBR)^2 - 1.43$$

where a_i is the strength coefficient of the ith layer, h_i is the thickness of the ith layer (millimetres), n is the number of pavement layers. *CBR* is the California bearing ratio of the subgrade at in situ conditions of moisture and density (percentage).

This method requires a record of pavement structures and subgrade CBR since construction, adjusted to take account of maintenance. If such information is not available then it is not feasible to evaluate the MSN by the above equation. An alternative way to assess pavement/subgrade strength is to measure the surface deflection – the vertical deformation of the pavement surface measured by a Benkelman beam or a falling weight deflectometer. The bigger the deflection or the deflection curvature the more readily the pavement deteriorates.

Falling weight deflection and deflection curvature, the difference between vertical deformations at 0 and 200 mm, were available in the maintenance study area. The structural number for pavement strength SNC could be calculated from the surface deflection but a better approach is to use the measured deflection or curvature directly as a variable in the roughness model.

Surface deflection is an excellent indicator of relative strength along a nominally homogeneous pavement. In the study region, the pavement, subgrade and environmental factors were reasonably homogeneous so that either the surface deflection or deflection curvature could be used as a strength indicator. Surface deflection gave the best fit when the roughness measure was aggregated over segments for use in the incremental model but deflection curvature showed a better fit when the raw roughness measure was the dependent variable in the aggregate model. Details are presented later.

Traffic loadings expressed as the cumulative equivalent standard axles (CESAs) in each lane are estimated from traffic composition and the equivalent standard axles of each vehicle classification. This was extracted from culvert strain gauge (CULWAY) data wherever such equipment was installed. Otherwise CESAs were estimated from average annual daily traffic and the percentage of heavy vehicles. The total number of equivalent standard axles (ESAs) to be applied to the pavement during the period between the two roughness-recording time points *t-1* and *t*, *ΔNE4*, can be determined with the formula:

$$\Delta NE4 = 365 * 1.1 * AADT \, / \, (\text{No. of Lanes}) * E * C\% * \Delta GF$$

where C is the proportion of heavy commercial vehicles, E is the estimated number of ESAs per commercial vehicle and ΔGF is the calculated growth factor according to the assumed annual traffic growth rate.

Usually a pavement covers more than one traffic lane. It was assumed that traffic is distributed evenly across a pavement so that each lane has the same number of standard axles.

Based on road traffic survey information, it was assumed that traffic volumes increased exponentially during the period from road commissioning to the roughness-recording year. An annual growth rate of 2 per cent was assumed on the basis of past traffic increases. Any changes in proportions of axle configurations and load sizes were ignored.

Maintenance treatments include routine maintenance, reseal, overlay and reconstruction. Routine maintenance is measured by area patched in square metres per lane-kilometre, while reseal is counted in number of times resealed. Overlay and reconstruction reduce roughness substantially and are discussed later.

Roughness is measured for each 100-metre road segment. International roughness indices (IRIs) are obtained at three positions across the pavement: the outer wheel path, inner wheel path and mid-lane. For an aggregate model the average of the outer and inner path values is used as the dependent variable but for the incremental model the individual averages had to be aggregated to match the segments for which other data were provided.

Maximum Likelihood Estimation

The available data for the dependent variable roughness is the IRI for each road segment in the study area. A major source of variation in roughness measures is the fact that a different (wheel) track on the road is being profiled each time. Other random influences as well as measurement errors result from traffic loading and subgrade/pavement strength. Because of the effects of unmeasurable variables and measurement errors, each measured roughness R_i^* is regarded as being composed of a deterministic term the estimated roughness R_i and a random term ε_i as follows:

$$R_i^* = R_i + \varepsilon_i \tag{9.2}$$

The random term ε_i is assumed to be independently and normally distributed with mean zero and variance σ_i^2.

A maximum likelihood method is formulated to estimate parameter values from the observed roughness counts. The probability of obtaining the value of an observed roughness R_i^* is expressed in terms of the estimated value R_i by $\phi(R_i^*, R_i)$. Let N denote the number of the valid records in which roughness and information on all independent variables are available. The joint probability of measuring the roughness R_i^* is then:

$$\Phi = \prod_{i=1}^{N} \phi(R_i^*, R_i)$$

The log-likelihood is defined as $L = \ln \Phi = \sum_{i=1}^{N} \ln \phi(R_i^*, R_i)$

Because each roughness is assumed to be normally distributed with mean R_i and variance σ_i^2 the probability of measuring roughness R_i^* is:

$$\phi(R_i^*, R_i) = \frac{1}{\sqrt{2\pi}\sigma_i} \exp\left[-\frac{(R_i - R_i^*)^2}{2\sigma_i^2}\right]$$

Then the maximum likelihood estimator is:

$$L = -\frac{N}{2}\ln(2\pi) - \sum_i \ln\sigma_i - \frac{1}{2}\sum_i \frac{(R_i - R_i^*)^2}{\sigma_i^2}$$

The first part $-N/2*ln(2\pi)$ is a constant and can be omitted, so that the maximizing problem for an aggregate model becomes:

$$\text{Max } L = -\sum_i \ln\sigma_i - \frac{1}{2}\sum_i \frac{(R_i - R_i^*)^2}{\sigma_i^2} \quad \text{s.t. } R_i \geq 0, \ i = 1,...,N \tag{9.3}$$

where R_i^* is the measured roughness and R_i is the value estimated. The roughness indices are strictly positive.

Previous work has indicated that random variation in measured roughness varies with the magnitude of the roughness itself. This was confirmed by experienced engineers in Main Roads Western Australia. Therefore the standard error of the random term is assumed to be proportional to the estimated roughness, that is $\sigma_i = \lambda R_i$. This heteroscedastic Normal distribution provides a realistic approximation in spite of the Normal distribution permitting negative values.

Equation 9.3 is modified for the incremental model by replacing R_i and R_i^* with ΔR_i^t and ΔR_i^{t*}, respectively. From equation 9.2,

$$R_i^{t*} = R_i^t + \varepsilon_i^t \quad \text{and} \quad R_i^{t-1*} = R_i^{t-1} + \varepsilon_i^{t-1}.$$

Thus the measured roughness difference ΔR_i^{t*} between two consecutive times consists of a deterministic term, the estimated roughness difference and a random term:

$$\Delta R_i^{t*} = \Delta R_i^t + \zeta_i^t$$

where:
$$\zeta_i^t = \varepsilon_i^t - \varepsilon_i^{t-1}$$

and
$$\varepsilon_i^t \sim N[0, (\sigma_i^t)^2] = N[0, (\lambda R_i^t)^2].$$

Superscripts *t* and *t-1* indicate values at those times.

Based on the heteroscedastic Normal assumption for absolute roughness, the random term ζ_i^t is still normally distributed with mean zero, the variance being derived as follows:

$$\begin{aligned}
\text{var}(\zeta_i^t) &= \text{var}(\varepsilon_i^t - \varepsilon_i^{t-1}) = \text{var}(\varepsilon_i^t) + \text{var}(\varepsilon_i^{t-1}) - 2\,\text{cov}(\varepsilon_i^t, \varepsilon_i^{t-1}) \\
&= (\sigma_i^t)^2 + (\sigma_i^{t-1})^2 - 2 r_i \sigma_i^t \sigma_i^{t-1} = \lambda^2 [(R_i^t)^2 + (R_i^{t-1})^2 - 2 r_i R_i^t R_i^{t-1}] \\
&= \lambda^2 [(\Delta R_i^t)^2 + 2(1 - r_i)(R_i^{t-1} + \Delta R_i^t) R_i^{t-1}]
\end{aligned}$$

Thus the magnitude of the variance of ζ_i^t is dependent on the correlation r_i between ε_i^t and ε_i^{t-1}. If these successive values have a perfectly linear relationship, that is, $r_i = 1$, then the variance of ζ_i^t will have the same form as in the residuals of the absolute roughness, that is $\text{var}(\zeta_i^t) = (\lambda \Delta R_i^t)^2$.

However the values of r_i are expected to be less than 1, so that $\text{var}(\zeta_i^t)$ cannot be simplified to a function of only ΔR_i^t.

Furthermore r_i varies from segment to segment, so that there is no stable relationship between the variance of ζ_i^t and ΔR_i^t. Therefore assuming a homogeneous Normal distribution, with constant variance for all random variables ζ_i^t, $\sigma_i^2 = \sigma^2$, is a simplified feasible choice for model calibration. This implies that the unexplained part of roughness change does not vary with the magnitude of the roughness itself. On this assumption the maximum likelihood function for the incremental model becomes:

$$\max \quad L = -N\ln\sigma - \frac{1}{2\sigma^2}\sum_i(\Delta R_i^t - \Delta R_i^{t^*})^2 \quad i = 1,...,N \qquad (9.4)$$

Equation 9.4 has the five model parameters of Eqn 9.1 (α, β, γ, θ, δ) plus a variance parameter σ to be calibrated in order to obtain the optimal ΔR_i^t s. Although the maximum likelihood function with five parameters is usually well behaved, a simple Newton method could not reach the optimum because the solution space is not strictly quadratic. The matrix of second derivatives or Hessian was not always negative definite. The quadratic hill-climbing method was used to solve this problem. In any iteration, if the Hessian was not negative definite then a positive number was subtracted from each diagonal element, the number chosen being large enough to make the corrected Hessian negative definite.

The asymptotic covariance matrix of the parameter estimates is calculated as the negative inverse of the Hessian of the log-likelihood function at its maximum likelihood. The diagonal elements provide the estimates of variances while the off-diagonal elements give covariances. The standard errors from the diagonal elements are used to calculate asymptotic 't' ratios. The likelihood ratio statistic is also used to test the significance of parameters. The coefficient of determination, R^2, is a measure of the extent to which the model fits the data.

Data for Model Estimation

The study area was the road network of Wheatbelt Southern Region of Western Australia. It includes 11 flexibly paved main roads and highways, the total length being 1598 km, and significant local roads. Most are two-lane roads, while there are some one or three sealed lane sections. One major highway had annual average daily traffic (AADT) ranging from 1000 to more than 3000 vehicles per day in 1998 while AADT on other roads ranged from

25 to 1020. This is a typical rural area with light traffic. The data for model calibration were mainly extracted from the Main Roads Western Australia databases. Four inventories have been compiled for the main roads in the Wheatbelt Southern region from surveys in 1996, 1997 and 1998:

- 1998 inventory. This includes roughness and strength data in different files but no traffic, road age or structure data. Each 100-metre road segment has a roughness record, while segments of about 800 metres each have strength records.
- 1997 inventory. This includes a file of traffic and roughness. Each 100-metre road segment has a record. There is no road age, structure or strength information.
- 1996 inventory. This includes, in a single data file, road structure, the construction and reseal years, traffic and roughness but no strength information. The length of a road segment, for which each row of items is recorded, ranges from 0.01 km to 8.15 km. Information on major items is missing from some records, being entered as zeros.
- CWOMS data. This database was developed to record routine maintenance history. Details include schedule items, work items, completion dates, quantities and costs. However maintenance costs were not provided due to confidentiality.

Matching and combining data

Data for the modelled variables, roughness, age, deflection, traffic and maintenance were extracted from different inventories, and these variables were measured at different road-length intervals. Thus they had different record numbers for the same road network in the study region. In addition roughness and deflection were measured for both left and right lanes while age, traffic and maintenance were recorded by entire sections. A summary of the data extracted is shown in Table 9.7.

Because the data were recorded at different intervals and saved in different files, it was necessary to match the records individually so that each observation used in estimating the model contained matching information. Data were combined by calculating weighted average values according to the location. That is roughness, deflection and age records were aggregated by applying weights that were the lengths of the road segments.

From a statistical point of view, a model should be calibrated directly from individual data. The procedure adopted was to preserve individual data as much as possible by matching the other data files to the deflection data files. Each measured right-lane deflection point was located midway between two measured left-lane points and vice versa so that the actual interval between any two neighbouring points (one being in the left lane and the other in the right lane) is roughly 400 metres. The example in Figure 9.5 shows a two-lane road with 100-metre segments separated by a line 'I', measured deflection points represented by '*', and corresponding roughness segments '~'.

Table 9.7 Data extracted for roughness model estimation

Variables	L/R	Number of records	Interval
Roughness	Left	24 167	100m
	Right	24 186	100m
Deflection	Left	3 092	≈ 800m
	Right	3 056	≈ 800m
Age		4 376	0.01~8.15km
Traffic		194	Link based
Maintenance		43	Sample based

From an engineer's point of view, each deflection measure indicates the strength of the pavement around the measured point. When the interval extends 200 metres on each side, the point measurement is not believed to reflect the strength of this 400-metre segment well. The closer to the point, the closer to the measured value is the strength of the pavement.

Therefore it is reasonable to assume that the strength of a 100-metre roughness segment is represented by the deflection of the corresponding measured point, extending about 50 metres on each side. Only those roughness segments in which there were deflection measures were selected for model calibration.

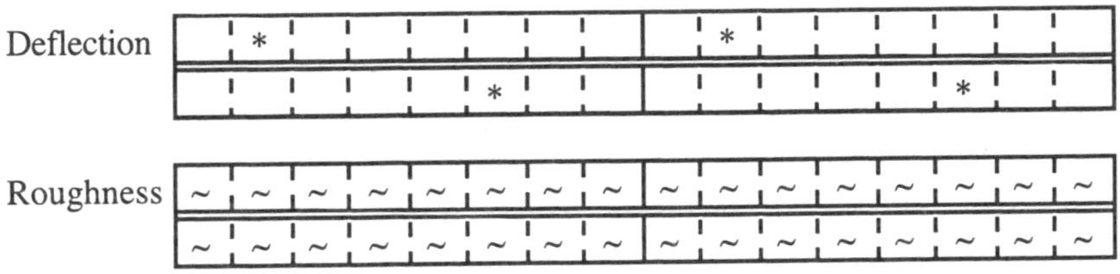

Figure 9.5   Points for measuring deflection and segments for measuring roughness

Age is recorded for various intervals ranging from 0.01 to 8.15 km while traffic is recorded on a link basis. The age and traffic of the selected roughness segments were matched according to location in straight line kilometres (SLK) and averaged over the relevant lengths. There were 6148 falling weight measuring points on the network but only 3689 valid records were left after deleting records for which there were no matching age or traffic records.

Inclusion of Routine and Periodic Maintenance Effects

Without reliable measures of the routine and periodic maintenance applied to the actual road pavement, the combined effects of various factors on roughness cannot be reliably predicted. Therefore it was essential to collect a set of well-specified data on these classes of maintenance.

The sampled road segments were distributed across the study area and were selected by experienced Main Roads engineers in the region. Relevant information, including road condition and maintenance history for each segment, was provided by the maintenance engineers. In addition, information about age, traffic and routine maintenance was extracted from the Main Roads databases.

Because the segment lengths were unequal, ranging from 0.33 to 10 km, the other data had to be aggregated from individual records so that they would match the maintenance segments. Thus roughness, which was measured in 100-metre lengths (left and right), deflection and age were aggregated into weighted averages based on the lengths of the maintenance segments.

The focus was on the periodic maintenance applied to each segment between time $t-1$, at some date in 1996 or 1997, and t, at some date in 1998. Δts are time differences between the two dates on which the roughness was measured, ranging from 1.382 to 1.866 years.

The sample included 43 road segments. Of these, only one had been given an overlay in the period. To deal with this treatment would require an overlay variable. However adding a variable for which there is only one observation would be the same as adjusting that observation to give it a perfect fit. It would contribute nothing to the estimation and the observation was eliminated from the data set.

In addition, roughness measurements on six segments of newly widened highway were made along widely different tracks from the previous observations, so that the segments were spuriously recorded as becoming rougher after reseal and widening. These were excluded, leaving 36 valid observations.

Calibration of the incremental roughness model
The model to be estimated is equation (9.1):

$$\Delta R_t = \alpha e^{\beta't} DEF^\gamma \Delta NE4 + (\beta\Delta t + \theta \text{ Reseal} + \delta \Delta RM) R_t$$

DEF is falling weight deflection and *RM* is routine maintenance. There is an implied parameter of 1 on *ΔNE4*, the incremental number of standard axles. Calibration of this model based on the 36 observations gave the results shown in Table 9.8.

All calibrated values are reasonable and the ρ^2 of 0.603 indicates a relatively high level of explanation for this kind of work, although the sample is small. The asymptotic '*t*' ratio for δ is significant at the 5 per cent level and the other coefficients are significant at the 1% level with 30 degrees of freedom.

The estimated value of 0.018 for β indicates that the annual increase in roughness due to ageing and environmental effects is about 1.8 per cent. This calibrated β of 0.018 is somewhat larger than the HDM tabulated value of 0.016 (Watanatada et al., 1987) for subtropical non-freezing semi-arid areas that is applicable to Wheatbelt South. However it is not significantly different. This refinement also follows from the separate specification of maintenance effects, which have tended to mask the traffic, ageing and environmental effects in previous models.

Table 9.8   Incremental roughness model: maximum likelihood estimates

Parameter	Parameter estimate	Standard error	't' ratio
Scalar (α)	6.7601	1.81931	3.72
Age–Environmental (β)	0.0180	0.00540	3.33
Falling weight deflection (γ)	3.2906	0.57894	5.68
Traffic (implied parameter)	1	–	–
Reseal (θ)	–0.0990	0.01697	5.84
Routine maintenance (δ)	–0.0013	0.00055	2.27
Variance (σ^2)	0.0865	0.01020	8.48

$\rho^2 = 0.603$

The estimate of –0.099 for θ indicates that each reseal decreases roughness by about 9.9 per cent. The estimate of –0.00126 for δ indicates that a square metre of patching per lane-kilometre decreases roughness by approximately 0.126 per cent. The estimated coefficient γ with respect to falling weight deflection of 3.2906 indicates the substantial effect of road weakness on deterioration. The scalar α of 6.7601 indicates how fast deterioration will be on weaker roads with more heavy trucks. The residuals plotted in Figure 9.6 appear to be randomly distributed and there is no evidence of heteroscedasticity.

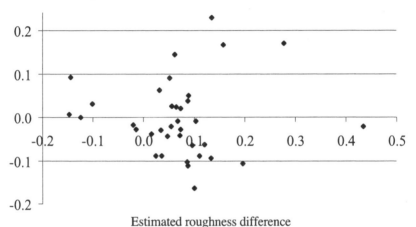

Figure 9.6   Residuals plotted against estimated roughness differences

Applicability of the Calibrated Model

Inclusion of actual maintenance distinguishes this model from most previous ones, making it more suitable for practical application. It depends on projection of maintenance activities, including routine and periodic, but that is precisely what is required in a model to prioritize and schedule maintenance. Such a model can be used to test hypothetical maintenance strategies.

The results confirm that routine maintenance such as patching not only reduces roughness but also maintains roads in good condition. This means that good maintenance practice can keep the road network to a lower annual deterioration rate. A given amount of maintenance on a rough road is more effective than on a smoother road.

Resealing, as one of periodic maintenance treatments, was carried out once or twice on each road aged up to 31 years in the study area. The estimate, indicating that roughness decreases by about 9.9 per cent following each reseal, is consistent with HDM3 for good paved roads with low traffic. The rougher the road, the more significant the resealing effectiveness.

The age–environment variable explains about 52.5 per cent of the roughness changes that would have occurred without maintenance, while traffic explains about 47.5 per cent. This shows a much greater contribution of traffic to deterioration than a number of previous results, partly because old and relatively thin pavements in the study area were easily damaged by heavy trucks and also because maintenance effects were specified separately.

In summary, the calibrated incremental model overcomes the key shortcoming of the aggregate model in that maintenance effects are separated from the effects of other factors, especially traffic. This model has the following advantages:

- it takes account of maintenance;
- it can employ the latest roughness measurements regardless of the initial roughness;
- it is suitable for prioritizing and scheduling maintenance activities.

Roughness and Strength with Overlay

The incremental maintenance model deals only with routine maintenance and reseal. Overlay and rehabilitation must also be modelled.

Thin overlay

Roughness reduction from thin overlay can be derived from an HDM model:

$$IRI_a = 3.9 - T/52 + 28*(IRI_b - 3.9)/T$$

where IRI_b and IRI_a are roughnesses before and after overlay (m/km), and T is overlay thickness (mm).

It has been found by Cox (1994) that this relationship underestimates the roughness reductions in Australia when the 'before' roughness (IRI_b) is less than 6 and to overestimate the roughness reduction when IRI_b is greater than 6. Based on case study results, the relationship has been modified to:

$$IRI_a = 2.4 + QCF - 0.008T + 10.0(IRI_b - 2.0)/T$$

where QCF is a quality control factor varying from –0.5 for good construction to +0.5 for poor construction.

Thick overlay

Roughness reduction from thick overlay was estimated from a model developed by Martin and Ramsay (1996):

$$\Delta R = 0.75R_b - 0.0005T - 0.0014D - 0.0016S - 0.43$$

where ΔR is the change in roughness after rehabilitation, R_b is roughness (IRI) before rehabilitation, T is thickness of a granular resheet (mm), D is the depth of pavement reworking/reconstruction (mm) and S is depth of pavement stabilization using cement, lime or bitumen (mm).

Strength increase

The increased strength resulting from a major overlay is estimated from a model also developed by Martin and Ramsay (1996):

$$\Delta SNC = 0.011T + 0.003D + 0.016S - 0.57$$

where ΔSNC is the change in strength after rehabilitation (modified structure number), SNC_b is strength before rehabilitation (MSN) and the other terms are as before.

After ΔSNC is evaluated by the above equation, the falling weight deflection is derived through the following relationship developed in HDM3 and used for Australia:

$$SNC = (6.5 \,/\, Def)^{0.625}$$

and the falling weight deflection after overlay is estimated by

$$Def_a = 6.5[(6.5/Def_b)^{0.625} + 0.011T + 0.003D + 0.016S - 0.57]^{-1.6}$$

where Def_b and Def_a are deflections (mm) before and after overlay.

Application of the Modified Roughness Model

The purpose of the maintenance study has been to develop a road roughness deterioration model suitable for prioritizing and scheduling maintenance and renewal projects on the highways and main roads. For the strength indicator, the commonly used modified structure number was replaced by the falling weight deflections not only because they are available but also because they are appropriate for reasonably homogeneous roads. They improve the model fit.

The most significant modification has been to include routine and periodic maintenance instead of rutting, cracking, patching and potholing terms. Good maintenance prevents the occurrence of significant ruts, cracks and potholes on roads. The calibrated incremental model was applied in this study for roughness prediction under the varying projected conditions.

APPENDIX 9B   SEGMENT LOCATION

Table 9.9   Segment location relative to link end nodes (see Figure 9.2)

Seg No	Link Start	Link End	Length (km)	Width (m)
1	1	2	5	8.24
2	1	2	5	9.22
3	1	2	5	8.88
4	1	2	5	9.47
5	1	2	5	8.93
6	1	2	5	9.87
7	1	2	5	8.88
8	1	2	4.62	9.08
9	2	30	5	7.74
10	2	30	5	9.09
11	2	30	5.5	7.93
12	30	3	5	9.04
13	30	3	5	8.58
14	30	3	5	8.19
15	30	3	5	8.2
16	30	3	5	8.11
17	30	3	5	7.76
18	30	3	5	7.89
19	30	3	5	7.94
20	30	3	5	7.6
21	30	3	6.5	7.64
22	3	4	5	9.12
23	3	4	5	8.6
24	3	4	5	9.57
25	3	4	5	9.48
26	3	4	5	9.4
27	3	4	5	8.62
28	3	4	5	8.61
29	3	4	3	8.76
30	4	5	5	8.62
31	4	5	5	10.21
32	4	5	5	8.63
33	4	5	4.5	8.71
34	6	7	5	8.8
35	6	7	5	8.88
36	6	7	5	7.19
37	6	7	5	7.1
38	6	7	5	6.02
39	6	7	5	6.9
40	7	8	5	7.02
41	7	8	5	8.2
42	7	8	5	8.15
43	7	8	5	9.88
44	7	8	5	7.85
45	7	8	5	6.31
46	7	8	5	6.02
47	7	8	5	6.63
48	7	8	5	7.82
49	8	9	5	6.3
50	8	9	5	6.41
51	8	9	5	7.43
52	8	9	5	7.44
53	8	9	5	7.32
54	8	9	4	7.3
55	9	10	5	7.4
56	9	10	3	7.4
57	10	11	5	7.48
58	10	11	5	7.14
59	10	11	5	7.21
60	10	11	3	7.45
61	11	12	7	7.48
62	12	13	5	7.01
63	12	13	5	7.48
64	12	13	7	7.02
65	13	14	5	7.16
66	14	15	5	7.17
67	14	15	3	7.11
68	15	16	5	7.43
69	15	16	5	6.99
70	15	16	5	5.04
71	15	16	3.3	4.62
72	16	17	4.7	4.17
73	17	18	5	4.63
74	17	18	5	4.59
75	17	18	5	4.01
76	17	18	6	5.07
77	18	19	4	8.84
78	19	20	5	5.89
79	19	20	5	5.25
80	19	20	5	4.35
81	19	20	5	4.69
82	19	20	5	4.66
83	19	20	5	5.78
84	19	20	6	4.67
85	19	20	6	3.75
86	20	21	5	5.23
87	20	21	5	3.92
88	20	21	5	4.32
89	20	21	3	5.21
90	21	22	5	8.2
91	21	22	5	8.2
92	21	22	6	8.2
93	21	22	6.3	8.2
94	22	23	5	8.47
95	22	23	5	8.2
96	22	23	5	8.2
97	22	23	5	8.2
98	22	23	5	8.2
99	22	23	5	8.2
100	22	23	6	8.2
101	22	23	6.7	8.2
102	23	24	5	6.81
103	23	24	6	6.8
104	23	24	6	6.8
105	24	25	5	6.92
106	24	25	5	6.8
107	24	25	5	6.82
108	24	25	5	6.9
109	24	25	5	6.83
110	24	25	5	6.98
111	24	25	6	6.85
112	24	25	6	6.77
113	25	26	5	6.3
114	25	26	5	6.28
115	25	26	5	6.28
116	25	26	5	6.27
117	25	26	5	6.72
118	25	26	5	6.38
119	25	26	4.17	6.23
120	3	27	5	6.9
121	3	27	5	7.13
122	3	27	5	6.8
123	3	27	5	6.73
124	3	27	5	6.53
125	3	27	6.4	8.06
126	28	29	5	6.2
127	28	29	5	6.2
128	28	29	5	6.22
129	28	29	6	6.2
130	28	29	6.86	6.2
131	17	32	5	4.28
132	17	32	5	4.63
133	17	32	5	5.15
134	17	32	5	4.51
135	17	32	5	4.71
136	17	32	6	5.99
137	32	33	5	5.04
138	32	33	5	3.87
139	32	33	3.88	3.96
140	33	34	5	3.79
141	33	34	5	4
142	33	34	5	4.38
143	33	34	5	3.98
144	33	34	5	4.33
145	33	34	5	4.13
146	33	34	5	4.36
147	33	34	4.8	3.87
148	34	28	5	5.7
149	34	28	6	5.51
150	34	28	6	5.61
151	35	36	5	6.28
152	35	36	6	6.42
153	36	8	5	8.84
154	36	8	5	6.24
155	36	8	5	6.65
156	36	8	5	6.12
157	36	8	5	5.71
158	36	8	5	5.76
159	36	8	3	6.32
160	8	37	5	7.65
161	8	37	5	7.4
162	8	37	5	7.4
163	8	37	5	7.52
164	37	38	5	8.17
165	37	38	5	7.42
166	37	38	5	7.4
167	37	38	3	7.91
168	38	39	5	7.6
169	38	39	5	7.62
170	38	39	5	7.65
171	38	39	4	7.6
172	39	27	5	7.64
173	39	27	5	7.6
174	39	27	4	9.86
175	27	40	5	7.1
176	27	40	5	6.82
177	27	40	6	6.8
178	40	41	5	6.8
179	40	41	5	6.83
180	40	41	5	6.84
181	40	41	5	7.38
182	40	41	5	7.4
183	40	41	5	7.4
184	40	41	4	7.88
185	41	42	6	7.23
186	41	42	6.24	6.8
187	43	44	5	7.01
188	43	44	5	7.11
189	43	44	5	7
190	43	44	5	7
191	43	44	5	7.05
192	43	44	6	6.94
193	43	44	6.78	7.16
194	44	4	5	7.2
195	44	4	5	6.72
196	44	4	5	6.78
197	44	4	5	6.86
198	44	4	5	6.88
199	44	4	5	7.05
200	4	41	5	7.43
201	4	41	5	7.59
202	4	41	5	7.46
203	4	41	5	7.49
204	4	41	5	6.89
205	4	41	4	8.3
206	41	45	5	7.79
207	41	45	5	7
208	41	45	5	7.05
209	41	45	5	7.08
210	41	45	5	7.32
211	41	45	5	7.22
212	41	45	5	7.84
213	41	45	4	8.03
214	45	46	5	7.8
215	45	46	5	7.4
216	45	46	5	7.51
217	45	46	5	7.4
218	45	46	4	7.46
219	46	47	5	7.48
220	46	47	5	7.4
221	46	47	5	7.44
222	46	47	5	7.4
223	46	47	5	7.4
224	46	47	5	7.4
225	46	47	5	7.4
226	47	28	5	7.4
227	47	28	5	7.4
228	47	28	5	7.4
229	47	28	6	9.48
230	28	48	5	7.24
231	28	48	5	7.4
232	28	48	5	7.46
233	28	48	5	7.4
234	28	48	5	7.5
235	28	48	5	7.58
236	28	48	5	7.6
237	28	48	5	7.6
238	28	48	5	7.6
239	28	48	6	7.41
240	48	49	5	7.49
241	48	49	5	7.44
242	48	49	5	7.66
243	48	49	5	7.43
244	48	49	5	7.4
245	48	49	5	7.4
246	48	49	5	7.4
247	49	25	5	7.4
248	49	25	5	7.4
249	49	25	5	7.38
250	49	25	5	6.8
251	49	25	5	7.01
252	49	25	3	7.4
253	27	51	5	8.42
254	27	51	5	5.96
255	27	51	5	5.83
256	27	51	6	5.77
257	27	51	6	6.09
258	51	52	5	5.74
259	51	52	5.59	6.41
260	52	100	5	6
261	52	100	3	6.3
262	100	53	5	5
263	100	53	5	4.05
264	100	53	5	4.26
265	100	53	5	3.82
266	100	53	5	4.86
267	100	53	5	4.61
268	100	53	5	4.13
269	100	53	4	4.76
270	53	32	5	5.65
271	53	32	5	5.3
272	53	32	5	4.86
273	53	32	5	6.28
274	53	32	3	6.52
275	32	19	5	6.04
276	32	19	5	6.03
277	32	19	5	6.2
278	32	19	5	5.91
279	32	19	3	6.03
280	54	55	5	6.8
281	54	55	4.5	6.8
282	55	56	5	6.8
283	55	56	5	6.8
284	55	56	6.7	6.8
285	56	57	7.7	7.4
286	57	58	5	6.8
287	57	58	5	6.05
288	57	58	5	5.6
289	57	58	5	5.95
290	58	59	5	6
291	58	59	5	6.04
292	58	59	5	6.07
293	58	59	5	5.66
294	58	59	5	5.94
295	59	60	5	6.06
296	59	60	5	5.6
297	59	60	5	5.55
298	59	60	5	5.2
299	59	60	5	5.69
300	59	60	3	6.62
301	60	61	4	10.38
302	61	62	5	5.73
303	61	62	4.1	5.6
304	62	63	5	5.62
305	62	63	6.39	5.75
306	31	65	5	5.91
307	31	65	5	4.24
308	31	65	5	4.32
309	65	66	5	6.28
310	65	66	5	7.03
311	65	66	3.7	8
312	66	3	6.3	7.03
313	66	44	5	6.09
314	66	44	5	5.7
315	66	44	5	6.1
316	66	44	5	6.2
317	66	44	5	6.02
318	66	44	5	5.67
319	66	44	5.49	5.6
Total			1598.7	

APPENDIX 9C   CALCULATING LOCAL TRUCK TRAFFIC

The maintenance study dealt with the road network in an area where the economy is based principally on agriculture and mining. There is also a small amount of tourism, manufacturing and fishing, as well as retail trade. The percentage breakdown in the value of the Region's various economic activities is shown in Figure 9.7.

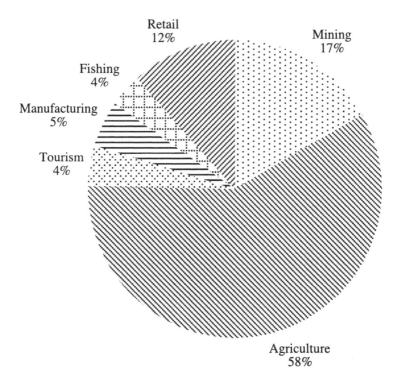

Source: Department of Local Government and Regional Development, W.A., 2005

Figure 9.7   Economic activity in the Wheatbelt South region of Western Australia

By far the largest freight task in the Wheatbelt South Region involves the transport of grain, fertilizer and agricultural products, the combined mass being in the order of about 3 million tonnes. Fuel is also a substantial contributor with over 0.1 million tonnes being transported annually by road.

All grain is transported from farm to the grain receival point by road. About 20 per cent of the region's grain is transported by road from grain receival points to either railheads or to port, the rest being transported by rail. Most of the grain receival points are located on rail but there are 12 receival bins (horizontal or vertical storage facilities) from which the grain is hauled by road to the nearest railhead. In addition, there are eight bins from which grain is hauled directly to port by road. Local carriers undertake most of the haulage from farms to the nearest bins whereas the linehaul from bins to railhead or port is generally performed by larger companies using road trains.

More than 0.35 million tonnes of fertilizer are distributed in the south of the region. Most of it is either carried by road in large trucks (40 tonnes) to depots, whence farmers purchase their supplies to be back-loaded when contractors or farmers bring grain to Perth. These depots were once serviced by rail but now most fertilizer is moved by road. Another part of local truck traffic is for fertilizer spreading.

Prior to the deregulation of transport, fuel was carried by rail to depots owned by oil companies in strategically located centres but only one such rail depot remains. All others are serviced by semi-trailers (29 tonnes – 40 000 litres) or B-double tankers (truck and trailer, 40 tonnes – 54 000 litres).

Modelling Local Traffic

Whereas general freight traffic in the study region could be modelled with the joint trip distribution and route assignment model (See Table 6.1) the local freight traffic could not. The local traffic is mainly for the transportation of the principal commodities within the zones, such as grain, fertilizer, fuel and general freight. Different goods are modelled separately.

For fuel and general commodities that are spread over whole areas, it is reasonable to model their transport as part of the general traffic. However some of the local movements of these commodities are so complex and there is so little information about them that they could not be modelled.

Grain traffic is seasonal and mainly occurs during a short period of about 50 days from December to February when grain is transported from farms during the harvest. Fertilizer transport is also seasonal but occurs over a shorter period.

Data included the grain sources and destinations, the locations of receival bins and the associated production $Prod_i$. Farmers transport their grain to the closest bins so that each bin serves a limited area. The grain transport vehicles are assumed to travel halfway from the approximate boundary of the bin collection area on roads N_i .

The available frequency distributions indicate that local trucks normally have a gross vehicle mass of about 16 tonnes with axle group mass of 4 tonnes, the average amount carried being about 12 tonnes. Thus the annual average daily local freight traffic volumes for grain transport on a link $f_i^{freight}$ can be calculated as:

$$f_i^{freight} = Prod_i \; / \; 12 \; / \; N_i \; /365 \qquad (9.5)$$

Fertilizer distributed over the grain producing areas was assumed to be proportional to the grain production. Total fertilizer tonnage is about 0.35 million while total grain received at bins is about 2.5 million tonnes. The average amount carried by vehicles from fertilizer supply points is about 40 tonnes but this part of the traffic is not local. The average local traffic load for distributing fertilizer is approximately the same as for transporting grain locally but the spreading period is assumed to be 30 days. Thus the local traffic for spreading fertilizer is estimated as:

$$f_i^{freight} = Prod_i \; * \; (350/2507.4) \; / \; 12 \; / \; N_i \; /365 \qquad (9.6)$$

The main and seasonal local traffic can be modelled by adding the results of equations 9.5 and 9.6. The modelled results indicate that this traffic is very small compared with the total truck traffic but it does contribute to road damage.

REFERENCES AND FURTHER READING

Optimal Maintenance Scheduling

Han, R. (1999), 'Optimising road maintenance projects on a rural network using genetic algorithms', *Australian Transport Research Forum*, Perth: Sands & McDougall, 477-491.

Han, R. (2002), *Genetic Algorithm to Optimise the Allocation of Road Expenditure Between Maintenance and Renewal*, PhD thesis, University of Western Australia.

Pavement Modelling

Bein, P., J.B. Cox, R.W. Chursinoff, G.H. Heiman and G.A. Huber (1989) 'Application of HDM3 pavement deterioration model in Saskatchewan pavement management information system', *Transportation Research Record 1215*, Washington: Transportation Research Board, 60-69.

Cox, J. (1994), 'Economic maintenance intervention standards', *Proceedings of 17th ARRB Conference*, Melbourne: Australian Road Research Board, 91-110.

Fwa, T.F. and K.C. Sinha (1987) 'Estimation of environmental and traffic loading effects on highway pavements', *Australian Road Research*, **17**(4), 256-264.

Goldfeld, S.M., R.E. Quandt and H.F. Trotter (1966), 'Maximization by quadratic hill-climbing', *Econometrica*, **34** (3), 541-551.

Greene, W.H. (1997), *Econometric Analysis*, London: Prentice Hall.

Han, R. (2000), 'A new road roughness deterioration model', in Wang K.C.P., Xiao G. and J. Ji (eds), *Traffic and Transportation Studies: Proceedings of ICTTS 2000*, Reston, Virginia: American Society of Civil Engineers, 776-783.

Han, R. (2002), *Genetic Algorithm to Optimise the Allocation of Road Expenditure Between Maintenance and Renewal*, PhD thesis, University of Western Australia.

Heywood, R.J., E.D. Ramsay, J.R. Mclean and R.M. Karagania (1996) 'Road roughness – infrastructure damage based standards', *ROADS 96: Combined 18th ARRB Transport Research Conference Transit NZ Land Transport Symposium*, Melbourne: Australian Road Research Board, 307-321

Martin, T.C. and E.D. Ramsay (1996), 'Rural pavement improvement prediction due to rehabilitation', *ARR 283*, Melbourne: Australian Road Research Board.

Martin, T.C. and S.Y. Taylor (1994), 'Life-cycle costing: prediction of pavement behaviour', *Proceedings of 17th ARRB Conference*, Melbourne: Australian Road Research Board, 187-206

Miller, M.J.E., and K.Y. Loong, (1990), *Pavement Management: Development of a Life Cycle Costing Technique*, Canberra: Bureau of Transport and Communications Economics.

Paterson, W.D.O. (1989), 'A transferable causal model for predicting roughness progression in flexible pavements', *Transportation Research Record 1215*, Washington: Transportation Research Board, 70-84.

Ramaswamy, R. and M. Ben-Akiva (1989), 'Estimation of highway pavement deterioration from in-service pavement data', *Transportation Research Record 1272*, Washington: Transportation Research Board, 96-106

Sayers, M.W. and S.M. Karamihas (1997), *The Little Book of Profiling: Basic Information about Measuring and Interpreting Road Profiles*, http://www.umtri.umich.edu/erd/roughness/litbook.html

Watanatada, T., C.G. Harral, W.D.O. Paterson, A.M. Dhareshear, A. Bhandari, and K. Tsunokawa (1987), *The Highway Design and Maintenance Standards Model*, Baltimore: Johns Hopkins University Press.

Local Truck Traffic

Department of Local Government and Regional Development, W.A. (2005) Indicators of Regional Development in Western Australia, http://www.dlgrd.wa.gov.au/

10. Optimizing with GA in Spreadsheets

The models used for the rural, urban and maintenance problems of Chapters 7, 8 and 9 were each coded specifically for the particular case. However it is possible to program a genetic algorithm project selection and scheduling problem up to a considerable size in a spreadsheet workbook. The spreadsheet format does impose some limitations on the size of the network to be analysed but there is little restriction on the number of projects to be evaluated. The capacity and dimension limitations are discussed later.

This chapter uses an example to give a fairly detailed explanation of how a genetic algorithm within a spreadsheet workbook can be used to optimize a construction programme. The simple example demonstrates the essential steps, which may seem complicated at first sight. However it is not expected that the reader will labour over the details, most of which are shown in Appendix 10A. The purpose is to show that modelling of this type is within the reach of anyone with some experience in using spreadsheets. The chapter concludes with a discussion of scaling up to a problem of realistic size – still in spreadsheets.

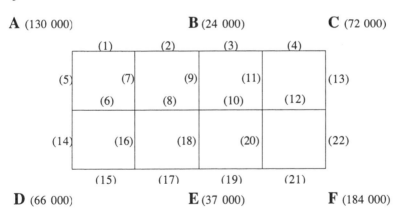

Figure 10.1   Populations and link identifiers for hypothetical network

The application uses the hypothetical uncongested interurban network and populations of Chapter 6. They are repeated in Figure 10.1. Populations of the cities A to F are shown in brackets and the identifier code number of each link is also shown in brackets. To reduce the calculations, traffic between cities is taken to be fixed for a 30-year period. This unchanging traffic is calculated with the gravity model of equation (6.8) and $\alpha = 0.53$. The constant total traffic makes route substitution the sole response by drivers to the time and operating cost changes resulting from road investments. However including traffic generation responses would not make the analysis any more difficult.

PROBLEM SPECIFICATION

The construction programme is for ten years, a forward planning period that is suitable for re-evaluation every three to five years. The benefits are calculated for individual years up to year 11 and then linearly projected for another 19 years to year 30. The budget is $10 million for each of the first nine years and $15 million in year 10. Evaluation has been simplified by not permitting projects to spread between years. Unused budget spills over to the following year until year 10. All costs and benefits are discounted at the rate of 7 per cent per annum.

The Project Options

One project has been specified for each one of the 22 links (Table 10.1).

Table 10.1   Potential projects and resulting travel-time improvements

Link/ project	Project cost, $m	Old time, hours	New time, hours	Link/ project	Project cost, $m	Old time, hours	New time, hours
1	14.00	2.00	1.93	12	3.25	2.09	2.01
2	14.90	2.15	2.07	13	10.00	1.88	1.84
3	9.20	1.88	1.83	14	6.55	1.87	1.84
4	10.90	2.01	1.95	15	11.50	2.01	1.95
5	9.50	1.96	1.92	16	1.54	1.84	1.80
6	1.57	1.85	1.82	17	8.15	1.95	1.91
7	1.60	2.09	2.04	18	5.95	1.92	1.87
8	2.15	1.97	1.93	19	14.60	2.01	1.95
9	7.75	2.05	1.98	20	1.55	2.09	2.04
10	2.93	1.96	1.90	21	20.30	2.19	2.11
11	1.56	2.06	2.01	22	17.90	2.12	2.05

The analysis would be no more difficult if there were multiple project possibilities for one or more links and no projects for others. In order to show how different is the optimal project schedule from one based on simple ranking, the projects were devised so that they would all give the same ratio of benefits to costs on the unrealistic assumption that each is implemented alone at the beginning of the 30-year period and there is no change in traffic on links. This method of setting up the projects made them all reasonably competitive and might be less likely to occur in real life.

Spreadsheet Construction and Calculations

The spreadsheet calculations are explained in summary form in Appendix 10A. The project cost, base time and project time (after completion) is specified in the spreadsheet for each link. When a project order has been selected the spreadsheet 'looks up' the link details and enters them as a project schedule, subject to the annual budget constraints. Benefits result from reduced travel times. However the aggregate benefit must be calculated in all years by multiplying time on each link by the traffic, which has been changed in response to the altered network conditions.

So the big task is to calculate route probability and traffic. Route travel times are summed over link times, some of which are reduced by projects while the rest are unchanged. Then it is a matter of applying the route choice probability equation to the route times, taking account of all specified routes between each city pair. The daily route traffic is the product of the total city pair traffic and the calculated probability.

The traffic on each link is found from the route traffic by an incidence matrix and summation. Then time is converted to cost and the discounted present values of the sum-products of link costs and traffic volumes are multiplied up to annual totals and summed. The cost conversion from simple time represents a composite of time-cost valuation and vehicle operating cost, on the assumption that a faster link travel-time also means a better road surface and therefore less vehicle wear.

User benefits are found by subtracting the sum of discounted annual user costs with projects from the discounted present value of a constant stream of annual base costs (without projects) for 30 years. The net present value of the whole investment schedule is equal to user benefits less discounted project costs. This simple example does not take account of the renewal and maintenance costs that would enter a more realistic assessment.

The complete set of calculations including traffic assignments can be done in the spreadsheet workbook for any arbitrary project sequence. However it is salutary to find how poor one's intuition can be in selecting an apparently good sequence even in such a simple case. The selection problem is addressed efficiently with a genetic algorithm.

THE GENETIC ALGORITHM SEARCH

The function of the GA is to rearrange the project string of 22 elements in order to obtain a progressively better result. There are 22 factorial (about 1.124×10^{21}) possible arrangements of this string so that the efficient GA search, using crossover, mutation and selection, is essential. However most of the computational task is performed in the spreadsheet operations. The GA – Evolver in this case – is embedded in the spreadsheet. The GA population was set at 80, the crossover rate at 0.6 and the mutation rate at 0.2.

When arranged in numerical order (1, 2,...,22), the string gives a project sequence with a negative net present value of $-278\,000$. This ordering was used as the start for each run or experiment.

Results

Ten GA runs were completed. A sequence of generations for one run is plotted in Figure 10.2. The upper line is the NPV for the best of the population of 80 GA individuals (strings) and the lower line is the average for the whole population. The plot illustrates a typical feature of such runs: the process will occasionally produce a superior solution that will not be bettered over many trials – a long horizontal segment – but then an even better one emerges.

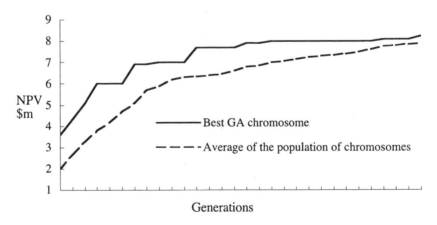

Figure 10.2 Convergence of the GA objective function (NPV)

The net present values of four of the ten results range from 96.1 to 96.6 per cent of the best result while the rest are between 90 and 93 per cent. Three of the very good results give investment schedules that are substantially different from the best. This topic was considered in some depth in Chapter 7.

The calculated net present value (NPV) for the best solution is $9.078 million. This is the result of subtracting from the discounted user benefits the discounted values of those projects in Table 10.1 that were actually chosen to be constructed. The ratio of benefits to costs is 1.13. The complete string found by the genetic algorithm to give the best solution is:

8 6 12 10 16 17 5 4 13 3 18 19 14 22 20 15 7 2 1 9 11 21

The first 14 projects shown in bold are the only ones that could be implemented within the budget. Although the remaining eight could not be included, they participated fully in the genetic algorithm search. Three of the projects discarded from the best result are included in two other relatively good solutions but fairly low in the rank order.

A summary final view of completed projects, with base and final traffic levels, is provided in Figure 10.3. Although this figure loses sight of project timing, it does show the diversion of traffic from the unimproved links.

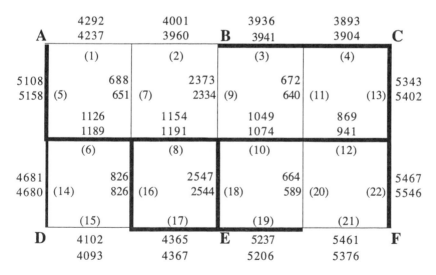

Note: Link identifier numbers are shown in brackets

Figure 10.3   Links upgraded in the optimum plan shown by heavy lines; traffic in base year above and year 11 below

It demonstrates that, with total traffic volume constant, the number of daily trips on the unimproved links declines as drivers are attracted to the improved links. Travel times for the best solution are shown in Table 10.4 and daily traffic year by year in Table 10.6 (both of these tables in Appendix 10A).

Converting the result into a road construction timetable gives the schedule shown in Table 10.2. This is in the same general format as the construction timetable in Chapter 7, Table 7.5 but the model formulation here requires each project to be constructed entirely within one year.

Table 10.2   The best solution formulated as a construction timetable

Proj. no.	Cost ($m)	Investments in road projects ($M) by years										Total ($m)
		1	2	3	4	5	6	7	8	9	10	
1	14.00											
2	14.90											
3	9.20						9.2					9.20
4	10.90				10.9							10.90
5	9.50			9.5								9.50
6	1.57	1.57										1.57
7	1.60											
8	2.15	2.15										2.15
9	7.75											
10	2.93	2.93										2.93
11	1.56											
12	3.25	3.25										3.25
13	10.00					10.0						10.00
14	6.55									6.55		6.55
15	11.50											
16	1.54		1.54									1.54
17	8.15		8.15									8.15
18	5.95							5.95				5.95
19	14.60								14.6			14.60
20	1.55											
21	20.30											
22	17.90										17.9	17.90
Total		9.9	9.7	9.5	10.9	10.0	9.2	5.95	14.6	6.55	17.9	104.2

In Table 10.2 it is the cumulative annual total that has been subject to budget control. Allowing construction to be spread over two or more years would not be difficult but providing for divisibility of benefits would require more complex specification. On the other hand specifying predecessor relationships as in Chapter 7 is not difficult in a spreadsheet formulation.

LARGER SPREADSHEET EVALUATIONS

Using a spreadsheet workbook imposes limitations on the size of network to be evaluated but does not limit the number of project options. The dimensions of one sheet in a workbook are at least 256 columns and more than 65000 rows. This is adequate for a fairly large problem. The following spreadsheet tabulations are required (as in Appendix 10A):

1. The basic tabulation to derive the annual investments and travel times from the link project order and then map the travel times into numerical link order. This has as many columns as there are network links, regardless of the number of potential projects, but relatively few rows: three repetitions of the number of investment years plus about eight. Appendix Table 10.4 (Appendix 10A) shows most of what is required except the travel times by year in link order.
2. The route time and traffic matrix (a small portion shown in Table 10.5) lists all links in each route and looks up the time on each to obtain the route time from which the route traffic is calculated. This is done for every year. There are as many columns in each year as there are links in the route with the most links, plus three more columns. Thus if the longest route has 15 links and there are ten construction years then there will be 197 columns (including the route labels and link numbers).
3. The link incidence matrix to map route traffic into links (portion in Table 10.6). Directly below it is the summary of link traffic by years. There are as many columns as network links and this tabulation can be located directly above the columns in Table 10.4.

Scaling up a spreadsheet to cope with a realistic network will face the problem of the number of routes becoming large. If all routes are enumerated, using a method such as that given in Appendix 6D of Chapter 6, then the route tabulations in points 2 and 3 above will require a substantial number of rows.

A network with 15 centres and 50 links would give a total of about 1700 reasonable routes, which could be handled readily by both the link-incidence and the route-time and traffic matrices but entering the 1700 rows would be tedious. Table 10.3 shows a fairly typical distribution of routes for such a case. The number of routes grows with the numbers of centres and links; for example 20 centres and 70 links would give more than 5000 'reasonable' one-way routes (the return route being assumed identical in each case).

Table 10.3   Indicative distribution of reasonable two-way routes in a hypothetical network with 15 cities and 50 links

Routes per city pair	City pairs	Routes
1	19	19
2	13	26
3	8	24
4-9	20	130
10-19	13	191
20-29	8	196
30-39	5	174
40-49	4	178
50	15	750
Total	105	1688

Note: The maximum number of relevant and reasonable routes is taken to be 50.

It is assumed that no city pair is joined by more than 50 relevant and reasonable routes. Others may be 'reasonable' in the sense of no backtracking but are likely to be unacceptably long. In one of the extreme cases in Figure 6.6 (Appendix 6D to Chapter 6), with 786 one-way routes, the fiftieth route is 14 per cent longer than the shortest. Although technically 'reasonable', the remainder could be ignored for practical modelling.

Satisfactory forecasts may well be obtained if only a small number of alternative routes are considered. A maximum of ten or 20 routes between an origin–destination pair may be sufficient to provide a model which responds appropriately to the upgrading of any link or group of links.

CONCLUSION: USING SPREADSHEETS TO SELECT AND SCHEDULE PROJECTS

The foregoing discussion indicates that a spreadsheet application of genetic algorithm to select and schedule projects is appropriate for networks of moderate size. Because the dimensions that have been discussed would not include minor roads, such an application could cover a fairly large region. The number of potential projects to be evaluated can be substantial and the GA would have no difficulty in selecting from 50 projects.

The time taken to compute is governed primarily by the magnitude of each traffic assignment for each evaluation year; a larger number of projects does not greatly increase computing time. In the simple example of this chapter, each GA run tested more than 5000 possible sequences and each run or experiment took 10 to 15 minutes. When the route traffic assignment task becomes large the computing time may be extended to several hours.

The simplification of assuming fixed traffic for each city pair can be relaxed by incorporating a growth factor. This will give a small table of traffic to be used in the calculations of route traffic in successive years. Another improvement would be to incorporate a more complete schedule of project costs, including renewal. This would affect the final NPV calculation and have a limited impact on travel times and consequently on traffic assignments.

Road deterioration as a function of traffic could also be incorporated. For the larger projects, a construction schedule spanning multiple years could be incorporated without much difficulty. This would break the simple identification of one project with one link, as would more than one potential project for a link, but would not be difficult to specify in the spreadsheet.

APPENDIX 10A   THE SPREADSHEET CALCULATIONS

The spreadsheet calculations are driven by the 'link project order' in Table 10.4. (Only the first 14 of the 22 links could be shown in Table 10.4.)

The top four numerical rows of Table 10.4 constitute a look-up table (HLOOKUP) and the elements in the next three numerical rows are obtained by 'looking up' the link numbers in the project order.

Both the investment and link travel time tabulations in the rows below the actual project order (numbers in bold) are obtained with simple 'if' statements to determine whether the cumulative project cost is less than the permissible total. If it is less than the permissible cumulative investment to the end of the particular year then the project cost is read into the investment schedule and the project time is read into the (next-year) time tabulation; if not then the base time is read in and there is no investment. The travel times that have been reduced by projects are shown in the lower left portion of the travel time tabulation.

Table 10.4   Initial steps in calculating the impacts of a sequence of project investments – portion of spreadsheet

Link	1	2	3	4	5	6	7	8	9	10	11	12	13	14
In link order:														
Project cost	14.0	14.9	9.2	10.9	9.5	1.57	1.6	2.15	7.75	2.93	1.56	3.25	10.0	6.55
Base time	2.00	2.15	1.88	2.01	1.96	1.85	2.09	1.97	2.05	1.96	2.06	2.09	1.88	1.87
Project time	1.93	2.07	1.83	1.95	1.92	1.82	2.04	1.93	1.98	1.9	2.01	2.01	1.84	1.84
In project order:														
Project cost	2.15	1.57	3.25	2.93	1.54	8.15	9.5	10.9	10.0	9.2	5.95	14.6	6.55	17.9
Base time	1.97	1.85	2.09	1.96	1.84	1.95	1.96	2.01	1.88	1.88	1.92	2.01	1.87	2.12
Project time	*1.93*	*1.82*	*2.01*	*1.90*	*1.80*	*1.91*	*1.92*	*1.95*	*1.84*	*1.83*	*1.87*	*1.95*	*1.84*	*2.05*
Cumulative project cost	2.15	3.72	6.97	9.90	11.4	19.6	29.1	40.0	50.0	59.2	65.1	79.7	86.3	104.0
Project order	**8**	**6**	**12**	**10**	**16**	**17**	**5**	**4**	**13**	**3**	**18**	**19**	**14**	**22**
Investments														
Year 1	2.15	1.57	3.25	2.93										
Year 2					1.54	8.15								
Year 3							9.5							
Year 4								10.9						
Year 5									10.0					
Year 6										9.2				
Year 7											5.95			
Year 8												14.6		
Year 9													6.55	
Year 10														17.9
Link travel time (in project order)														
Year 2	*1.93*	*1.82*	*2.01*	*1.90*	1.84	1.95	1.96	2.01	1.88	1.88	1.92	2.01	1.87	2.12
Year 3	*1.93*	*1.82*	*2.01*	*1.90*	*1.80*	*1.91*	1.96	2.01	1.88	1.88	1.92	2.01	1.87	2.12
Year 4	*1.93*	*1.82*	*2.01*	*1.90*	*1.80*	*1.91*	*1.92*	2.01	1.88	1.88	1.92	2.01	1.87	2.12
Year 5	*1.93*	*1.82*	*2.01*	*1.90*	*1.80*	*1.91*	*1.92*	*1.95*	1.88	1.88	1.92	2.01	1.87	2.12
Year 6	*1.93*	*1.82*	*2.01*	*1.90*	*1.80*	*1.91*	*1.92*	*1.95*	*1.84*	1.88	1.92	2.01	1.87	2.12
Year 7	*1.93*	*1.82*	*2.01*	*1.90*	*1.80*	*1.91*	*1.92*	*1.95*	*1.84*	*1.83*	1.92	2.01	1.87	2.12
Year 8	*1.93*	*1.82*	*2.01*	*1.90*	*1.80*	*1.91*	*1.92*	*1.95*	*1.84*	*1.83*	*1.87*	2.01	1.87	2.12
Year 9	*1.93*	*1.82*	*2.01*	*1.90*	*1.80*	*1.91*	*1.92*	*1.95*	*1.84*	*1.83*	*1.87*	*1.95*	1.87	2.12
Year 10	*1.93*	*1.82*	*2.01*	*1.90*	*1.80*	*1.91*	*1.92*	*1.95*	*1.84*	*1.83*	*1.87*	*1.95*	*1.84*	2.12
Year 11	*1.93*	*1.82*	*2.01*	*1.90*	*1.80*	*1.91*	*1.92*	*1.95*	*1.84*	*1.83*	*1.87*	*1.95*	*1.84*	*2.05*

Another tabulation in the spreadsheet – not shown but directly above the top row of Table 10.4 – uses the link project order and the rows of link travel time (project order) as another look-up table to map the travel times back into normal link order. (The fact that the first row of this look-up table, link project order, is not in ascending or descending numerical order does not matter because the setting is 'FALSE', so that exact values must be read.)

The next step is to calculate route probability and traffic. The tabulation just created itself becomes a look-up table for the route-time calculation sheet (Table 10.5). The links in each route are listed in the route row and the times are looked up and summed for each year. The core calculation is to apply route-choice probability equation (6.2) (Chapter 6) to the route-times, taking account of all specified routes between each city pair:

$$p_{rs}^k = \frac{e^{-15.0\left(C_{rs}^k / C_{rs}^{\min}\right)}}{\displaystyle\sum_{k \in K_{rs}} e^{-15.0\left(C_{rs}^k / C_{rs}^{\min}\right)}}$$

The sum in the denominator is conveniently obtained by having a column ('Exp') to calculate separately for each route: $e^{-15.0\left(C_{rs}^k / C_{rs}^{\min}\right)}$. Thus the probability of a motorist taking a route is the ratio of the 'Exp' for that route to the sum of the 'Exp' values for all routes between those two cities. The daily route traffic is the product of the (fixed) total city pair traffic and the calculated probability.

Table 10.5 Small portion of route time, probability and traffic matrix

City pair	Route		Link numbers						Link times in year 2 (after year 1 investments)						Total time	'Exp'	Route traffic
A-F	1	1	2	3	4	13	22	2.00	2.15	1.88	2.01	1.88	2.12	12.04	2.17E-07	66
	2	1	2	3	11	12	22	2.00	2.15	1.88	2.06	2.01	2.12	12.22	1.72E-07	53
	3	1	2	3	11	20	21	2.00	2.15	1.88	2.06	2.09	2.19	12.37	1.42E-07	43
	4	1	2	9	10	12	22	2.00	2.15	2.05	1.90	2.01	2.12	12.23	1.7E-07	52
	5	1	2	9	10	20	21	2.00	2.15	2.05	1.90	2.09	2.19	12.38	1.41E-07	43
	6	1	2	9	18	19	21	2.00	2.15	2.05	1.92	2.01	2.19	12.32	1.52E-07	46
	7	1	7	8	10	12	22	2.00	2.09	1.93	1.90	2.01	2.12	12.05	2.14E-07	65
	8	1	7	8	10	20	21	2.00	2.09	1.93	1.90	2.09	2.19	12.20	1.77E-07	54
	9	1	7	8	18	19	21	2.00	2.09	1.93	1.92	2.01	2.19	12.14	1.91E-07	58

Each year is represented in the spreadsheet tabulation shown partly in Table 10.5 by a block of columns with as many columns as there are links in the route that has the most links, plus three more columns. This is repeated for every year. (The link identifier numbers in each route row can be derived from the link-incidence matrix in Table 6.3 by transposing and using 'data sort' to eliminate empty cells.)

The next step is to calculate link traffic, costs and NPV. The route traffic is copied back into the first sheet; the bottom right of this tabulation is shown in the top left of Table 10.6.

Table 10.6   Mapping route traffic to links – portion of spreadsheet

	Daily route traffic (part only)					Link incidence matrix (part only) by links									
Route	Yr 7	Yr 8	Yr 9	Yr 10	Yr 11	1	2	3	4	5	6	7	8	9	10
CD 7	38	37	37	36	36								1		1
CD 8	31	30	30	29	29			1					1		1
CD 9	34	34	33	33	33		1	1					1	1	
CD10	24	24	24	23	23	1	1	1				1			
CD11	44	44	43	44	44					1			1		1
CD12	36	35	35	36	36			1			1		1		1
CD13	40	39	39	40	40		1	1			1		1	1	
CD14	28	28	28	28	28	1	1	1			1	1			
CD15	28	28	27	28	28	1	1	1	1	1					

		1	2	3	4	5	6	7	8	9	10
Base traffic on link:	Yr 1	4292	4001	3936	3893	5108	1126	688	1154	2373	1049
Summed daily link traffic:	Yr 2	4265	3969	3881	3833	5120	1179	677	1229	2372	1157
	Yr 3	4251	3951	3876	3831	5127	1175	679	1193	2365	1149
	Yr 4	4227	3945	3873	3830	5163	1197	658	1193	2354	1148
	Yr 5	4230	3950	3902	3881	5162	1195	658	1190	2353	1133
	Yr 6	4231	3951	3904	3880	5160	1194	656	1189	2337	1130
	Yr 7	4237	3962	3951	3905	5156	1190	656	1183	2330	1101
	Yr 8	4240	3961	3947	3905	5150	1187	654	1199	2351	1105
	Yr 9	4234	3953	3925	3891	5155	1189	655	1194	2352	1074
	Yr 10	4232	3954	3925	3892	5163	1192	652	1191	2348	1073
	Yr 11	4237	3960	3941	3904	5158	1189	651	1191	2334	1074

The SUMPRODUCT function is applied to the route traffic columns in Table 10.6 and the link incidence matrix of Chapter 6, Appendix 6B, Table 6.4 (portion shown in Table 10.6). This gives the daily link traffic by years shown in the lower part of Table 10.6. The Year 1 row shows the base-year traffic which is unaffected by the investments.

Then time is converted to cost and the discounted present values of the sum-products of link costs and daily traffic volumes are multiplied up to an annual total for each year. The cost conversion from simple time represents a composite of time-cost valuation and vehicle operating cost on the simplifying assumption that a faster link travel-time also means a better road surface and therefore less vehicle wear.

User benefits are found by subtracting the sum of discounted annual user costs with projects from the discounted present value of a constant stream of annual base costs (without projects) for 30 years. In the project case the year 11 costs become a constant stream for the next 19 years and are then discounted.

The net present value of the whole investment schedule is equal to user benefits less discounted project costs. This simple example does not take account of renewal and maintenance costs which would usually be included in a realistic assessment.

11. Concluding Comments

This chapter has two purposes. The first is to quickly review some key aspects of evolutionary computing as applied to the selection and scheduling of road projects. In this context the significance of multiple solutions is explored a little further than in Chapter 7.

The second purpose is to raise some broad issues about optimal road investment plans that have not been raised earlier in the book. One of these is making optimum investment scheduling the key to a continuous planning cycle. Another is the condition of a whole network and how it may be related to the marginal benefit–cost ratio as approximated by the ratio for the last project. This is followed by a limited comparison of an optimal maintenance timetable with current planning and expenditure.

COMPLEXITY OF ROAD PLANNING

The inter-relations between projects in a network are so complex that a subset of them in a particular combination or pattern (that is construction activities over years) may or may not contribute to an increase in the net economic benefit. The impact depends on the construction schedule for the other projects and the substitution and complementarity effects. To capture all of these it is necessary to take into account every project throughout the network. Evaluating only some of them may lead to a conclusion that is invalidated when all projects are considered. On the other hand the study network must be circumscribed for practical reasons but the boundary should not cut across important interactions.

Some network effects are readily seen at a broad level but are not easy to identify at the project level. Identification of complementarity and substitution effects between projects in the full study network would usually be impossible. Furthermore projects are distributed through time as well as space and the network effects and budget constraints make projects interdependent in both dimensions.

SOLUTION BY GENETIC ALGORITHM

The robustness and efficiency of genetic algorithm has made it ideal for optimizing a road project construction timetable. It is the first adequate and realistic method of solving this problem. An ancillary application has been to use another version of GA to calibrate the parameters of the travel models needed in the search for the optimal sequence. The following key features of genetic algorithm for road investment selection and scheduling summarize points made in Chapter 4:

- The GA encodes each potential solution to a problem as a string of numbers and treats the string as an entity rather than a collection of separate decision variables.
- The GA evaluates a population of solutions to the same problem at each generation.
- Solutions are scattered over the solution space and so give a broad view of the space and a high degree of immunity to the danger of being trapped at a local optimum.
- GA uses the actual value of the objective function rather than derivatives with respect to decision variables to guide the search. This makes it possible to model a complex system without sacrificing realism or key aspects of the system.
- GA uses probabilistic transition rules in the search but it systematically compares, combines and evaluates information as the search progresses.

The project search begins by randomly initializing a population of individuals in the first generation, assigning a value to each position on every individual string. The values assigned are in the domain range with no repetitions. The example is an individual representing 5 road projects to be selected and scheduled. It might be randomized as (2, 3, 5, 1, 4) which maps into the construction sequence:

$$project_2 \rightarrow project_3 \rightarrow project_5 \rightarrow project_1 \rightarrow project_4.$$

The information on each individual is decoded and evaluated to give the value of the objective function or fitness of an individual. The GA individual in the example above would be translated into a construction timetable and the corresponding net present value calculated and compared with those for individuals with other project sequences. The search and improvement process would then begin.

Objective Function and Constraints

The objective is to maximize net present value and the decision variables are the project investments by years. The solution is constrained and modified by the annual budgets. It may also be subject to limits to annual expenditure on individual projects, preferred project investment profiles over years and staged construction. The specification involves multiple years, complex constraints, travel demand elasticities and an adequate representation of driver route choice in response to changing road conditions.

If divisibility and indivisibility of project benefits is an issue then it is modelled according to effects on the level of service provided by a new road link during construction. When equally beneficial projects are competing for limited resources, one with indivisible benefits is expected to be completed as soon as possible. However some of the benefit indivisible projects in the regional solutions would not be completed as soon as possible because benefit divisibility is only one of many factors taken into account in developing the project timetable.

The dominant influence or constraint on the solution is travel behaviour, modelled to represent the ways in which travellers and truck operators react to network changes. This is the main source of complexity in the road investment timetabling problem.

Urban traffic modelling

The first task in urban traffic modelling is to find shortest routes between zones. Vehicles are allocated to these and then traffic is distributed away from congested routes. The major computational task is to find quickest routes repeatedly.

It is assumed that drivers seek the routes which minimize their individual travel times so that the journey time on all routes actually used are equal and less than those which would be experienced by a single vehicle on any unused route. Traffic is loaded on to the least-cost routes, the effects of congestion on travel times are calculated and traffic is efficiently reassigned. Convergence generally takes a small number of iterations even for a large urban network.

This deterministic user equilibrium (DUE) model is highly responsive to network conditions as they are modified by road projects.

Non-urban traffic modelling

Two travel models have been jointly estimated to capture travellers' responses to changes in the rural road network. The first is a direct demand gravity model to predict traffic volumes between centres. The theoretically preferred representation of impedance is an exponential function with the logsum of travel costs over all reasonable routes connecting each pair of centres. However it gave results implying that trips are not significantly influenced by distance in the composite model whereas the minimum travel time gave sensible results.

The second model is a multiple path logit for route choice and traffic assignment. The ratio of travel time by any reasonable route to the minimum travel time has been found to be a good modelling specification. Its merits have been discussed in Chapter 6, Appendix 6A. All parameters have been estimated jointly, first by genetic algorithm and then by more precise methods. This was done on the basis of a limited number of road traffic counts.

The formulation of the combined gravity and logit model implies that if there is no change in link costs then traffic will always increase as population and economic activity grow. However new links, road widening and variations in roughness change the route costs and this results in redistribution of traffic between routes as well as changes in the total volume. Different project combinations result in different traffic volumes on individual links as drivers respond to variations in operating costs and travel times. Thus the demand models build connections between costs and demands and so make investment optimization achievable.

Multiple Solutions

A GA starts with a population of potential solutions which evolve into better ones. At the end of the study there is a pool of possible solution timetables with which the planner can work. This has some similarity to the approach taken in multicriteria analysis:

> Expression of preferences in decision-making processes is an activity which is greatly facilitated if it is done with some background knowledge concerning the set of feasible solutions. (Nijkamp et al., 1990)

Examination of the top 100 regional road project GA solutions in terms of the Euclidean distance between them leads to the following conclusions:

* The search space has multiple peaks.
* Very good solutions with similar NPV may have highly dissimilar project schedules.
* Conversely similar solutions may range from very high NPV to negative NPV.

Multiple good solutions
The presence of multiple almost equally good solutions to the road project problem provides valuable information for decision makers. They are interested not only in narrowly defined efficiency of resource allocation but also in wider impacts such as environment protection and development of the local economy. From a group of equally good solutions, in terms of road user benefits, decision makers can choose the solution which is also most effective on other criteria. In other words, they can choose a solution that is as good as other solutions in terms of narrowly defined allocation efficiency but better when environmental, developmental and other impacts are taken into account.

Similar but inferior solutions
The presence of similar construction timetables with radically different payoffs, some being large and positive while others are negative, has an important implication for practical road investment decisions. Modifying an outstanding road construction timetable for any reason may well cause a substantial decrease in benefits. This is due to the complex network effects.

Complementarity between road projects
If a road project timetable contains complementary projects then it is likely that collectively they will have a high pay-off. It has been noted that sequential projects are likely to be complementary. This is a general observation in a particular study and an investigation of complementarity would be needed to isolate the effects of the sequential projects individually. This could be done by calculating the marginal benefit–cost ratio as they are deleted one by one (Chapter 9).

Substitutability between road projects
Although it is difficult to isolate cases of partial duplication of project effects, comparison of regional project solutions has indicated that any construction schedule involving a degree of substitution between routes will tend to give poor results. Two solution schedules may be fairly similar but if substitution and duplication effects are evident in one then its NPV will be much lower than the other.

A PLANNING CYCLE WITH REPEATED OPTIMIZATION

Because project optimization is based on forecasts of traffic and road conditions, the reliability of the optimized timetable is influenced directly by the accuracy of traffic forecasts and budget projections. When actual trends diverge from forecasts the solution becomes sub-optimal. Consequently as forecast accuracy declines into the future, the firmness of the timetable's optimality decreases year by year. This difficulty is overcome by using a rolling process to adjust the original plan. The plan is updated with the new information every few years or whenever there are significant changes.

When incorporating new project information, it may be found convenient to seed a GA run with a small proportion of high-performing strings from previous runs in order to hasten convergence. To balance exploration and exploitation it may be advisable to replace only a fraction of the entire population with good strings. A diverse range of high-performing strings (that is strings of diverse genotype but comparable performance) should be chosen so that multiple peaks in the search space are more effectively explored.

On the basis of the results obtained in this study, the rolling programme would have the following features:

- Road projects in the first half of the programme are firmly scheduled and the corresponding budgets are exhausted. In contrast, budget forecasts for the second half of the programme period are less accurate, limits to yearly expenditure on individual projects less precise, and there may be projects which are unfinished because their benefits are indivisible, leading to unused resources.
- In the next round of programming, the second half of the previous plan becomes the first half of the following one. All information is updated, including more accurately predicted budgets and more specific limits.
- The unfinished operations in the previous plan and newly identified undertakings are pooled to form a new set of road projects to be scheduled in the new full programme period. The new schedule overlaps the previous one by half a programme period and the timing of construction of the unfinished projects may or may not be the same as in the previous timetable.
- The rolling process for developing road construction timetables is repeated regularly.

THE COMPREHENSIVE OBJECTIVE FUNCTION

In the case of the maintenance study, the average roughness values over the whole network shown in Figure 11.1 indicate that the road condition in the optimized network would get worse during the planning period under the constraints imposed by the specified budgets. This projected deterioration appears paradoxical in view of the fact that the marginal benefit–cost ratio for the programme (Chapter 9, Table 9.5) is less than one, a result which seems to imply that the funding is somewhat more than adequate.

This is certainly surprising in view of the progressively increasing roughness. The worsening network condition suggests that the given budgets are insufficient to control roughness whereas the marginal cost–benefit analysis indicates that the proposed budgets may be too large in terms of economic effectiveness.

This apparent paradox arises from taking too narrow a view. Simply concentrating on roughness (Figure 11.1) is to ignore the benefit side. Much of the optimized expenditure would be spent on widening narrow roads. This would not reduce average roughness over the whole network but would achieve substantial benefits.

Thus a conclusion based only on roughness would be misleading because the widened roads would make the entire service level better and the results of the marginal cost–benefit analysis are correct. To put it another way, the objective function takes account of all benefits: it is not simply set to minimize average roughness. The goal of the GA is to maximize net present value.

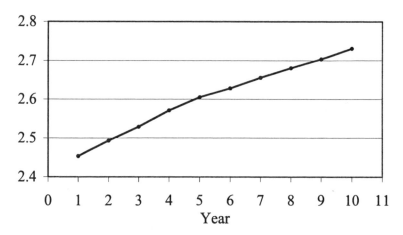

Figure 11.1   Change in average roughness over the optimized network: maintenance study

Taking an even longer view, it is clear that the emphasis on widening narrow pavements in the optimized programme represents a phase in development. Subsequent expenditure would arrest and even reverse the deterioration in roughness.

MAINTENANCE SOLUTION COMPARED TO ACTUAL PLANS AND OUTCOMES

There is usually little opportunity to compare optimal schedules with practical plans or actual outcomes and possibly not much interest in doing it. However there was a plan for the area covered by the maintenance modelling of Chapter 9 and two years had actually been completed. These provide the basis for a limited comparison.

The main objectives of the ten-year maintenance plan for the study area are to preserve ageing pavements and to widen single-lane sections of main roads to two lanes. Although the periodic maintenance and widening projects determined by the best solution from GA optimization are represented by small segments about 5 kilometres long, they become projects spanning large segments when summed over the ten-year planning period.

It was found that the optimized schedule corresponded approximately to the road authority plan when viewed over ten years. However some inferior solutions would also fit the plan approximately. All projects identified in the plan are on long road segments and priorities have been broadly allocated. A comparison has been made for years already completed. Actual expenditure has been close to the budgets imposed in Chapter 9 and the actual and modelled expenditure allocations are fairly similar (Table 11.1).

Table 11.1   Actual and modelled maintenance allocations in completed years

Treatment	Actual allocation %	Modelled allocation %
Routine maintenance	21.11	12.66
Periodic maintenance	18.01	22.37
Renewal and widening	60.88	64.97
Total	100.00	100.00

However these figures merely indicate a similar composition of total expenditure and it has been demonstrated that achieving maximum benefits depends on the sequence of treatments. Detailed information down to the project and segment level for routine and periodic maintenance is not available. A comparison of the modelled results with the actual at this detailed level can only be made for widening. Half of the widening projects are similar while the other half are at different locations. There are apparently two reasons for the differences:

- The modelled (optimized) results were achieved by maximizing benefits.

- The actual practice has been to rank projects by a sufficiency rating method based on current road conditions combined with multi-criteria evaluation. The rating criteria are social, economic, environmental and safety. The economic merit is measured by benefit–cost ratio and is given a heavy weight.

In summary the actual practice is not entirely driven by net benefit maximization. It may meet short-term requirements but would lose a lot of benefits over a long period.

A NEW PLANNING PARADIGM

Chapter 1 started by saying that genetic algorithm can radically improve road planning and overcome the faults in current methods of selecting projects and ordering them into a construction timetable. It was noted that a standard evaluation procedure can assess a programme of projects but it cannot tell how much better an alternative programme might be. We have shown that the task is not merely to evaluate a set of projects but to select the right ones and at the same time find the right construction sequence.

It was also noted that to assess every possible sequence of only ten projects it would be necessary to evaluate more than 3 million cases and the number is much greater if there are more projects. So an efficient search method is needed. Genetic algorithm is a form of evolutionary computing able to conduct a search in an efficient and seemingly intelligent way.

Questions Addressed

A number of key issues have already been reviewed in this chapter. We finish with a summary review of the answers that the book has provided to the set of questions posed in Chapter 1.

- What is different about a programme-optimizing approach to road investments ?

  The GA optimum is the result of a directed search through the immense number of possible project timetables. It is this systematic search which enables GA to avoid the trap of sub-optimizing with single evaluations, whether these evaluate one project at a time or a specified project timetable. Such single evaluations may take account of all network effects but they are still sub-optimizing.

- How difficult is it computationally ?

  A full GA application to select and schedule road projects still imposes a considerable computing load but increasing computer speed is whittling this down from many hours or even days to a matter of minutes or perhaps an hour or two for large problems.

- How are standard evaluation methods and criteria incorporated ?

  The objective function built into the GA calculates the net present value of costs and benefits. This standard evaluation procedure is appropriate because all of the alternatives assessed by the GA use the same budget. The benefit–cost ratio is also calculated as a measure of capital efficiency and the internal rate of return is calculated. Benefits are calculated from the traffic impacts of the projects throughout the network on the basis of costs in the project and base cases. It is possible to use a multi-criteria objective function.

- How are planning and budget constraints handled ?

  The various planning constraints include limits to the expenditure allocated to any one project, preferred construction profiles and staged construction. When each alternative ordered sequence is generated by the GA, such constraints are imposed by a heuristic process as the sequence is transformed to a construction timetable. Budgets are usually annual; as each is exhausted the partially completed and subsequent projects spill over into the next and following periods. When the total budget is exhausted the remaining projects are omitted from the timetable.

- What is genetic algorithm and how is it used to select and schedule projects ?

  A GA for scheduling contains a string of projects to be arranged in an optimal sequence. Any string or 'chromosome' decodes to an objective function value (NPV in this case). Recombinations and mutations of the elements on parental chromosomes create different offspring.

Successive generations are populated by randomized competition so that strings giving high NPVs tend to survive and combine. The initial population is drawn randomly and to find the best solution the randomized but directed search tests many possible sequences.

- How is traffic generation and assignment handled ?
  Each project sequence generated by the GA is a potential solution. When the sequence has been transformed into a construction timetable which satisfies budget and planning constraints the corresponding traffic is generated and assigned by an appropriate method. In a city the traffic is assigned by the deterministic user equilibrium (DUE) method. Rural and inter-urban traffic is generated and assigned by a simultaneous gravity and stochastic network loading (logit) model.

- To what extent can standard software be used in optimization ?
  Each of the three applications reported in the book (Chapters 7, 8 and 9) was coded specifically for the particular problem. However GA packages are available and some are embedded in spreadsheet (Excel) software. Chapter 10 used a hypothetical example to demonstrate that the problem of optimally selecting and scheduling a considerable number of road projects in a network of moderate size can be handled by such software.

- How is the method applied to regional road networks ?
  Chapter 7 reported on an application of GA to optimize the selection and sequence of projects in a rural road network. In this case traffic generation and assignment was done with a combined gravity and logit model.

- How is it applied to urban road networks ?
  Chapter 8 reported on an application of GA to optimize the selection and sequence of projects in an urban road network. Traffic assignment was done with a deterministic user equilibrium (DUE) model.

- How is it used to optimize maintenance ?
  Chapter 9 reported on a maintenance-optimizing application of GA in a rural network. There were 319 road segments to be scheduled and any treatment was determined by a heuristic. Again traffic generation and assignment was done with a combined gravity and logit model.

- To what extent does the method give the decision maker latitude to choose between solutions of similar merit ?
  The GA method generates a variety of solutions of approximately equal merit. The final choice among these may well take account of other factors without losing any net benefit so long as the chosen solution is not modified.

REFERENCES AND FURTHER READING

Han, R. (1999), 'Optimising road maintenance projects on a rural network using genetic algorithms', *Australian Transport Research Forum*, Perth: Sands & McDougall, 477-491.

Nijkamp, P., P. Rietveld and H. Voogd (1990), *Multicriteria Evaluation in Physical Planning*, Amsterdam: North-Holland.

Qiu, M. (1997), 'Prioritising and scheduling road projects by genetic algorithm', *Mathematics and Computers in Simulation*, **43**, 569-574.

Taplin, J.H.E. and M. Qiu (2001), 'Using GA to optimise the selection and scheduling of road projects', in Chambers, L. (ed.), *The Practical Handbook of Genetic Algorithms: Applications*, Boca Raton, FL: Chapman & Hall/CRC, 99-134.

Index